Volume Two

Basics of Christian Thought

Todd Brennan, General Editor

CATHOLIC THINKERS IN THE CLEAR

Giants of Catholic Thought
from Augustine to Rahner

William A. Herr

THE THOMAS MORE PRESS

Chicago, Illinois

Portions of this book appeared in different format in the newsletter of the same title published by the Thomas More Association.

ISBN 0-88347-239-2

Contents

Introduction
9

Chapter 1
TERTULLIAN, CLEMENT, ORIGEN
12

Chapter 2
PLATO AND AUGUSTINE
24

Chapter 3
AUGUSTINE
36

Chapter 4
ANSELM AND ABELARD
49

Chapter 5
BONAVENTURE
63

Chapter 6
ARISTOTLE
75

Chapter 7
ALBERT AND THOMAS
87

Chapter 8
THOMAS AQUINAS
100

Chapter 9
DUNS SCOTUS
113

Chapter 10
WILLIAM OF OCKHAM
126

Chapter 11
ERASMUS AND THOMAS MORE
139

Chapter 12
CAJETAN AND SUAREZ
DOMINICANS VS. JESUITS
THE COUNTER REFORMATION
153

Chapter 13
TERESA OF AVILA
167

Chapter 14
DESCARTES AND PASCAL
181

Chapter 15
GILSON AND MARITAIN
THE THOMISTIC REVIVAL
195

Chapter 16
GABRIEL MARCEL
207

Chapter 17
TEILHARD DE CHARDIN
220

Chapter 18
JOHN COURTNEY MURRAY
233

Chapter 19
KARL RAHNER
247

Chapter 20
BERNARD LONERGAN
EDWARD SCHILLEBEECKX
HANS KUNG
260

Conclusion
275

Index
277

Suggested Readings
284

Publication of this volume of
BASICS OF CHRISTIAN THOUGHT
is made possible in part by a
ROBERT E. BURNS GRANT
from the Claretian Fathers and Brothers

INTRODUCTION

SEVERAL years ago, officials at the Lincoln Park Zoo in Chicago began constructing buildings to house some exotic new species, the likes of which had never been displayed there before: cows, chickens, pigs, and sheep. Many city children, it had been discovered, knew more about the animals of the jungle than about those of the barnyard. All the youngsters knew about milk and eggs is that they came from the grocery store.

Something similar often happens with ideas. We tend to assume, at least implicitly, either that they have always existed or else they come from books. Our way of thinking seems "natural"; it may even seem the only possible way to think. In a similar fashion, the English language seems the "natural" way to speak, or even the only way, until we learn to express ourselves in other ways.

In fact, of course, all the ideas we use, all our ways of looking at things and thinking about them, were fabricated by someone, usually as responses to specific problems or situations. At the time, they were appropriate responses. But ideas, like bureaucratic structures, often acquire a life of their own and continue in existence long after their usefulness has passed. Sometimes these ideas can hinder understanding rather than facilitate it. Learning how and why certain ideas arose can help us to recognize those situations.

This is as true with respect to religion as it is to anything else. The Gospels contain a message, a truth. But a truth cannot be transmitted unless it is expressed, and it cannot be expressed without being put into a certain form. The same truth can be expressed in many different forms, but each form will color, restrict, interpret, or otherwise change the truth in a different way. There can be no "pure" content—a message

9

without an expression—any more than there can be a physical body without a particular shape, but we can learn to distinguish one element from the other.

You cannot express an idea, for example, without using a language. It is possible to express the notion that freedom is a basic human right in French, in Russian, and in Swahili, but each of these three expressions will have subtle associations and shades of meanings which the others do not. This is unavoidable. And the more abstract the notion being expressed, the more likely it is to happen.

Even within the same language, a given truth or fact will be experienced and expressed differently by people with different ways of looking at the world. A human body, for example, means something different to a beauty contest judge than to a chiropractor; the evergreen seen by a poet is not the same as the evergreen seen by a tree surgeon. This also is unavoidable.

Jesus came to earth with a message. Had he been born in 5th-century B.C. China, let us say, or in 12th-century Persia, this message would have been expressed in terms of the way people looked at the world in those times and places; and it would have reached us in a much different form than it did. As it happened, he was born at a time when most of Western civilization expressed its ideas in the vocabulary and basic worldview of classical Greek philosophy, so that is how the Christian message came to be explained. The union of scriptures with Greek thinking—something that took centuries to accomplish—is what created traditional Christianity. This process began at a very early stage: even the beginning of St. John's Gospel, for example, shows very strong Greek influences. This particular manner of expression came about essentially through a historical accident. It could have happened differently. Whether or not this is still a good way to explain the Christian message in a world where that vocabularly and that worldview are no longer so familiar to us—and, if not, how it should be explained—is for the reader to decide.

What we are going to investigate is how and why some basic Christian concepts received their traditional formulation, and how more recent thinkers are attempting to reformulate them. We will try to distinguish the content from the forms by seeing how the forms were created. And we are going to meet the people who created them.

It will be like a journey through history, to see how we got to where we are now, and some glimpse of where we might want to go in the future. But this journey will not be a free ride: the reader will have to provide his or her own transportation. In the absence of a time machine, you will have to imagine yourself in the times and places we will be visiting, and you will have to try to think as the people we will be visiting thought, to see the world through their eyes.

Chapter 1
TERTULLIAN, CLEMENT, ORIGEN

CHRISTIANITY did not come into existence with a theology of its own. It did not need one. It considered itself simply as the fulfillment of Judaism; and so long as it remained basically a Jewish sect, it could explain and defend itself in purely Jewish terms. Jesus, for example, could be presented as the fulfillment of Isaiah's prophecies. When the decision was made to baptize Gentiles, however, and to preach the Gospel to them, this was no longer sufficient. If you want to explain something to someone, you must explain it in terms of something he or she is familiar with; and Isaiah was hardly a household word in Italy or Asia Minor.

As Christianity spread through the Roman Empire, it had to deal with questions and challenges posed in non-Jewish terms. It was, to a large extent, through this process that the implicit content of Christianity was made explicit. And, as usually happens, the way the questions were asked had a great deal to do with the way they were answered.

Let us pause here for a moment and mentally travel backward through time. We are going back past the Second World War, past the First World War, the Civil War, past the Revolution; back past Columbus to Europe and the Reformation, back before the Renaissance, before the Middle Ages; before Charlemagne, before Attila, before the fall of Rome; back to an age further removed from the age of Thomas Aquinas than that of Aquinas is from ours. We are going to look at the beginning of the synthesis of traditional Christianity.

We are in the Roman world of the second century A.D. The Empire has reached its greatest extent, stretching from Britain and Holland across almost all of Western and a good

part of Eastern Europe. Turkey, parts of Russia, Palestine,
Syria, Egypt, and the whole of the North African coast are
all under Roman law. Marcus Aurelius is emperor, and at
the moment is campaigning against the barbarians on the
Danube frontier.

For the first time in history, the Western world has a common culture (as we shall see, this would happen only once
again), and this culture is based on a mature and firmly
established worldview which has been developing for five
hundred years. Christians, scattered in widely dispersed set-
tlements within this immense empire, have to decide, at least
implicitly, what attitude to take toward this worldview.

It was more than just a matter of agreeing or disagreeing
with Plato, or any other particular thinker. What in those
days was called "philosophy" encompassed practically the
whole of systematic human knowledge. In part it was an issue
—one which Christians have had to face a number of times
since—of what attitude to take toward secular learning,
toward science. It was a question of the value of human
reasoning.

But there was more to it even than this. For many in the
Roman world, the great philosophical systems served virtually as religions, providing a moral code and even a kind of
salvation, in this life or the next, for those who followed it.
Were these systems of belief compatible with Christianity?
Was speculation based on reason alone necessarily a threat
to faith?

The first outstanding Christian thinkers were not professional philosophers or theologians. They were bishops,
priests, or simply articulate laymen who were concerned with
explaining and defending their faith. Out of their individual
efforts, a consensus would eventually emerge, a consensus of
enormous importance for the future not only of the church
but of Western culture as well. It was a process which literally

helped determine the way of thinking which we find so "natural" today.

One possibility, then as now, was to maintain that faith supercedes reason. Chief among those who championed this view was the Roman lawyer Quintus Septimus Florens Tertullianus, better known as Tertullian, the first major Christian thinker to write in Latin. Born around 160 in Carthage, in present-day Tunisia, the son of a Roman centurian, he was baptized in his late thirties and devoted his considerable intellectual and literary talents to the defense of Christianity. He had a remarkable gift for the well-turned phrase. "The blood of Christians is the seed of the Church" was one of his aphorisms. "It is certain because it is impossible" was another.

Like many others of his profession, past and present, Tertullian was not a particularly broadminded fellow. Once he had entered into combat he tended to see very little merit in the other side's position. With all the vehemence at his disposal, which was no small amount, he condemned pagan culture as pernicious and Greek philosophy as dangerous and foolish.

Jesus Christ was the only true philosopher, Tertullian maintained; others can only lead people astray from the truth he taught. Whatever of value might be found in the writings of the pagan Greeks had been stolen from the Hebrew scriptures. Had he done no more than rail against pagan philosophers, however, Tertullian would never have acquired a reputation as one of the leading theologians of the early church. In fact, he made some essential contributions to Christian doctrine.

He was the first one to use the term "Trinity" (one of Tertullian's typically clever word-plays, it is, of course, simply a variation of the word "unity"), and in his discussion of the Trinity he was the first writer to use the word "person" in its technical philosophical sense. His treatise on baptism was the first systematic work written on any of the sacraments before the Council of Nicaea, and many of the dogmas defined at Nicaea were expressed in formulas originally used by Tertullian. In opposition to the Docetists he insisted on the reality of Christ's human nature; and, in a characteristic but bizarre burst of overenthusiasm, he reinforced this contention by insisting that Jesus was physically ugly.

It is intriguing to speculate on what influence Tertullian's legal training and his uncompromising personality, appearing at a time when basic Christian attitudes were still being formed, may have had on the growth of the legalistic tradition in Christian thinking. The Gospels, after all, are not legalistic documents, and yet somehow that tradition appeared and flourished within Christianity.

Certainly Tertullian did not hinder this trend. His writings are filled with such legalistic concepts as debt, guilt, satisfaction, and compensation. He insisted that all women should be veiled. His puritanical leanings became more and more extreme as time went on, and before long—only about fifteen years after his baptism, in fact—he joined a heretical group which shared his rigorous views and never returned to orthodoxy.

Tertullian died in Carthage at an advanced age. He was one of the most compelling, if not always one of the most attractive, figures in early church history, and his influence on the development of Christian doctrine, for better or for worse, was enormous. So indispensible were his contributions that the church was forced to preserve his writings for its own use even after it had condemned him as a heretic—a case perhaps unique in history.

His views on the value of human reason may have been determined by his conception of the church as a small, elite, charismatic group, governed and inspired directly by the Holy Spirit, which must constantly guard against any possibility of contamination by pagan influences. Thus he taught that Christians must have as little contact with the Roman government as possible: they may not serve in the army or even teach in public schools. It was precisely this obsession with eliminating all traces of contagion which led to Tertullian's break with the church—he refused to accept the possibility that serious sin could be forgiven.

This same logic induced him to hold that wisdom imparted by the Holy Spirit made study of secular—that is to say, pagan—learning totally superfluous. Why should one read the Greek philosophers, when the Spirit communicates directly with the church through prophets and prophetesses? As he himself expressed it, "What has Athens to do with Jerusalem?"

Tertullian's hostility toward speculation by unaided reason and his insistence that all wisdom comes from revelation are attitudes which appeared very early in Christian history— there are traces of them, for example, as far back as St. Paul —and they are still held by some Christians today. They are unspoken presuppositions of fundamentalist religion. Had these views prevailed, the great Christian philosophical and theological systems would never have been developed—nor, perhaps, the great scientific systems.

But the possibility of a union of philosophical speculation with Christian revelation eventually won general acceptance. Of the many places in which this possibility was explored and tested, one was of paramount importance, the Egyptian city of Alexandria; and of the many who contributed to the development of this union, two men deserve particular attention.

Why Alexandria? In part, because all the necessary elements were there. As the intellectual center of the Hellenistic world, and as one of the great commercial crossroads of the

Mediterranean, Alexandria was a place where a wide variety of religious and philosophical beliefs—Greek, Roman, Jewish, Christian and oriental; speculative, scientific, magical and mystical—met and interacted.

Titus Flavius Clemens, Clement of Alexandria, who was born in Athens around 150, came to Egypt as an adult, was baptized, and taught for a number of years in Alexandria as a layman. He refused to accept the choice between an unthinking fundamentalism and esoteric speculation which abandoned the apostolic tradition.

At a time when pagan intellectuals were asking (and not for the last time) how any intelligent person could be a Christian, Clement provided the answer. In a sense, he played the same role for Christianity in the second-century Greek-speaking world that John Henry Newman did for Catholicism in nineteenth-century England: he made it intellectually respectable. He was the right person for the job, just as Newman was. Cultured, well-educated, an accepted member of the intelligentia, he had sought intellectual satisfaction in vain in the existing philosophical schools and finally found it in Christianity. He was living proof that such a thing was possible, and his audience respected him too much not to take him seriously.

To the charge that Christians wished to abandon the glorious heritage of Greece and Rome in favor of the inelegant and unsophisticated Hebrew scriptures, Clement replied that there is only one wisdom and one truth; it comes from God and is to be found everywhere, by Greek and Hebrew alike. Reason is humanity's greatest gift; and it tends to lead all sincere people, pagan or Christian, to God. There is no need, then, for Christianity to be hostile to pagan culture, only to the diabolical religious practices which many pagan writers themselves had deplored.

In response to the contention that Christianity violates

human dignity by demanding acceptance on faith of propositions which offend rationality, Clement developed an important (and controversial) explanation of religious faith. It is
not a mindless commitment, he said. It is an assent, an act of
the will, which is subsequently verified by experience. Since
there is only one truth, faith and reason cannot be contradictory; they must be complementary.

Reversing Tertullian's position, Clement taught that philosophy—that is, unaided human reason—is the teacher
which leads us to Christ. Philosophy prepares the pagan mind
to accept the message of Jesus just as the Mosaic law prepared the Jews. Furthermore, once we have accepted the
faith, human reason helps us to acquire a clearer understanding of its truth. "I believe in order that I might understand"
was Clement's motto. One who simply believes without making an effort to understand what he believes, he insisted, is
like a child in comparison to an adult.

Clement was eventually ordained, but was forced to flee
Alexandria in the persecution of 202 and died in Cappadocia
(in present-day Turkey) in 215. He was long considered a
saint in the Western church (his feast day was December 4);
but his name became associated with several heretical doctrines, and in 1586 he was dropped from the list of saints by
Pope Sixtus V.

Clement tried to do one thing and actually accomplished
something different—and something much more important.
He wanted to prove that Christianity was not a radical rejection of Greco-Roman culture (and in this he was correct, as
we are seeing); but in the process, and perhaps without realizing it, he developed the conception of faith and reason as two
valid and independent means of acccss to a single, indivisible
truth. It is a theory which we shall be meeting again.

Clement was succeeded as the leading teacher in Alexandria by one of his pupils, a man named Origen. Origenes

Adamantus was probably the most learned and influential teacher in the first four centuries of Christianity. Born in Alexandria around 185 ("Origenes" is the Greek form of an Egyptian name meaning "Child of Horus"), the son of a Christian martyr, Origen was in his teens when he began teaching philosophy and rhetoric, and he continued teaching in Alexandria for twenty-eight years.

Although perhaps a bit extreme in some respects—he is said to have castrated himself, for example, out of a desire to remain pure—Origen had none of Tertullian's obstinate closed-mindedness. He pursued learning wherever it was to be found, studying philosophy under such teachers as Ammonius Saccas, a fallen-away Christian who also taught the neo-Platonist Plotinus, and learning Hebrew in order to advance his scriptural research.

Origen's reputation for scholarship transcended both religious and geographic boundaries. His lectures in Alexandria attracted learned pagans as well as catechumens; and he accepted invitations to teach and debate in Rome, Arabia, Greece, Palestine, and Antioch. He was a spectacularly prolific writer, especially after a wealthy man he had converted to Christianity hired scribes to take shorthand from him; and he is credited with the authorship of over 800 separate works.

He made so many contributions to the interpretation of scripture that he has been called the founder of biblical theology. But he also insisted that God has written his truth in our hearts as well as in the bible.

As a result, Origen considered Christian faith to be not a static set of beliefs but a progressive ascent to God. The beginning of this ascent, and the only stage which most Christians ever achieve, is what might be called traditional faith—the beliefs of the masses, based on a literal interpretation of scripture. This is sufficient for salvation; but it is still inferior to Christian belief based on a foundation of philosophy, an assimilation of all human knowledge into a kind of Christian wisdom. Above both of these, however, he saw a mystical "perfected faith," a divine illumination made possible only by a grace which is given to very few.

While acknowledging that Christians are obliged to accept the teachings of the apostles, Origen insisted that they are otherwise free to speculate as their reason prompts them. Following his own suggestion, and building on the foundations Clement had established, he constructed the first complete Christian philosophico-theological system, of which the main features were the goodness of God, the freedom of the will, and the dignity of reason.

God, he taught, can be known only in a negative manner (that is, statements about what God is not—such as "incorporeal" and "unlimited"—are more accurate than statements about what God is). The created world is eternal, like the divine will which produced it, because it is impossible for God ever to be inactive.

Vehemently opposing the contention that salvation and damnation are predestined, Origen replied that human souls differ in goodness because of their behavior in a previous existence (this had its roots in Plato), but that because rationality implies freedom to choose, no one—not even Satan—is ever totally beyond redemption. Through a process of purification, all eventually will be reunited with God: the "restitution of all things" which is spoken of in Acts 3:21.

To think of damnation as eternal, Origen argued, would be to admit that Lucifer's rebellion had succeeded, that the devil had indeed been able to set up a permanent empire of evil in opposition to God's goodness. Besides, if God's mercy is truly infinite, how can it stop at the gates of hell? Are we more powerful than God, that our stubbornness can withstand his love for all eternity? Origen was repelled by the attitude of those Christians who found joy in the prospect of a salvation conceived in contrast to the eternal torment of others.

But at that point, the freedom which rationality implies begins to cut the other way. Even heaven is not necessarily absolute; and the souls of the blessed can fall from grace just as the rebellious angels did, suggesting that the whole process might repeat itself. A common feature of pagan philosophies was a cyclical theory of history based on necessity: Origen managed to develop a cyclical theory based on freedom.

Notice that none of these ideas is found in scripture, nor do they necessarily conflict with scripture. They simply constitute one of the rational forms in which the content of scripture can be explained. Scripture itself, Origen held, must sometimes be interpreted in an allegorical sense in order to capture its true meaning.

Even in that relatively tolerant era, however, the notion that the devil himself might be saved was more than some people could accept. The bishop of Alexandria initiated a formal condemnation of Origen, who was forced to flee to Palestine. He died in 254 at Tyre (in present-day Lebanon) during the persecution of Decius.

Many of his ideas, particularly on the nature of free will, had a great influence on later thinkers. More important than this, however, was the example given by him and by Clement —and by those whom they trained—that the human reason is not only not the enemy of Christian faith but is actually essential for its full understanding and development.

It seems safe to say that none of the participants in this long series of debates on how to express the content of Christianity could have realized the full implications of the issues they were discussing, and no formal vote on the validity of philosophical speculation was ever taken.

As time went on, however, a consensus developed: the le-

gitimacy of reason and speculation was implicitly acknowledged simply because its advocates appealed so irresistibly to
that part of human nature that wants to understand things.

It helped, probably, that church authorities had not yet
acquired the apparatus to impose a more fundamentalist position. It also helped that most of the disputants themselves
were highly educated people, thoroughly steeped in the tradition of intellectual discourse. It is difficult for a rational
person, even one like Tertullian, to construct a rational argument against rationality; and people like Clement and Origen
asked questions and proposed answers which forced even
those who disagreed with them about the proper place of
unaided reason to respond with reasoned arguments.

The effects of this outcome are almost incalculable. It
freed Christianity from a literal and sterile fundamentalist
approach to scripture. It permitted the development of
Christian philosophy and theology as we understand them today. It helped to keep Western culture, at a critical stage in its
history, from becoming actively hostile to science and learning. It made it possible for the church, for more than a
thousand years, to attract the best minds in Europe into its
service.

At the same time, it is also true that as the church turned
toward the intellectual it tended to turn away from the emotional and the mystical; the more avidly it pursued abstract
truth, the less it tended to value individual concrete experience. Emphasis gradually shifted from the God of
Abraham and Isaac to the God of the philosophers, as
Kierkegaard once put it—from a loving, creating Father to an
unmoved mover and an uncaused cause.

It must be admitted that this union between faith and
reason of its very nature has always been an uneasy one. The
idea that there are two valid sources of knowledge, reason
and faith, rather than just one, is perhaps the single most

volatile idea in our intellectual heritage. Certainly it has been at the root of some of the most fundamental conflicts in Western culture. It is the ideological foundation, for example, for the separation of church and state. It provided the rationale for insisting on the freedom of scientific inquiry. We shall be examining some of the reasons that these issues came to be phrased in the way that we hear them discussed today.

By the middle of the third century, the legitimacy of attempting a rational exposition of the content of the Christian faith had been generally accepted, at least in principle; and apologists, polemicists, and writers of various descriptions were exploring and expounding—in an era without lists of forbidden books—every facet of Christian belief.

But although they prepared the way, none of them was able to develop a systematic exposition of the Christian worldview in a manner to rival the classical worldviews of paganism. This would require time—until the new faith had firmly established itself and a specifically Christian system of values had begun to develop—and it would require an absolutely first-rate philosophic and literary genius.

At the end of the fourth century, at the very moment when the supposedly imperishable Roman Empire was collapsing before the onrushing barbarians, such a person appeared. He was born in the African province of Numidia, and his name was Augustine.

Chapter 2
PLATO AND AUGUSTINE

SOME of the most commonplace things are devilishly difficult to explain. One of these is the phenomenon of change. Take the case of a ball dropped off the roof of a tall building. At every given moment as the ball falls it occupies a certain space. But whenever it occupies a certain space, it must be at rest. And if at every given moment it is at rest, how does it ever get from the top of the building to the ground? It seems to be true that the ball is moving and also true that it is not moving, and yet these are contradictory.

A similar problem exists with all other forms of change. Consider the page these words are printed on, for example. The ink is fading before your eyes—fading very slowly, it is true, but fading nonetheless. The paper is slowly turning yellow and disintegrating. If you are sitting in a room, your chair is slowly collapsing and the walls are slowly falling down. And yet it is also true that each of these things seems to have a stability, a permanence. This is true of everything in the world. On the one hand it is true that everything changes; on the other hand it is true that everything stays the same. How can this paradox be resolved? And how can any of our statements ever be true if the objects we are speaking about are changing even as we speak?

Understanding and explaining this problem of change was perhaps the single biggest challenge for the pre-Christian Greek philosophers. Eventually it became clear that in every case of change there is an element which remains the same (it is the same object after the change as before) and an element which alters. But what are these two elements, and what is the relation between them?

The first one to provide a really coherent answer to this

question was Plato, and he used his answer to construct a complete worldview, a worldview which is important for our purposes because it had the most profound impact imaginable on the development of Christian thought. Plato found the key to his answer in mathematics.

Take out a sheet of paper and draw five circles on it. Now look at them carefully. Is any of the five really a circle? That is, does any of them have all points on its circumference an absolutely equal distance from the center?

Try again if you wish—trace around the edge of a coin, perhaps, or use a drawing compass—but the fact is that you can never draw a real circle, one that really fits the definition, and neither can anyone else. If you do not believe this, take the most perfect-looking circle you can find and look at it under a magnifying glass or a microscope.

As a matter of fact, neither you nor I nor anyone else has ever seen a real circle. No saucer, no coin, no manhole cover has all points on its circumference absolutely equidistant from the center. Why is this? Simply because they are physical, and no physical object can ever be made absolutely straight, or absolutely round, or absolutely flat. It just cannot be done.

But look again at your sheet of paper. You can see that some of those figures come closer to being a perfect circle than others do. And you could not see that unless you knew what a perfect circle is. The geometric circle which no one has ever seen is more real than the markings on your paper, because it sets the standard against which they are judged. It is the model which they are, in a way, trying to imitate, some more successfully than others.

This is really quite remarkable, if you stop to think about it. What we are saying is that an idea—which is what our geometric circle really is—has more reality than any physical representation of it. We are saying that physical things, or some of them at least, are only imperfect imitations of non-physical ones.

Plato went on to extend this line of reasoning to the entire physical world. He argued that there must be some kind of permanent realities underlying the multiplicity of changing objects in the physical world in the same way that a geometric circle underlies the markings on your page; otherwise we would not be justified in calling these objects by the same name.

What is it, for example, that a sunset, a piece of music, and a fashion model have in common which allows us to call all of them "beautiful?" Whatever it is, each of these examples has some of it, but none has it all. It is beauty which makes a flower beautiful, to the extent that the flower possesses it; and beauty will continue to exist after the flower has crumbled into dust, just as the geometric circle existed before you drew on your sheet of paper and will continue to exist even after your paper disintegrates. So the existence of beauty must be separate from the existence of any physical object.

There must be one of these permanent, immaterial objects for each class of things which are called by a common name, according to Plato, each one more real than the physical objects which strive to imitate it. In fact, this physical world of our everyday experience is but a pale, imperfect, temporary reflection of the perfect and permanent world which these immaterial objects make up. This world is like a shadow compared with that other one, for material things are always less perfect and less real than the immaterial things which they imitate.

But if we have never seen a geometric circle, or pure beauty itself, how do we know what they are? How are we able to judge that one of its reflections is more accurate than another? Because, says Plato, we saw these perfect models in a previous life. Or, more accurately, our spirit, or soul, existed in that other world and saw those perfect objects before we were born. When we see a physical object, then, it reminds our spirit of the immaterial model which it resembles.

What we think of as knowledge is not really new information but a remembrance of what we experienced before birth. Learning is not a process of transferring knowledge from one person to another but a process whereby one person draws out from another person knowledge which that person already possesses but has difficulty in recollecting without assistance. (Our word "education" recalls this concept of Plato: it comes from a Latin word meaning "to lead out.")

For Plato, this other world, immaterial and perfect, is our soul's natural home, the place to which it longs to return. In the physical world the soul is in a truly wretched state, trapped inside a body much less perfect than it is, a body whose needs and tendencies are the exact opposite of its own. In fact what you really are is one of these immaterial souls, trapped for a time within the body of an animal. The effect would be about the same as if your brain, with all your intelligence, sensibilities and aspirations, were transplanted inside the body of a jackal or a pig, and you were forced to eat offal and filth and live like a brute inside that body until finally death released you.

Human life is an unmitigated calamity for the soul, says Plato; and death should be the happiest moment of our lives, since it will free us from an unnatural union with the body which draws us downward toward brutish, sensual pleasures and will allow us to escape back to that perfect and unchanging world we originally came from. In the meantime, we should live as far removed as possible from the body and its desires. Otherwise, when death finally releases us, our spirit may find itself too much attracted by physical pleasures to leave this world and achieve its true destiny.

The idea that there is an unchanging world, more perfect

than this physical one, which is our eternal destination; that physical desires are a hindrance to one's perfection; that there is a rational soul whose existence is independent of the body's; that God must be unchanging because change implies imperfection—these were not Christian inventions. They are all found in Plato, and were familiar to every educated person in Europe long before Jesus was born.

It would have been as difficult for any philosopher or theologian of the early Christian era not to be influenced by these ideas as it would be for a modern physicist not to be influenced by Newton. But the way in which these ideas became an explicit part of the Christian worldview requires some explanation. Part of what happened was determined by sheer chance, because there was another, a competing worldview— that of Aristotle—which was lost to Europe for a thousand years through a bizarre set of circumstances, as we shall see later on, leaving Plato's view more or less unchallenged until the twelfth century. But another part of the story involves one of the most interesting and most influential thinkers in European history.

No one since St. Paul has made anywhere near as much impact on the development of Christian doctrine as St. Augustine. For more than half of the time span between the era of Jesus and our own, his has been the dominant voice— and much of the remaining period occurred before his birth. Catholicism and Protestantism alike, until relatively recently, have drawn their inspiration mainly from the scriptures and from him.

Part of the reason for his influence is the fact that he lived during the period when Christianity was developing from a persecuted sect into the dominant force, both culturally and politically, in Europe. The backdrop to this development, and one of the factors accelerating it, was nothing less than the end of a world: the destruction of the Roman Empire.

But a more important reason for Augustine's influence is that he was a truly extraordinary person, a man of incomparable natural gifts, charismatic personality, and inexhaustible energy and determination. And then, of course, he was also a saint.

Aurelius Augustinus was born in the village of Tagaste, in present-day Algeria, on November 13, 354, the oldest of three children. His father, who owned a small amount of land and a number of slaves, was a member of the village council.

Even the circumstances of Augustine's birth seem to symbolize the role he would play as the key figure in the transition between a world dominated by pagan Rome and one dominated by the Christian church. He was born forty-one years after the Edict of Milan had given Christianity legal status, but eight years before the last great wave of persecutions, that of Julian the Apostate. Monica, his mother, was Christian; his father, Patricius, was a pagan. As a child he spoke both Latin and the native language of the area, Punic (a dialect of Phonecian).

More is known about the life of Augustine than about the life of any other early Christian writer, primarily because in the midst of an incredibly active career he somehow found the time to write his life story, the *Confessions,* thereby inventing the autobiography as a literary form. It was quite a life. Augustine was Thomas Merton, Thomas More, and Thomas Aquinas all rolled into one, with touches of Thomas Hobbes and Thomas Jefferson thrown in.

As a boy, Augustine was the kind of student that infuriates teachers and parents alike: highly intelligent, but willing to study only what interested him; articulate and a natural leader, but more concerned with the playing fields than the classroom; a tireless worker, but strong-willed and hard to motivate—the kind of son about whom hundreds of generations of mothers and fathers have said in anguished tones,

"Now if that boy would only apply himself . . . . "

But he had one outstanding talent. He was good with words, so good that a wealthy neighbor gave his family money to send him for advanced studies in Carthage, a major Mediterranean city. Free now to concentrate on the field of his choice, rhetoric, he excelled at his studies and began to prepare for a teaching career. He began living with a woman who would remain his mistress for ten years; soon she gave birth to a son whom he named Adeodatus (literally, "Gift of God," a Latin translation of the Punic name Iatanbaal, "Gift of Baal").

It was also in Carthage that Augustine encountered the Manichaeans, a sect of Eastern origin which claimed to possess rational answers to questions for which Christianity could offer only contradictory formulas and a vague reference to mysteries. Chief among these questions was the metaphysical problem of evil. Christianity holds that everything that exists was created by God, and that everything created by God is good. But without any question there is evil in the world. Now either God is the creator of evil, or else God is not the creator of all things. In either case, Christianity is wrong. Also, if God is almighty and all good, as the Christians claim, why does he permit evil to exist?

For their part, the Manichaeans had a seemingly straightforward answer: there are two supreme beings—one the creator of good and the other of evil—which are engaged in a constant struggle. The material world and human life and history are reflections of that struggle. This was the best answer to the problem Augustine had yet heard; he accepted it and persuaded a number of his friends to accept it as well.

After finishing his studies Augustine began teaching, first in Tagaste and then at Carthage, and launched his literary career by winning a prize for a dramatic work. In 383 he decided that he needed a larger stage to display his talents and moved to Rome, where he discovered, too late, that Roman students had a disconcerting habit of cancelling their courses just before the tuition payment was due. Not long afterward, he interviewed for and received a teaching position in Milan.

He was about thirty when he settled in Milan with his mistress and son. His mother, now a widow, arrived soon afterward and moved in with them. Before long she began insisting that Augustine turn the mother of his son out of his house and marry a respectable girl. Finally, reluctantly, he sent the woman back to Carthage, keeping Adcodatus with him. He also made arrangements to marry; but, facing the prospect of a long engagement, he soon found another mistress to tide him over until the wedding. It was during this period that he uttered one of the most famous of all prayers: "Lord, make me pure; but not yet."

Meanwhile he was beginning to fall under the influence of St. Ambrose, Bishop of Milan, who was able to convince him that the tenets of Christianity were not as outlandish as the Manichaeans had made them out to be. At the same time, his philosophical investigations led him to read the works of the neoplatonic writer Plotinus. This introduced him to the concept of God as a spiritual substance (Manichaeanism was a thoroughly materialistic religion) and to the idea of evil as a privation, an absence of good—not something with a positive existence which needs a creative force to explain it.

The combination of these influences gradually made Augustine intellectually receptive to orthodox teachings. But no true religious conversion was ever totally intellectual: an essential element was still missing. He would later devote a major portion of his *Confessions* to this period, painting in the most intimate detail a classic portrait of a soul in torment. He wanted to believe, for his mind was already convinced of the truth; but, unwilling to renounce the allure of sensual pleasures, he was unable to make the act of the will, the leap and surrender of faith, to accept it emotionally. He was like a man who knows that he desperately needs love, but is unable to make the simple act of acknowledging his need and accepting it.

At last, in the midst of an intense spiritual and emotional struggle in the garden of his house in the summer of 386, Augustine heard a child's voice chanting over and over, "Take and read." Interpreting this as an omen, he opened a copy of the Bible and read the first verse his eyes fell upon: "Let us behave properly as in the day, not in carousing and drunkenness, not in sexual promiscuity and sensuality, not in strife and jealousy. But put on the Lord Jesus Christ, and make no provision for the flesh in regard to its lusts" (Romans 13:13-14).

This was the same conclusion his intellect already had reached. Before he finished reading the verse all his doubts and reservations had melted away, and he felt the peace and certainty he had been seeking so long. He was baptized, along with his teenage son, by St. Ambrose on Holy Saturday, 387.

About a year later Augustine returned to Tagaste and established a monastic community. Adeodatus became a member, but he died about a year later. Some two years after his death, Augustine was ordained a priest and founded another monastary, this one at Hippo (the modern Algerian city of Bône), a seaport about 150 miles from Carthage. This community was destined to become a virtual seminary for northern Africa: ten future bishops were trained there and countless priests, many of whom founded similar communities. Had Augustine done nothing else in his life, he would have won a place in history as one of the founders of monasticism in the Western church.

In 395 he was consecrated a bishop. But writings of every variety continued to stream from his pen, as they would for the rest of his life: scriptural commentaries (Augustine discussed the finer points of biblical interpretation with St. Jerome, who was not always receptive to his views), polemics on various heresies, philosophical treatises, expositions of systematic theology, dissertations on the sacraments—more than two hundred books in all. Among the most important of these writings were a fifteen-volume work on the Trinity, a twelve-volume literal commentary on Genesis, and a thirty-three volume attack on Manichaeanism.

Augustine devoted special attention to attacking the doctrines of the Pelagians, a group which denied that the effects of original sin are totally corrupting and held that a person can gain salvation through his or her own efforts. He was so determined to refute this view, in fact, that some of his more extreme statements caused acute embarrassment to the Catholic Church centuries later: Luther contended that Augustine believed in salvation through faith alone; Calvin quoted him in support of predestination; and the founder of the seventeenth century Jansenist heresy entitled his major theological work *Augustinus* in his honor. In the year 400 Augustine published his *Confessions*.

He also spent twenty years attacking the Donatists, followers of an African bishop who insisted that no one who had committed a serious sin could ever validly administer the sacraments. Eventually this movement grew into a full-fledged schismatic church, which in many places—including Hippo—gained the allegiance of the majority of Christians. The position of Donatus really amounted to saying that a sacrament is not efficacious if the person who administers it is unworthy. In refuting this claim, Augustine developed some of the key concepts of sacramental theology, particularly the idea that since grace is caused by God and not by humans, the effects of a sacrament are transmitted by the very act of administering it, regardless of the personal merits of the minister. *ex opere operato*

In the midst of these controversies, he continued to carry out the normal administrative and pastoral duties of a bishop, plus taking a leading part in church councils and settling ecclesiastical disputes far from his own diocese. He preached on Sundays and feast days, while scribes took down his words (about five hundred of these sermons still exist); and he maintained an active correspondence. People with disputes brought them to him to settle; the sick, the poor, the disconsolate came to him for help.

Meanwhile the disintegration of the Roman Empire continued at an ever-quickening pace. In 410 a Visigoth army captured Rome itself. Partly to refute the accusation that this disaster was a punishment inflicted by the pagan gods because of the spread of Christianity, and partly as a means of developing his own Christian worldview in its fullest scope, Augustine began writing his greatest masterpiece, *The City of God*. It took him thirteen years to complete this work, which was destined to become the theoretical blueprint for the emerging political order that would arise from the ruins of the Roman world.

The City of God is basically an exposition of human history from the time of Adam and Eve. Augustine saw this history as a conflict between the Divine City (those who live according to the laws of God) and the Human City (those ruled by self-love and self-will). Although he did not explicitly make the comparison, many of his readers in subsequent years identified the Divine City with the church and the Human City with the state. This had the extremely important consequence of justifying—of almost requiring—the raising of the church to a position of superiority over the state.

Near the end of his life, Augustine wrote an unusual book called *Retractions,* a listing of his written works along with the errors and shortcomings he could see in each of them from the perspective of greater age and experience. It was the act of a faithful servant giving a final accounting of his stewardship.

In 430 an army of Vandals, one of the barbarian tribes which were carving out for themselves whole sections of the collapsing Roman Empire, laid seige to Hippo. Shortly before they captured the city, Augustine died, at the age of seventy-five. He had written no will, for he left no material possessions.

Chapter 3
AUGUSTINE

ALTHOUGH different people want many different things for many different reasons, there is only one thing that everyone wants for its own sake and that is happiness. To ask a person why he or she wants wealth or fame or anything else is a meaningful question, but to ask why a person wants to be happy makes no sense. We do not want happiness for any reason; we want it for itself.

The problem, of course, is how to find happiness, and why we keep doing so many things that make us unhappy. From his answers to these two questions, St. Augustine formed the core of his entire philosophy.

The principal reason for our unhappiness, he says, stems from the fact that we are built in such a way that we want things to last—we yearn for the security of permanence and stability—and we cannot be satisfied with anything which does not last.

No one is content with being only partly happy, and happiness which we know must end is always less than complete. Our most fervent wish in the moments of our greatest joy is that the joy would last forever. And this desire, which sometimes approaches desperation, leads us to seek lasting joy in transient objects.

In his *Confessions,* Augustine analyzes the bitterness of his grief at the death of a close friend in a remarkable figure of speech: he had poured out his soul, he wrote, like water on sand, by loving a mortal being as though he were immortal. The soul desires a resting place and cannot find one, because it seeks its rest in things which pass away.

This is the primary reason for the basic frustration we all experience: nothing in the world can give us what we want most, permanent happiness, because nothing in the world is permanent. Life cannot satisfy our greatest need and most powerful desire, and we know it. Are we, then, condemned to a warped, frustrated existence? Or is there a way out of this dilemma?

From the fact that nothing in this world can satisfy us, Augustine drew the conclusion that it is not this world that we were made for. Our problem is that we keep trying to make ourselves believe that it is.

What can make us happy? In the final analysis, only God can. As rational beings we desire knowledge, we seek to understand things; and we can be content with nothing less than the answer to all questions and the explanation of all things, which is God. At the same time, as we have seen, perfect happiness requires a permanence, and only God will endure forever. Just as the mind seeks a permanent object of knowledge, such as the ideal Forms of Plato, so the heart seeks a permanent object of desire. Or, as Augustine put it, our hearts were made for God, and they are restless until they rest in Him.

The basic choice we face in life is between God and creatures, between what will satisfy our deepest needs completely and what will give only a temporary illusion of satisfaction. This is not, however, a choice between good and evil, as the Manichaeans taught, but a choice between a greater good and lesser goods.

To understand Augustine's thinking here we have to examine the concept of a hierarchy of being, an idea he took from the neoplatonists. The foundation of this position is the belief that not everything is equally real, because not all things are totally and completely what they are. This goes back to the phenomenon of change. For something to change means for it to become other than it is. But this is possible only for something which is not completely identical to itself.

If something were totally and entirely identical to itself, it would have a kind of reality which a changeable thing does not have. And this is true, in the final analysis, only of God. Only God never changes, cannot change—a concept, by the way, which causes a number of problems when one attempts to explain creation. Only God possesses the fullness of being; and creatures possess more or less of it, depending on whether they are more or less changeable. And since being is a perfection—it is better to exist than not to exist—this hierarchy of being is also a hierarchy of goodness. Complete evil would be complete nonbeing.

To choose a creature (even ourselves) over God, then, is to reject the fullness of goodness and reality in favor of something less real and less good. This is objectively wrong—wrong not because it goes contrary to a law or a commandment but because it offends the very order or nature itself.

And Augustine felt that this is precisely what occurs every time we take pleasure in a creature, whatever it be, for its own sake. Thus he writes in *Confessions* that as a schoolboy he sinned by studying literature because he enjoyed it, rather than concentrating on subjects which were more useful.

Why is this? Because to derive pleasure from a creature in its own right rather than from that creature's usefulness in leading us to God is to treat the creature as an end in itself, whereas in fact only God is an end in himself. In that sense it is to treat the creature as though it were God. It is almost a form of idolatry. The fact that the wrong is objective explains how a child, even an infant, can sin—in Augustine's sense of the word.

This theory found its most striking application, and had perhaps most far-reaching effects, in the area of sexual morality. In *The City of God*, Augustine describes sex as he believed it was intended to be and as every virtuous person would still prefer to have it: without physical excitement or mental distraction. The description is quite specific but thoroughly businesslike, more "Platonic" by far than Plato himself (Book XIV, Chapter 26, if you care to look it up). Even a husband and wife, in his opinion, commit sin—in Augustine's sense of the term—if they have sexual relations for pleasure rather than for the purpose of producing children, or even if they do it for the proper reason and enjoy it in the process. To understand this in context, one should remember that he also wrote that someone listening to vespers sins if he takes more pleasure in the sound of the music than in the meaning of the words. The "sin" in both cases is the same—taking pleasure from a creature rather than solely from God.

too much!

Lust, or inordinate desire, leads to wrongful habit, which eventually controls our minds even against our will. But the prisoner of habit is still responsible for the consequences of his habit, because the habit was voluntarily adopted.

Such a choice is not natural to us, since we are naturally attracted to goodness, and more attracted to greater goodness than to lesser goodness. It is possible only if we lie to ourselves, only if we make believe that what we know not to be true really is true. For Augustine, every sin is essentially an act of self-deceit.

This was one reason why he believed that there is no such thing as a wrong which does no harm: at the very least, it harms the person who does it, since it violates his or her own dignity as a rational being. By the same reasoning, he held that obedience, far from being a humiliating subservience, is actually the characteristic virtue of a rational person. Properly understood, it is nothing more than an acknowledgement of reality.

But even this lying to ourselves is difficult to explain, since our minds desire truth, not error. Why would we want to deceive ourselves? Why would we prefer something which

will make us less happy to that which alone can make us completely happy? Who would prefer an illusion to the reality?

The explanation, says Augustine, is that while it is true that
the mind will always tend toward truth when undistracted,
things which cannot satisfy us—creatures—make a stronger
impression on us than God. By yielding to pleasures which
strongly appeal to us at the moment, we keep ourselves from
obtaining what we really want most.

Anyone who has ever been interested in dieting—or simply
in good nutrition—should find no difficulty in understanding
what Augustine is saying here. No one would really rather be
ill than well, yet most of us eat and drink things that are not
good for us, and do so to excess, because at the moment they
appeal to us more strongly than the idea of health. By eating
and drinking things that taste good, we prevent ourselves
from maintaining good health. The taste and the health are
both good, but the first is a lesser good compared to the
second.

Augustine's meaning is that we need to exercise the same
discipline in the moral order that a dieter uses in the physical
order, and for an analogous reason: valuing creatures for the
pleasure they give us rather than for how they relate to our
final happiness is like valuing foods on the basis of their taste
rather than on the basis of their effect on our bodies.

If we were really as completely rational as Plato had believed, of course, we would naturally do the right and
reasonable thing and choose greater goods over lesser ones.
But Augustine did not share Plato's conviction that we automatically accept and act on the truth once we see it clearly.
On the contrary, he believed that we are quite capable of
analyzing a situation logically, seeing all the pros and cons
clearly, determining that alternative A is much more to our
advantage than alternative B, and yet choosing alternative B
anyway.

If Augustine's basic view of the world could be expressed in two words, those words would be "love" and "sin." These concepts sometimes led to conflicting conclusions, particularly in his ethical theory.

"Love" is a word notorious for meaning different things to different people. The Latin term which Augustine used was *diligere,* which comes from the same root as our word "election." It literally means to choose out, to pick something over something else. Augustine was not speaking of an emotion, but of the act by which we commit ourselves to one thing rather than to other things. It is this act of choosing, of loving, he says,—and not an act of knowing—which determines whether or not we achieve happiness.

Not only did Augustine use his conception of love to understand and explain individual behavior, but he expanded it into a whole theory of history. A society, for him, is basically a group of persons who agree about the things which they love. This object of love can either be God, or something else. In *The City of God* he describes the development of two societies, one springing from self-love and the other based on the love of God. In the first, people rule over other people, driven on by a desire for domination; in the second, God rules, and people serve one another. Since self-love, as we have seen, is based on a lie, on self-deception, there can be no justice in the first kind of society—only brute force and exploitation. Ignatius Loyola used the same basic idea a thousand years later in his *Spiritual Exercises,* in what he called the "Meditation on the Two Loves."

So certain was Augustine that well-founded love determines how a person lives that he did not hesitate to offer as a rule for moral guidance the famous phrase *"Dilige et quod vis fac,"* which might be loosely translated as "Once your love is properly placed, do as you see fit."

This formula, obviously, was not legalistic: it is an invitation to a total personal commitment, not a list of rules. But at the same time, Augustine was also convinced that we are incapable of placing our love properly through our own efforts, and thus that rules are absolutely essential in practice.

Sometime during his seventeenth year, Augustine and some of friends amused themselves with a typical boyhood prank: they stole some pears from a neighbor's tree. None of his friends, in all likelihood, ever thought about the episode again. But Augustine did, many times, and he recounts the story at great length in *Confessions*. He saw in this incident something which Plato (and most modern criminologists) could not accept. He saw a completely motiveless crime.

As Augustine tells the story, he and his companions decided one day to take the fruit even though they already had all the pears they could eat and ended up by throwing what they had stolen to the pigs. What fascinated—and repelled— him was the realization that they had not committed the theft for the sake of the pears; they had done it simply because it was wrong, for the sheer joy of doing evil.

But why would anyone want to do evil for its own sake? For Plato, such a thing would be a contradiction and therefore impossible; for evil harms the one who performs it, and no one would deliberately do something to harm himself or herself. Augustine also considered it a contradiction, but quite possible. Experience shows it to be possible.

The reason one takes joy in doing an evil deed just because it is evil, he says, is that it is an act of rebellion. It is a way of playing God, of pretending to be subject to no restrictions and thus justified in imposing one's will on others. This desire to be like God was, of course, the sin of Adam. It is, literally, the original sin, the sin of self-deceit.

For Plato, what we call evil was an intellectual mistake. Since he could argue logically that no one would choose evil knowingly, he concluded that evil is the same as ignorance and therefore not blameworthy, even if regrettable. You do evil because you do not know better. Augustine insisted that you *do* know better—but you choose not to act better. The difference between the two is crucial. If someone does wrong out of ignorance, then—as Socrates argued at his trial—he should be instructed, not punished. But if the wrong is done deliberately, then we are subject to punishment.

Adam's sin of disobedience had as its consequence that his body no longer obeyed his will, a consequence that has been passed on to each of us at birth like a genetic defect and which results in a perversity of the will, a tendency toward evil for its own sake. Augustine says explicitly that no human being has ever been born who was less a sinner than Adam and Eve.

This perversity Augustine thought he could detect even in *dark,* the newly born. Even a nursing child, he says, with plenty of *views!* milk for itself, will become angry if another child shares the same milk. There is no such thing as youthful innocence; there is only physical inability to carry out the evil intentions.

Perversity of the will, the effect of original sin, cannot be changed or corrected. All we can do is trust that God will give us the strength to overcome it, for we cannot do so by ourselves. This help is absolutely necessary for our salvation, and yet we cannot attain it by our own efforts. In a similar fashion, we might say that an alcoholic will always be an alcoholic; but if he admits his weakness and seeks help he may find the strength to stop drinking, even though he might not be able to do so without assistance. Just as we cannot maintain ourselves in existence without external nourishment, Augustine wrote, even though we are able to end our lives without assistance, so we can fall from grace by our own power but need God's help to stay there.

This position obviously calls into question the freedom of the will, and it was precisely on this point that Augustine took issue with Pelagius.

Augustine contended that, as a result of Adam's sin, the soul is totally incapable of making even the most tentative approach to God unless it has received a divine grace; that this grace is made available only to a limited number of people; and that, as a consequence, the others are irrevocably predestined to damnation in spite of any efforts they might make to lead virtuous lives. If this grace is received, on the other hand, it cannot be resisted and invariably produces its redemptive effects on the soul—although it does not destroy human freedom because the acts of the will which it elicits are performed with our consent.

Pelagius attacked all four of these positions. He insisted, in particular, that God never commands us to do the impossible, and therefore that everyone is capable of seeking salvation through his or her own efforts. To say that sin has become inseparable from human nature, so that it is shared even by infants, seemed to him to imply that God produced evil creatures or else that the devil had a hand in making us. And he was totally repelled by the notion that some people are never given a chance to be saved. (On this last point, at least, the church eventually decided that Augustine had been mistaken.)

But Augustine, who had based many of his views on sin and grace on an analysis of his own experience, was totally unmoved by these arguments. He saw them, in fact, as a denial of and a rebellion against God's omnipotence; and through the force of his reputation and his eloquence he eventually succeeded in having Pelagianism condemned. Furthermore, since he was convinced that nothing but fear can overcome people's inborn desire to sin for its own sake, he

finally concluded that punishment is a necessary means to
moral goodness.

In the end, it seems, Augustine's belief in the power of sin
proved stronger than his belief in the power of love.

Someone once wrote that Plato was responsible for both
the best and the worst elements of Western culture. One
could reasonably argue that Augustine had a similar effect on
Christian culture.

To unite Christianity, as Augustine did, with an other-
worldly philosophy such as Platonism—one which considers
the physical world and what takes place in it as far less real
and less important than an eternal and perfect world for
which our souls are destined—necessarily increased Christianity's concern with the afterlife and diminished its interest
in this life. If this world is but a shadow of a higher reality, as
Plato claimed, what does it matter what happens here?

There are benefits, no doubt, in lifting people's minds and
hearts up from the pains and frustrations of mortal existence
to the promise of something better to come; and this has been
the inspiration of some of our greatest literature and art. But
the price that had to be paid for this in the case of Christianity was a lessening of the urgency people have felt about such
things as social justice and human suffering.

The whole orientation of Christianity, its basic attitude
toward life in this world, would have been profoundly different had Augustine been, let us say, an existentialist rather
than a Platonist. But of course it would have been as impossible for Augustine to have been an existentialist as for Galileo
to have been a nuclear physicist: in both cases, the necessary
ideas simply didn't yet exist.

Another characteristic of Platonism was its sense of certainty, its confidence in knowing and possessing the absolute

and unchanging objective truth. The introduction of this element into Christian thought encouraged the construction of
impressive philosophical and theological systems, but it also
encouraged attitudes of intolerance and closed-mindedness.
When the truth is already known, dissent can only lead to
error; why tolerate it? It was Plato himself who pointed out
that censorship of art and music as well as of ideas was a
logical implication of his position. It did not take the church
long to decide that the same logic applied to its own doctrines. Augustine's concept of the City of God, a community
of true believers set off from and opposed to all others—if
not actually besieged by them—did nothing to lessen this
tendency. And it was he who wrote the first Christian treatise
in favor of using torture and repression to fight heresy.

There are passages in his writings where a sense of serenity
in the possession of truth and salvation leads to conclusions
which seem to fly in the face of common sense and even of
common decency. In the *City of God,* for example, he ad-
dresses the question of why, if death is the punishment for
Adam's sin and if baptism removes the effects of this sin, it
still happens that baptized persons die. He answers that if
people did not die even after baptism, faith would be weakened—that is, since people could see the effects of the sacrament with their own eyes, they would no longer need to rely
so completely on the virtue of faith. Furthermore, if baptism
removed the penalty of death, the martyrs would not have
enjoyed the glory of suffering death for Christ's sake. Also,
everyone would have demanded to be baptized if the sacrament prevented death. Why this would have been a bad thing
he does not say.

Augustine's adoption of the Platonic worldview, combined
with the lingering effects of his years as a follower of
Manichaeanism, resulted in a remarkably negative attitude
toward the human body in general and sex in particular.

(Since the Manichaeans believed that matter was evil, it followed quite logically that they disapproved of bringing new matter into the world, and therefore of the birth of children, and therefore of the generative act.)

The result was a tradition of guilt, repression, shame, and frustration which was directly opposed to the explicit teaching of scripture and of Augustine himself that the body and all of its functions are gifts of God and good in themselves. It is true that much of this came from later commentators rather than from Augustine's own words, but it is also true that these commentators found in his works an abundance of material they could use to support their own views.

Augustine's teaching that the primary purpose of sexual relations is the procreation of children—a view which has become the foundation of the church's position on birth control—is so familiar to us now that it comes as something of a shock to realize that other fathers of the church held that the primary purpose of sex is to express the love between husband and wife. Had that second view prevailed, one of the most difficult and painful issues to confront the church in this century—and perhaps in its entire history—might never have arisen. It was primarily the immense prestige of Augustine which pushed these other views far into the background, with consequences which continue to affect millions of people in a most intimate manner.

We have already talked about a number of reasons for the unparalleled influence of Augustine's teachings. One additional element contributing to that influence was the fact that the normal processes of historical development were shattered after his death. Under ordinary conditions, commentators would have criticized his work, followers would have developed and modified it, and rivals would have formulated alternatives to his positions; all of this would have tended to soften the impact of his ideas. The disintegration of cultural life which followed the fall of Rome prevented that.

One of the main reasons that Augustine had such enormous influence on succeeding generations is that circumstances did not permit the appearance of any thinker capable
of challenging his views for a long, long time.

Chapter 4
ANSELM AND ABELARD

TRY to imagine that the United States has been overrun and occupied, not by Russians or Chinese but by roving armies of Indians drifting northward from the jungles of the Amazon.

The conquerors take what they want from the defenseless civilian population—food, money, sex, or anything else that strikes their fancy—and destroy whatever displeases them. Then they move on to repeat the process somewhere else.

We try to resume our normal patterns of living, but with our army scattered, our leaders dead, and our police and other social services in disarray, the fabric of civilized life slowly begins to disintegrate. Five or ten years later a new army overwhelms us, then a third and a fourth. Eventually the newcomers find land and women that please them, and the great armies melt away. The invaders intermarry with the conquered population, forgetting their own language and customs and adopting ours.

By the time the killing and looting have stopped and a primitive kind of order is restored, it is too late to repair the damage. Too much has been destroyed, too many leaders and technical experts killed, too many skills lost. People believe the end of the world is coming, and wait apathetically for death.

There is no government, for our own system has collapsed and the invaders are not interested in establishing a new one. The networks of communication and transportation that supported our way of life have been smashed beyond repair. Our cars, trucks, trains and airplanes become useless, and the road system falls into ruins.

There is no way to transport food into the populated areas, so many of the people in our cities starve to death, and most

of the others flee into the countryside in search of something
to eat. Millions of these also starve.

Gradually our cities turn into wastelands; wild animals
prowl the streets. People tear down office buildings and use
the bricks and fixtures to fashion shelters of their own. As the
centuries go by, people even forget how the buildings were
constructed. Skyscrapers, they tell each other, must have
been the homes of a race of giants. Since the fastest mode of
transportation is on horseback through a countryside filled
with outlaws and other deadly perils, there is little travel.
Each community becomes an isolated entity, almost a country of its own.

Through all this devastation, one institution continues to
function: the church, since it possessed no army, was not
considered a threat by the invaders and was spared. It had its
own system of administration and government; and since its
officials were not elected, its structure survived the civil
turmoil.

As the possessor of the only surviving administrative apparatus, the church gradually takes over many of the functions previously performed by civil government: caring for
the sick and the poor, maintaining food and water supplies,
sometimes even running the government and organizing military operations.

Since it needed to train young people for its service, the
church had maintained its own schools; and these also have
survived. Before long, the clergy and those in church schools
are almost the only ones who can read and write. These people form, whether they realize it or not, the only link between
the civilization of the past and whatever civilization might
develop in the future.

This apocalyptic fantasy gives some idea of what happened
after the fall of Rome. The far-flung provinces of the Empire, cut off from trade with the capital and with each other,

withered away. Rome itself shrank to the size of a modest town; prosperous cities became mere villages; thriving towns simply disappeared.

It was almost the end of European civilization. Everything that had been built up over the centuries in Greece and Rome was almost lost, just as the Assyrian and Hittite cultures were lost, and we almost had to start all over again. Such a thing may sound impossible, but it has happened many times in history. What our world would be like today if it had happened after the fall of Rome is literally impossible to imagine, because the ideas we use to think about things today would not exist. They would be lost to us, just as the ideas of ancient Babylonia are lost to the modern inhabitants of Iraq.

In time, things began to improve. The cities that managed to survive became fortified towns, a fraction of their former size. The territory around them was controlled by warring bandit chieftains, some of whom were strong enough to extend their realms of influence and even to hand down their power to their descendants. Those who tilled the land survived by placing themselves under the protection of one of these chiefs: he promised to defend; they promised to serve.

Weaker chiefs consolidated their positions by placing themselves under the protection of stronger ones. Operating in a society controlled by these arrangements was the church, at the same time a spiritual power and a landowner, and often an actual civil ruler as well.

Every individual in Europe, from an abbot in Sicily to a peasant in Saxony to a nobleman in Gascony, was bound by a web of relationships to everyone both above and below him. Everyone knew his place—his rights and duties with respect to others—and everyone knew everyone else's as well. All but those at the very top of the hierarchy were under an obligation to serve someone, and all except those at the very bottom were under an obligation to protect someone. Anyone who failed to perform his duties automatically forfeited the corresponding rights.

This arrangement corresponded so closely to economic and social realities that it seemed entirely natural to everyone involved. It was this pattern of rights and duties which defined a person's identity, and to be excluded from this pattern, if such a thing were possible, would have been like being cast adrift into nothingness. It would almost have been like ceasing to exist as a human being.

A succession of dedicated individuals kept alive the spirit of inquiry during those dark centuries—people like Boethius, Alcuin, Bede, John Scotus Eriugena, and others who are but dimly remembered today. Then, in the eleventh and twelfth centuries, two remarkable men made original contributions to the development of Christian thinking which overshadowed anything that had been done since the time of Augustine. Their names were Anselm and Abelard.

St. Anselm was born of noble parents in Aosta, a town in the Italian Alps about fifty miles northwest of Turin, in 1033. His father wanted him to enter politics, but at the age of twenty-four Anselm left home to further his education. After studying for three years at several monasteries, he arrived in 1060 at the Benedictine monastery of Bec in northeastern France, one of the most famous of early medieval schools, to study under the renowned theologian Lanfranc. Before long he joined the Benedictine order, and in 1078 he was unanimously elected abbot of Bec.

His writing and teaching brought great prestige to the abbey, and Anselm probably would have spent the rest of his life quite happily at Bec had it not been for the convolutions of medieval politics and the fact that William of Normandy had insisted on marrying his own cousin, a Flemish noblewoman named Matilda. In response, Pope Alexander II placed Normandy under an interdict.

It was Anselm's mentor, Lanfranc, who had resolved the conflict by persuading the pope, who had been one of his students at Bec, to lift the interdict and approve the marriage. William was suitably grateful, and, after the conquest of England in 1066, Lanfranc was made Archbishop of Canterbury. After Lanfranc died, Anselm was named to succeed him by the Conqueror's son, William II.

Right from the start there were problems, and Anselm's tenure as archbishop was marked by such bitter disputes that he was forced to spend almost half the remaining sixteen years of his life in exile. He had not even taken up his new duties before he found himself embroiled in one of the great political controversies of the Middle Ages, the question of lay investiture.

The issue was whether a new bishop should receive the symbols of his office from religious or from secular authorities, and what made the problem especially difficult to resolve was the undeniable fact that medieval bishops were both spiritual and temporal rulers. If a bishop owed obedience to the pope in the spiritual order, did he not owe obedience to the king in the civil order? If the pope gave in, how could the church maintain its independence from the state? If the king gave in, how could he govern when those who controlled a large percentage of the land and wealth in his country owed him no allegiance? The stalemate continued for two years, until finally Anselm yielded and left the country.

He spent the remainder of William's reign on the continent, taking a leading part in the Council of Bari, which attempted to reunite the Greek and Latin churches, and writing theological works. In 1100 William was killed in a hunting accident, and his brother Henry seized power. As part of an attempt to add legitimacy to his reign, Henry invited Anselm to return to England.

Anselm proved useful to the king in a number of respects, such as arranging his marriage with a Scottish princess—also

named Matilda, as it happened—and supporting his claim to
the throne. When Henry demanded that he take an oath of
allegiance, however, Anselm refused. The contest of wills
began again, and Anselm, who by this time must have been
suffering from an acute case of *deja vu,* was exiled for three
more years.

Eventually a compromise was worked out: new bishops
would receive the symbols of office from their ecclesiastical
superiors but would swear loyalty to the king before being
consecrated. This solution seems so reasonable that one mar-
vels that it was not thought of years earlier; it set the pattern
for similar arrangements in other countries.

Anselm spent the next two years in relative peace, and died
in 1109. A little more than fifty years later, he was recom-
mended for canonization by another Archbishop of Canterbury, Thomas a Becket, who was well able to appreciate the
difficulties Anselm had experienced in dealing with kings.

In his writings Anselm followed the lead of Augustine by
trying to understand and explain in rational terms, so far as
was possible, the content of the Christian faith. We are guilty
of negligence, he argued, if we do no try to understand what
we believe. He is generally considered the founder of scholasticism because of his attempts to unite faith and reason in a
formal and systematic manner rather than merely collecting
the opinions of previous authorities.

In his book *Cur Deus Homo* ("Why God Became Man"),
Anselm developed a theory of redemption which took its
inspiration from the structure of feudal society and which has
survived to our own time.

Justice in the Middle Ages relied heavily on the concept of
compensation, in money or property, and the amount of
compensation which had to be paid depended on the status of
the injured party. One would have to make a greater reparation for having injured a nobleman than a serf, for example,

and a greater reparation yet for having injured a representative of the king.

Using the same logic, Anselm argued that Adam's sin required infinite reparation. Its seriousness was determined not by the nature of the act itself but by the status of the one who had been wronged, and since the injured party was God, the offense was infinitely grievous. And because no human being can perform an infinite act, there would be no possibility for anyone to attain salvation unless God himself became human and made reparation on our behalf.

This theory was adopted by later writers, and is still taught today. It is probably safe to say that few of those who teach or who learn it realize that the logical foundation of the argument is based on a social order which ceased to exist five hundred years ago.

Anselm is best remembered for having developed, in a book called *Proslogion,* a new and quite controversial approach to investigating a problem which even today should give the thoughtful believer pause: in the face of the many proofs for God's existence which have been constructed and refined for centuries by the finest of philosophical minds, why are there still people who do not believe in God? How is it possible for someone to remain unconvinced?

Taking as the starting point of his investigation the fool who, according to scripture, says in his heart that there is no God (Psalm XIV:1), Anselm proceeds to argue, not directly that God exists, but that it is impossible for anyone really to believe that he does not.

What is God? For Anselm, God is that being than which nothing greater or more perfect can be conceived. If you have an idea of God, and are still able to imagine something greater or more perfect than that, then you are not really thinking of God at all, but of something less than God.

This is precisely the case with the fool mentioned in the

Psalms. When he hears the word "God," he knows what the word means—he knows whom it refers to—but he does not understand the word in its true fullness. He might understand it, for example, in the sense of a "god" of ancient Egypt or Greece, and find no difficulty in denying the existence of such a being. But for someone truly to have an idea of God as the being which is the greatest and most perfect that can be thought of and still maintain that such a being does not exist is a contradiction—at least if one is operating within the Platonic tradition.

Why? Because, since existence itself is a perfection, a being who is the most perfect that can be conceived has to exist. If it did not, then it would be possible to think of that same being as existing, and therefore more perfect, which would mean that it could not really have been God that one was thinking of in the first place. Thus the fool's—or the atheist's—idea of God is not an accurate one. By definition, any accurate idea of God must be an idea of an existing being.

It is impossible to think of the most perfect conceivable being as not existing. Or, to put it yet another way, it is possible not to think of an all-powerful and all-perfect being. But it is not possible to think of such a being as not existing. Anything which can be thought of as not existing cannot be God.

There are some logical problems with Anselm's formulation of his position, and his critics were not slow to point them out. (One of them wrote a reply entitled "On Behalf of the Fool.") But it is possible to reformulate Anselm's arguments so as to avoid those problems, and his basic insight—that the existence of God cannot be doubted in the same way that the existence of everything else can be—remains valid and has been used by numerous writers.

St. Bonaventure and Descartes, for example, used arguments very similar to Anselm's, and Spinoza and Leibniz constructed different formulations of the same fundamental

idea. In our own time it has received more thoughtful attention than ever before.

The late Paul Tillich, for one, argued that one can
"prove" the existence only of those things one can doubt the
existence of, and that it is no more possible to doubt the existence of God than it is to doubt the existence of existence.
God is not the conclusion of a particular logical argument;
God is the necessary presupposition of all logical arguments.

Hans Kung, as we shall see later on, has adopted an argument for the existence of God whose logical underpinning is a
direct descendent of Anselm's argument. So did Karl Barth.

As we said earlier, ideas acquire lives of their own: once
formulated by one person, they can be used by others for
quite different purposes. What was for Anselm an attempt to
satisfy the obligations of his faith by better understanding
something he believed with all his heart has become for many
people in our day the best way, perhaps the only way, to construct an effective argument against atheism.

There are some people who seem to find it impossible to
keep their mouths shut. Call them troublemakers, if you will,
or nuisances, or perhaps even heroes—for some reason they
feel compelled to make an issue about things when more
prudent people might keep silent. They make things hard on
themselves and on everyone else as well. They just seem to be
built that way. Peter Abelard was like that. He was that, and
he was a great deal more: the most famous teacher of his
time, the most skillful master of logic and dialectic in Europe,
a talented poet and musician, an innovative theologian, and a
philosopher who made brilliant contributions to the analysis
of language. Abelard, who was born in 1097, did not have the
makings of a saint. If he had unquestioned faith in anything,
it was in logic; if he had an overwhelming passion, it was for a
woman.

In his autobiography—which, with typical flamboyance, he entitled *The Story of My Misfortunes*—Abelard says he began the study of logic at age fifteen, starting in his native Brittany and continuing on to any town where there was someone who could teach him. Eventually he was drawn to the cathedral school of Notre Dame in Paris, already one of the most famous in Europe. There he studied under one of the most renowned philosophers of the day, William of Champeaux, defeated him in a public debate, and left Paris to start a school of his own. A few years later he returned, again studied under William, and again defeated him in a public debate.

He then turned his attention to a new field, studied under one of the most prominent theologians in France, and quickly decided he could teach the subject better. To prove his point he gave a lecture on a passage from scripture with only one day's preparation. Sure enough, his fellow students found Abelard's presentation far superior to those given by their professor. The reason was that Abelard had discovered a new method of theological inquiry, one perfectly suited to his contentious temperament.

Basically what he did was to select a theological passage and then analyze it logically. This might involve pointing out apparent contradictions, evaluating how well the author had succeeded in proving his point, and testing the author's statements and arguments against those of other writers.

The difference between Anselm's technique and the more traditional procedure was roughly analogous to the difference between the approach to teaching literature which emphasizes the "message" of the work, "what the poet was trying to say" (in the opinion of the teacher), and the approach which objectively compares the literary forms and techniques different authors use. To students, Abelard's method was like a breath of fresh air; to many of his colleagues, it was arrogant, impudent, and superficial.

Soon Abelard was teaching both dialectics and theology at the cathedral school and also at Mont Sainte-Genevieve, on the left bank of the Seine near where the Sorbonne stands today. At a time when students were free to follow any professor they chose, Abelard's lectures drew huge crowds.

So famous had be become, in fact, that one of the priests assigned to the cathedral considered himself quite fortunate when Abelard accepted his invitation to move into his house and tutor his young niece, Heloise.

Heloise was, by all accounts, a remarkable girl; and the handsome and charismatic Abelard, the idol of the student community, must have been a totally irresistible figure. Soon he was teaching her things that would have made her uncle's head spin. Events followed their natural course, and Heloise gave birth to a son whom they named, for some unfathomable reason or other, Astrolabe. They then were secretly married. She was approximately eighteen at the time; he was about forty.

Everything might have worked out well had it not been for Heloise's family, who decided she had been shabbily treated. They wasted no energy on harsh words: they simply hired a gang of men to break into Abelard's bedroom and castrate him. Heloise entered a convent. Abelard, after considering his options, became a Benedictine monk.

Anyone who expected that Abelard's misadventure would take the fight out of him did not know the man. While residing at the monastery of St. Denis, he took it upon himself to prove that the patron saint of the community could not possibly have been the same Denis who had been converted by St. Paul, as the monks claimed. He resumed teaching, and wrote an intriguing book called *Sic et Non* ("Yes and

No"), a compilation of contradictory quotations from scripture and the Fathers on a variety of topics.

This was a convincing demonstration that in philosophical and theological writing, words could not always be taken at face value: the different senses in which a word could be used had to be distinguished, and rules had to be developed for resolving apparent contradictions. He and Heloise continued to exchange love letters, many of which still exist.

He also wrote a book on the Trinity which in 1121 was declared heretical at the Council of Soissons and burned. This was a heavy blow to Abelard. He left Paris and, apparently determined never to teach again, accepted election as abbot in an obscure monastery in Brittany. But a man of his temperament was not intended for community life. He found it impossible to get along with the other monks, and things deteriorated to such a point that several attempts were made on his life.

So back he came to Paris, to Mont Sainte-Genevieve, and resumed lecturing. Again he drew crowds of students, but the enemies he had been making all through his career were beginning to get the upper hand. Some of them complained about him to St. Bernard of Clairvaux, who at the time was perhaps the most influential man in Europe; and Bernard decided that Abelard was a dangerous influence. By this time, the church had developed procedures for dealing with dangerous influences.

A council was held in the town of Sens in 1141 to consider the issue; and Abelard, eager for what he thought would be a chance to debate Bernard, attended. He was condemned without a hearing.

Abelard was on his way to Rome to personally appeal to the pope when the abbot of the monastery of Cluny persuaded him to give up the fight. He may have known, as Abelard did not, that Bernard had taken the precaution, even before the council was convened, of insuring that the pope would not interfere. Already a sick man, Abelard died not long afterward.

Abelard's importance is due not to any of his specific ideas as much as to the method of inquiry he utilized, a method which was essential to the development of theology into a science in the sense that we know it today. (Whether or not it was a good thing for this to happen is another question.)

In a sense, Abelard was too far ahead of his time. The approach he took to theological writings was precisely what goes on today when a theologian publishes a new book or article: the positions he sets forth are analyzed logically and tested against the positions of other writers in the same way that the writings of historians and sociologists are.

In the twelfth century, however, this aroused a great deal of criticism, and the critics did have a valid point. The full content of scripture or the writings of the fathers might exceed what any logical analysis could reveal. By ignoring these additional elements, Abelard might be seriously distorting the meaning of the texts he was working with. One might just as well use logical analysis to try to "understand" a lyric poem.

As often happens in disputes of this nature, both sides were right. Ultimately, however, it was Abelard's approach which prevailed. What happened, to a great extent because of his work, was that the nature of theological writing changed: theologians concentrated more on constructing logically sound arguments and less on producing an emotional response in the hearts of their readers. When the great theological works of the thirteenth century were written, most of them clearly showed Abelard's influence.

The saga of Heloise and Abelard is one of the world's most famous love stories, and you may wish to pay your respects to their memory.

Take the Paris Metro to the Pere Lachaise stop and walk
across the street to the cemetery entrance. Follow your path-
way, bearing always to the right, and you will find a grey
stone canopy, carved in the Gothic style, supported by stone
pillars. Under it, the bodies of Heloise and Abelard lie side
by side.

Chapter 5
BONAVENTURE

ONE of the most characteristic institutions of the medieval world was the professional guild. Through this organization, certified craftsmen in a particular field set prices, enforced quality standards, drew up codes of professional ethics, and ensured that no one who was not a guild member practiced that craft.

Anyone wishing to become a goldsmith, let us say, had first to work for several years for little or no money to learn the rudiments of the craft under the guidance of a recognized master. If his work was satisfactory, he became a journeyman and was employed by a master to do the more routine tasks while improving his command of the fine points of the craft. When he and his master felt he was ready, the journeyman produced a "masterpiece," a particularly intricate piece of jewelry, perhaps, and submitted it to the judgment of a committee of master craftsmen. If the committee agreed that the masterpiece met the highest standards of their craft, the journeyman was admitted into the guild as a master in his own right, with all the privileges of membership. The medievals had a word for this type of professional guild. They called it a *universitas*.

One of the recognized crafts, more or less on the same level as stonecutting and leather tanning, was teaching. Around the middle of the twelfth century, guilds of teachers and guilds of students began joining together to form a new kind of educational institution. Since this new organization was, in essence, a professional guild, it adopted the structure and practices of a guild and was called a "university." Just as many guild customs survive today in the modern labor union, so also do they survive in the modern university.

Medieval students were considered to be the equivalent of apprentices, working without pay under the direction of a certified expert in the teaching field. After several years of basic studies, the most promising apprentices, or "bachelors," were allowed to teach for pay under supervision; these were like journeymen, the rough equivalent of our graduate assistants. When they had mastered all the skills of their profession, they produced a sample of their best work (analogous to today's thesis or dissertation) under the direction of a master. If this was accepted by a committee of other masters, the young scholar was accepted into the brotherhood of teachers and licensed as a "Master of Arts." As a symbol of his release from the tutelage of his master, a hat was placed on his head; this recalled the cap given to emancipated slaves in ancient Rome and survives in our time as the mortarboard worn at college graduation ceremonies.

Like other legal entities such as towns and corporations, a university officially came into existence when it received a charter of privileges, something like our articles of incorporation. This charter made the university a self-governing entity, almost an independent country. It established its own laws, with its own police and a court to enforce them. Many universities had their own jails; some of these, such as the one at Heidelberg, still exist.

Since the early universities were practically religious communities—all students and professors were legally considered clerics whether or not they had actually received orders, a concept which our language still recalls whenever we refer to paperwork as "clerical" labor—it was only natural for many of them to seek their charter from the pope. This had an important consequence, since those holding a diploma issued by any university chartered by the pope were able to teach at any other university with a similar charter. At the same time, a medieval version of Latin became the language of academic instruction throughout Europe.

The result was the development of an international network of academic centers, within which professors were free to teach and students to study more or less wherever they pleased. The Western world was a community united by a common faith, a common language, and a common set of values and ideals. Nothing like these conditions had existed since the time of ancient Rome, and in all likelihood they never will again.

The university was an institution perfectly suited to the conditions and spirit of its time, and the idea spread rapidly. By 1500 there were more than 75 universities scattered throughout Europe. In the high Middle Ages, though, one stood far above the others in size, fame, and influence. The University of Paris, formed not long after the death of Abelard by an amalgamation of several older institutions including the cathedral school of Notre Dame and the school of Mont Sainte-Genevieve, was the intellectual center of Europe.

All medieval universities were rowdy places by modern standards, but Paris was a virtual free-for-all. Rioting and mayhem were common, and one spectacular beerhall brawl caused a national political crisis. It also resulted, indirectly, in the admission into the theology faculty of two of the most important characters in our story.

What made the incident so serious was that soldiers of the king had intervened to restore order and had killed several students. No one was too upset about the loss of the students, but the intrusion of military forces into the university's territory was a gross violation of the independent status guaranteed by its charter. It was like the invasion of a neutral country. Many professors were outraged, and to dramatize their anger they went on strike. A number of them left the country. This created an interesting situation. For some time there had been friction between the established university professors—monks and diocesan priests—and representatives of the new mendicant orders, the Franciscans and Dominicans. One point of contention was whether the mendicants should be allowed to teach theology, and for twenty years the established professors had been able to keep them out. With many teachers on strike, however, there suddenly were more courses to teach than there were professors to teach them. The Dominicans received their first chair of theology the year the strike started, 1229; the Franciscans received one two years later.

Eventually the strike was settled, but this in turn caused another dispute. The returning professors, naturally enough, wanted their old jobs back; the mendicants, just as naturally, wanted to hold on to what they had gained. In 1256 Pope Alexander IV was forced to intervene to insure the granting of degrees to two mendicants. One was Thomas Aquinas. The other was Bonaventure.

St. Bonaventure seems to have had an extraordinary effect on everyone who met him. The formal announcement of his death declared, "The Lord gave him this grace, that all who saw him were filled with an immense love for him." Pope Gregory X attended his funeral, and ordered every priest in the world to say a mass for the repose of his soul. One of his professors, the theologian Alexander of Hales, said Bonaventure seemed not to have been touched by original sin.

He was born John de Fidanza around 1217 near Viterbo, in west-central Italy. He was about nine years old when Francis of Assisi died, so his boyhood coincided with the great wave of religious fervor which the preaching of Francis had unleashed. He himself credited the intercession of St. Francis for having saved him from death during a childhood illness.

At the age of about seventeen he enrolled at the University of Paris; eight or nine years later, having received the master of arts degree, he joined the Franciscan order and took the religious name Bonaventure.

As a Franciscan, Bonaventure studied theology under Alexander of Hales and others who followed the Augustinean tradition, and was accepted as a master of theology. Then he found himself caught up in the dispute between the established professors and the mendicants.

In order to understand this one must remember that the mendicants were something of a revolutionary movement. "Mendicants," after all, is nothing but a fancy word for beggars; and that is precisely what Francis intended his followers to be. He took his inspiration from the command of Jesus to his apostles (Matthew 10:7-10) to wander from place to place preaching the Gospel. They were to accept no pay for this work, and to have no other possessions than one suit of clothes.

Francis was the first one to found a religious order to put these principles into literal daily practice. Its members were not to "work and pray" in the manner of St. Benedict within a monastery governed by an elaborate Rule; they were to be itinerant preachers, supporting themselves by occasional labor and begging, and animated by the same spirit of humility and poverty, the same love of all God's creatures, the same spiritual joy, that Francis himself radiated.

As the order grew—which it did at a spectacular rate—it caused considerable concern and resentment, especially on the part of diocesan priests and of monks from wealthy and powerful abbeys, many of whom interpreted the mendicant way of life as a reproach to their own and were worried about what this kind of radicalism might lead to.

The opposition was particularly strong in Paris, and there was some legitimate reason for concern. Some Franciscans believed they were the vanguard of a purifying movement which would create a new church of the spirit, and in 1254 a Franciscan named Gerard wrote a book called *Introduction to the Eternal Gospel*. A group of university masters, jumping at the chance to discredit the new movement, extracted several score of supposed errors from the work and a commission of cardinals condemned it the next year.

Even the Franciscan Minister General, the head of the order, seems to have shared some of the discredited views, and so disruptive did he become that Pope Alexander IV ordered him to resign. Obeying, he proposed Bonaventure as his successor—because, he said there was no one more qualified in the entire order. Bonaventure at the time had been a Franciscan less than fifteen years and had occupied the chair of theology which the pope had allotted to the Franciscans less than a year. It was the end of his teaching career.

Bonaventure devoted the rest of his life to the guidance of the Franciscan order—he is known as its second founder—to preaching, and to theological writing. About three years after his election as Minister General he visited La Verna, the mountain upon which Francis had received the stigmata, an experience which seemed to impel him strongly toward mysticism.

One of Bonaventure's greatest accomplishments was to heal the rift between Franciscans who took a rigorous view of how poverty should be lived in the order and those who held a more liberal attitude. Each group considered itself just a little better than the other, which was not conducive to harmonious community life. True to his reputation as a master of reconciling opposing views, Bonaventure struck a middle course and won both sides to it. Pope Clement IV named him Archbishop of York, but Bonaventure persuaded him to withdraw the nomination.

Bonaventure resided in Paris from 1266 until 1273, with

the exception of a visit to Italy, and in his sermons he frequently denounced what seemed to be dangerous philosophical and theological ideas being propagated by some professors. His sermons were one of the factors which, in 1270, led the Bishop of Paris, Etienne Tempier, to condemn eighteen doctrines then being taught at the university, an event we will hear more about later.

In 1273, Gregory X named him Bishop of Albano and a cardinal; he resigned as Minister General and was consecrated at Lyons while helping to prepare for the ecumenical council held there the following year. Bonaventure took an active part in the workings of this council, particularly in negotiating a reconciliation between the Greek and Roman churches and in mediating conflicts between mendicant orders and the diocesan clergy, and it was while engaged in this labor that he died unexpectedly on July 15, 1274. He was buried the following day in the Franciscan church in Lyons.

Think of Bonaventure as something of a cross between Augustine and Francis of Assisi.

Like Augustine, he held that the quest for union with God should include the whole person, the emotional as well as the intellectual sides of our natures; like Francis, he insisted that physical objects and natural phenomena can help us to accomplish this by drawing our minds and hearts upward, toward their creator. Like Augustine, he adopted a modified form of Plato's philosophy; like Francis, he believed that direct experience of God, particularly through contemplation, is a source of knowledge about God far superior to speculation.

It is a superior form of knowledge because, like all forms of experience from sensation to the beatific vision, it is immediate and undeniable, and unique to each person who experiences it. No one, to use an unpleasant but classic example, need tell me when I have a toothache, and no one can convince me that my tooth is not aching if I can feel it throb. All toothaches may appear similar when described in a dental school textbook, but the most important characteristic of my toothache is that it is *mine,* not another person's, and there is none like it anywhere else. Experiential knowledge is privileged; it cannot be shared with or passed along to anyone else as theoretical knowledge can. Like wisdom and virtue, it can be encouraged and cultivated, but it cannot be taught.

Experience is superior because it is a richer, fuller, more authentic way of learning than that afforded by logical reasoning: compare a verbal description or a syllogism, for example, to the taste of a hot fudge sundae or the sound of wind rustling dry leaves. In addition, experiential knowledge of God is equally accessible to all, the illiterate peasant as well as the most learned scholar.

Most important, perhaps, the knowledge of God which comes from experience, particularly that achieved through contemplation, is a superior form of knowing because the process of acquiring it perfects and fulfills one's life. Professors of ethics are not necessarily more ethical than anyone else, nor are theologians necessarily more godly; but the contemplative advances himself or herself spiritually through the very act of contemplation. Bonaventure insisted in sermons to everyone from the king of France on down that contemplation should be practiced by everyone, as an essential element in any truly Christian life, even though the heights of mysticism (such as the ecstatic raptures of St. Francis) are reached by only a few.

But even granted the desirability of experiencing God first-hand, how is such a thing possible? At the most elementary level, we can experience God through his reflections (Bonaventure calls them *vestigia Dei*—literally, "footprints of God") in the physical world.

Just as the medieval cathedral, with its statues of saints,

portrayals of biblical scenes and personages, and allegorical representations of moral lessons, served as a sort of textbook in stone for the edification and education of the faithful, so the physical world and the various manifestations of nature served, for Bonaventure, both as mirrors reflecting various aspects of God's nature and attributes and as a sort of ladder (the metaphor is Bonaventure's own) by which the soul can rise to union with its creator.

Think of the hundreds of thousands of different species of animals, plants, insects, birds, and fish in the world and of all the different varieties of perfections they embody and the different ways they embody them. Think of the different types of knowledge, of beauty, of power, of gracefulness. Then think of all of these different manifestations as so many hundreds of thousands of different imitations of the divine perfection and you will have the material world as it appeared to Bonaventure.

The foundation of this position had been laid long before. We saw earlier that Plato taught the existence of eternal and immutable Forms, the perfect examples which material objects only imperfectly imitate. Christian neoplatonists had conceived of these Forms as actual ideas, models which God had in mind, so to speak, when he created the world. Augustine had accepted this concept; so had most theologians after him. Bonaventure expanded it considerably.

According to his view, God the Father's knowledge of himself, his divine Word, contains the Ideas or Forms of all actual and possible creatures. These are infinite in number, but although we can rationally distinguish them one from another, in fact they are identical to each other and to God. It is through these Forms, through the Word of God, that all things were made, as the prologue of St. John's Gospel teaches, and only through the Word that they can be truly known.

Thus the natures of different creatures have their origin in Jesus, the Word incarnate, who is the embodiment of all perfection. Since no one type of creature can adequately reflect the totality of this perfection, God created a multitude of species, each one of which manifests different aspects of the divine nature in different ways. (Bonaventure used a similar argument in defending the existence of the mendicant orders, contending that there must be a variety of forms of religious life within the church because no single order can fully imitate the perfections of Jesus.) And while every creature reflects God in some manner, only a human being is an actual "image of God," imitating the creator through the exercise of our intellect and will.

It is this relationship between God the Son and physical things which makes it possible for the material world to serve as "a ladder for ascending to God." It is a ladder, however, which we are not capable of climbing all the way without assistance.

Reason and experience show us that the creatures of the world are contingent: they do not contain the principle of their own being. Real truth for Bonaventure, as for Plato, meant an apprehension of something that cannot be other than it is, of an unchangeable object. In opposition to Plato, however, Bonaventure held that the fallible human mind is not capable of grasping these unchangeable, immaterial objects through its own efforts. It requires divine "illumination," the Light which, again in the words of the Gospel, enlightens everyone who comes into the world. This divine help, of whose operation we are unaware, permits us to apprehend the immaterial essences (similar to Plato's Forms) which underlie the transient phenomena of the material world. It also permits us to perceive basic moral truths.

In short, consideration of material things leads us to God the Son, whose perfections they reflect; the Son then illuminates our minds so that we can proceed to a clearer knowledge of God. We are born with a dim and indistinct awareness of God; through "The Mind's Journey to God" (the title of one of Bonaventure's most famous works) this becomes more distinct and explicit.

But knowledge is only one form of union with God, and not the highest or most perfect. Love, Bonaventure insisted, can attain what the intellect cannot. Experience of the physical world leads to abstract knowledge which leads to God; at this point, the experience of contemplative union with God leads to a different form of knowledge and to love.

The ascent from the material world to God was one of affirmation, of positive knowledge; now the soul knows God negatively, as beyond all concepts and all understanding, in "the darkness of the mind." This is the path of mysticism, and to travel it requires the practice of various forms of detachment and self-denial. Precisely how all this happens is necessarily vague—it must be experienced to be understood.

Bonaventure's worldview is, in a somewhat unusual sense of the word, empirical: it is based on an appeal to direct experience rather than on theoretical arguments. It goes beyond reason, although Bonaventure would be the first to insist that it is in no way contrary to reason. It is also, again in an unusual way, a "philosophy" in the same sense that Socrates used the term—a reasoned manner of living which has as its aim the pursuit of wisdom, a process of purification which frees the soul to follow its natural tendency toward goodness and truth.

It is, to use a possibly far-fetched comparison, somewhat analogous to a technique that a music appreciation teacher might use. "There are certain things you should do and not do," such a teacher might say, "in order to discover what a symphony really is. First you must learn to listen, and there are exercises which will help you learn this. In order to appreciate sounds, you must grow accustomed to silence. Then start with the sounds of nature—in an open meadow, let us say—and notice how they sometimes blend and sometimes contrast with each other.

"Now listen to a peformance of the symphony and allow yourself to absorb its beauty, not just once but many times. The enjoyment it will produce, if you are receptive to it, is the purest form of musical knowledge and the best possible incentive to develop even more your capacity for appreciating it. And, in the process, you will learn to hear the music going on all around you."

An alternative approach, of course, would be to have the student read a textbook on musical theory, with classroom exposition of the subject's more arcane aspects and perhaps a true-false test at the end.

Christianity it its fullest sense is more than a theory, more than an abstract theology. It is also a vision of reality as having spiritual as well as physical significance and a conception of daily living as a means of achieving union with God. No one ever integrated these elements with speculative theology, mysticism, and a philosophical worldview more successfully than Bonaventure, who was aptly described by Pope Leo XIII as the theologian "who leads us by the hand to God." This was not, however, the channel through which the mainstream of Catholic thinking was destined to flow.

Chapter 6
ARISTOTLE

IN 385 or 384 B.C., a son was born to Nichomachus, court physician to the king of Macedon.

The boy began learning his father's trade at an early age, as was then the custom, and in the process he acquired what would prove to be a lifelong interest in biology. In time he became the foremost biologist of antiquity, the first person to classify animals by genus and species, and the founder of a museum with specimens from all over the known world. His name was Aristotle.

Of course, biology was not his only strong suit. Aristotle may have mastered more different fields of knowledge than anyone else ever has; he was probably the most influential teacher in history. It is said that the *Encyclopedia Britannica*, at least before it was taken over by Americans, devoted far more column inches to Aristotle than to anyone else, simply because Aristotle had more to say about more subjects than anyone else. Dante, no slouch himself when it came to learning, called Aristotle "the master of those who know."

His family life was a bit bizarre by modern standards. After his father died he was adopted by a man named Proxenus, who had a son whom Aristotle later adopted as his own son and who eventually married Aristotle's daughter. This meant that Aristotle's son was his brother and his daughter's husband was both her brother and her uncle—but this need not concern us here. What matters for our purposes is that Aristotle, after studying philosophy under Plato for more than twenty years, went on to develop a worldview of his own, one which was suddenly rediscovered in the middle of the thirteenth century, just in time to be incorporated into

Christian philosophical and theological systems as an alternative to the worldview of Plato.

Histories of philosophy almost invariably emphasize the
differences between Plato and Aristotle rather than their
similarities. This is not conducive to proper understanding of
Aristotle, nor is it accurate: it would be hard to think of two
original philosophers who had more in common than Plato
and Aristotle. Where they mainly differed was in their point
of view.

To get a general idea of the difference, it might be helpful
to make a gross oversimplification and think of Plato as a
mathematician and Aristotle as a biologist, both looking at
the same phenomena and trying to discover the general principles which would explain them.

As a mathematician, Plato tended to look for the unchanging, immaterial unity underlying things. As a biologist, Aristotle tended to think of things in terms of their functions and
of the final state toward which they were developing. It was
probably this orientation which led Aristotle to develop the
concepts which enabled him to explain change much more
successfully than Plato had.

When you come upon an unsolvable problem, it is usually
a good idea to examine your presuppositions. What made the
phenomenon of change so difficult to explain was the quite
natural supposition that a thing either exists or does not exist.
Aristotle's solution, like most brilliant ideas, was basically
quite simple: let us suppose that in addition to existence and
nonexistence there is a sort of intermediate state.

And experience, in fact, does indeed show that there are
two quite different ways of not being something. An acorn is
not an oak tree. A marble also is not an oak tree. But the
acorn has something which the marble does not: it has the
power of becoming an oak tree, while a marble can never become one. What Aristotle discovered was the concept of
potentiality.

In every instance of change, something which has the ability to acquire a new characteristic passes from a state of merely having that ability to a state of actually possessing the characteristic. This capacity to acquire new characteristics cannot be seen or heard or tasted or weighed. Anyone who doubts its existence, however, to use an age-old example, need only walk into a powder magazine with a lighted candle. But where does a thing's potentiality come from?

All physical objects, says Aristotle, are composed of two quite different elements. One element has the ability to acquire many different determinations, and the other element specifies the determination which the first element will have at any given moment. Think of a piece of modeling clay: the same material can be given almost any shape. One shape vanishes and another takes its place, while the material itself remains unchanged. Put another way, matter has the capacity to receive an almost infinite number of forms. The clay—the matter—is potency; a given shape—the form—is a specific actualization of that potency. Clay, as long as it exists, must have some shape: there can never be matter which has no form at all.

Most of the changes we experience involve material which changes its characteristics—size or shape or color or smell—while remaining the same kind of material. But other changes are considerably more profound. Our bodies, for example, change fruit and grain into flesh and blood.

This fact, that one kind of material can be changed into another, suggests something quite remarkable: that material itself is a composite, that there must be a kind of common material—pure "stuff," so to speak—which can be changed into different specific kinds of material just as clay can be changed into different specific shapes.

In other words, if this common material, or "prime matter," is joined with the form of stone, it becomes stone; if it is joined with the form of water, it becomes water. A silver candlestick, then, contains two levels of matter/form composition: prime matter united with the form of silver makes silver material; silver material united with the form of a candlestick makes a silver candlestick. Form is the determination of matter, the fulfillment of potency. It is act.

It was this belief in prime matter—which implies that any kind of substance can be transformed into any other kind—which gave rise to the medieval fascination with trying to turn ordinary metals into gold. (As it turns out, the medievals were on the right track: nuclear physicists can turn small amounts of lead into gold right now. It is simply too expensive to be worth doing on a large scale.)

In a living being, the form is what makes the organism one kind of being rather than another—different forms result in different species. This means that all horses, for example, have identical forms: what distinguishes one horse from another is that the two identical forms are united with different matter, just as the only thing that differentiates two statues made from the same mold is the fact that their material is different.

As that which makes something the kind of thing it is, the form of a living being is its soul, the act of the body, the principle of life. Just as matter and form unite to make every physical object, so body and soul unite to make a human being.

This makes all the difference in the world compared to Plato. For Aristotle, a person was not a soul imprisoned in a body, but a composite of body and soul. Union with a body was not harmful to the soul, as with Plato; it was a positive good for the soul, since only through the body can the soul exercise its powers and thus realize its perfection.

So all physical objects are composed of a permanent element (form) and a changeable element (matter). Aristotle agreed with Plato that real knowledge consists in apprehending the forms of things—that science studies the forms of species, rather than studying specific individuals. They agreed that matter is essentially unknowable. They agreed that individual things are unknowable in the strict sense of the term.

Where they disagreed (at least on the surface—experts still argue about how different Aristotle's position really was from that of Plato) was that Aristotle believed forms have existence only within individual objects, not separate from them.

If it seems strange that science would be concerned with forms of species rather than with individuals, consider the case of a biology teacher who gave her students frogs to study. She would not be satisfied, on asking them what they had learned about frogs, if one student were to say this his specimen was blind in one eye, had a misshapen left leg, and displayed a strange brown marking on its back. That would not be biology. Science is not interested in what makes one frog different from all others, but in what it has in common with the others. This is another way of saying that science is not interested in the individual but in the species—or, in Aristotelian terms, with the essence of frogginess.

Since he held that intellectual knowledge consists in the apprehension of forms, and that forms exist only in matter, Aristotle had to explain how the form gets from the object into the mind.

There must be two principles involved, he reasoned. Since the intellect receives forms, there must be a receptive principle which is in potency to receive them—like a canvas, if you will, ready to be painted upon. But then there must also be an active principle to abstract the form from the individual object and impress it on the passive intellect. This second principle is the mysterious-sounding "agent intellect" of Thomistic philosophy. It is a concept which has mystified and amused generations of Catholic college students, and for an excellent reason: it makes absolutely no sense in isolation from the

Aristotelian metaphysics—and specifically the notion, adopted from Plato, that the reality of a thing consists primarily in its form—which made it necessary.

This is not an example which would have occurred to Aristotle, for obvious reasons, but the whole process might be compared to the operation of a photocopying machine. An image must be reproduced from an original, and this image must be transferred to a blank sheet of paper. These are separate processes; different machinery is needed to perform them. The example of photocopying is particularly apt because of a quirk in Aristotle's thinking that was to have serious repercussions centuries after his death: he believed, or at least strongly suggested (the text is ambiguous), that there is only a single, eternal active intellect for all people, existing separate from them, which abstracts forms and imprints them on the passive intellects of everyone. That would be like a single machine reproducing an image on millions and millions of sheets of paper. We shall see some of the problems this idea eventually caused.

It was again probably because of his interest in biology that Aristotle emphasized another important fact about change: it is not random. Change occurs with respect to some purpose or final state.

An obvious example would be an architect, who has a purpose in mind when he builds a house. For Aristotle, however, this principle also was exemplified throughout nature: an acorn develops, not into just anything, but into an oak, and a calf into a cow. Everything tends naturally toward its fulfillment, and Aristotle saw this state of fulfillment, or final cause, as actually producing the change—causing it, as it were, through the power of attraction. The form of an oak tree is like the final state which an acorn strives to attain, somewhat in the same sense that, for Plato, a geometric circle is like the model which physical circles strive to imitate.

Aristotle's most ingenious application of this principle was to the universe as a whole. We can observe motion in the heavens; this implies the existence of a mover. In fact, explaining the observed circular motions of all the planets and other celestial bodies around the earth requires assuming the existence of 55 heavenly spheres, one inside the other, ranging from that of the fixed stars to that of our moon, moving independently of one another and each requiring a mover. It was basically this concept which became known as the Ptolemaic system of astronomy and which reigned until the time of Galileo, Copernicus, and Kepler.

Since the universe is eternal (a belief which Aristotle shared with most other ancient philosophers, and which also caused a great deal of trouble later on), these movers also must be eternal. In fact, they are divine, and each moves its sphere not by the servile and decidedly ungodly process of pushing it around and around through space but by attracting it to himself, drawing it after him as its final cause, its object of desire.

Aristotle never did solve the minor problem of what keeps the 55 different movers in perfect synchronization with each other, so that the universe does not fly apart at the seams, but the medievals did solve it. They made the celestial movers into angels, cheerfully pushing their appointed spheres under the benevolent supervision and coordination of God himself. A number of medieval artists painted the scene.

It was, incidentally, speculation about what sound must be produced when these spheres rubbed against each other, and the conclusion that it must be beautiful beyond all description, which gave rise to the concept of "the music of the spheres."

No other part of Aristotle's scientific works had anywhere near as much influence in the Middle Ages as his writings on astronomy, the only science in which the medievals showed much interest. By an unfortunate coincidence, this was precisely the field in which Aristotle was most mistaken.

If Aristotle was a contemporary of Plato, why have we not mentioned him sooner? The reason, strange as it may seem, is that he played next to no part in our story until now. His works, with one major exception, were practically unknown to the Christian world until shortly before the time of Bonaventure.

How this came about is one of the stranger stories in our cultural history, filled with more unexpected twists and narrow escapes than most modern suspense films. It also helps to answer a number of intriguing questions, such as why Aristotle's books make such dull reading and why some of the writings of Thomas Aquinas were condemned as heretical.

The works Aristotle himself published were greatly admired in the ancient world for their clarity and eloquence. They were so widely distributed that no one took any special care to preserve them, and as a result not one of them exists today.

His unpublished writings, however—what might best be described as his lecture notes, filled with corrections, repetitions, outright contradictions, and later ideas inserted into passages containing earlier ones—were inherited by one of his followers and transported to Turkey. There they lay in storage for a century or more. Then a collector of old books named Apellicon bought the manuscripts, which by this time were torn, soiled, moldy and rotted through in places. Being a helpful sort of person, Apellicon took it upon himself to fill in what he thought the missing words must be and to have the results recopied.

Eventually these altered texts turned up in Rome as part of the plunder brought back by the victorious general Sulla. There, as a result of a bizarre rivalry between competing scholars which saw teams of scribes racing to copy down Greek words they did not understand as fast as their fingers could move, new texts, containing all the old mistakes and a multitude of new ones, were rushed into publication.

All this is worth recounting because it is important to our story to understand that the texts published in Rome were, to put it bluntly, a complete mess. But they were a mess of great interest to professional philosophers—despite the fact that their being personal notes not intended for publication and bereft of stylistic grace made them quite unattractive reading for the general public—and the manuscripts were carefully preserved.

(This did not necessarily prevent their disappearing again. Aristotle's *Constitution of Athens,* for example, somehow got misplaced and was not rediscovered until 1890, when it turned up in a collection of unrelated papyrus manuscripts. Nothing, no matter how impressive or important, is guaranteed to survive. Aristotle's entire writings might easily have been lost forever, as were those of so many other famous writers of antiquity. In philosophy and literature as in architecture, what we have today is a small number of miraculously preserved works, not necessarily the best of what there was, and large collections of ruins.)

The problem with Aristotle's writings, particularly after the fall of Rome, was that fewer and fewer people could read them. Knowledge of the Greek language simply died out in Western Europe.

The obvious solution was to translate the Greek texts into Latin, and about a hundred years after the death of Augustine, a philosopher named Boethius set about translating all the extant works of both Plato and Aristotle. As it turned out, he was able to complete only a small part of Aristotle's writings before meeting an untimely death. (An advisor to the Ostrogoth king Theodoric, Boethius was executed for treason. It was one of those eras when thinking was considered a subversive activity.)

Boethius was one of the few scholars of his time with a sufficient command of Greek to carry out his project, and after
his death no one else took up the work. As a result, the few
works Boethius had been able to translate were the only part
of Aristotle's philosophy that Western Europeans were able
to read until the twelfth century. Most of Plato's works remained untranslated until the Renaissance.

What Boethius had translated, as it happened, were Aristotle's logical writings. These works, appearing at a time when
post-Roman culture was in its formative stages, were enormously influential. It is not exaggeration to say that they were
chiefly responsible—for better or for worse—for our
culture's emphasis on syllogistic reasoning and our typically
dichotomous (true/false, yes/no, is/isn't) way of thinking.
They contributed greatly to the remarkable medieval fascination with logic, and it was through studying them that
Abelard gained his formidable skill in dialectics.

But while most of Aristotle remained unknown in Europe,
Europe was not the total civilized world—or even the most
civilized part of it. While the Dark Ages were descending
upon the West, a far more advanced Arab culture was making enormous strides in mathematics, medicine, philosophy,
and the sciences. And the works of Aristotle, translated into
Arabic by Greek-speaking Syrians, were widely read and
commented on. When the Arabs conquered Spain they
brought this knowledge with them, and it was chiefly through
Spain, often in translations from Greek into Arabic into
Spanish into Latin, that the ideas of Aristotle again made
their way into Western Europe.

This also is important to our story. For one thing, the
error-filled Greek texts had been even further corrupted by
multiple translations by the time they appeared in the West.
For another, the fact that Aristotelianism was rediscovered
through the medium of a non-Christian culture tainted it in

the minds of some people—somewhat as though Charles Darwin's works had been lost, and then reintroduced to the West by Chinese Communists.

Finally, generations of Arabian commentators had developed some interpretations of Aristotle which caused serious problems in Christian Europe. For example, the Spanish-Arab philosopher Averroes (Arabic name: Ibn Rushd) took Aristotle's idea that there is only one active intellect for all people and went Aristotle one better: he held that this unique intellect absorbs the passive intellects of individual people. This means that the process of knowing universals, or forms, really takes place completely outside the individual person, although the individual person shares in that knowledge. His reason for proposing this was that only an intelligence separated from matter—and thus from the human body—is really capable of apprehending an immaterial form.

When the remainder of Aristotle's major works were translated into Latin and reintroduced into Western Europe in the last half of the twelfth and first half of the thirteenth centuries, accompanied by the Arabian commentaries, Christianity was suddenly confronted for the first time since its earliest days with a comprehensive worldview developed entirely through natural reasoning. Many of the leading minds of the day were quick to make use of it.

It was not so much a decision that Plato had been wrong and Aristotle right as that Aristotle had developed concepts which were extremely useful in dealing with the kinds of problems these men were interested in, somewhat in the same way that evolution and relativity are powerful explanatory tools today, ways of looking at the world which are particularly helpful in analyzing certain kinds of phenomena.

But there were problems. Many of the ideas in this body of translation seemed to be opposed to church teaching. It was not even clear until the last half of the thirteenth century (when an authoritative translation of Aristotle's entire *Metaphysics* was produced at the request of Thomas Aquinas) which ideas were really Aristotle's and which represented errors in translation or interpretations of commentators.

There were acrimonious debates as to which of the Arabs had interpreted Aristotle correctly—or whether perhaps they had all been mistaken on some essential points and a new interpretation was necessary. In general, the philosophers at Paris followed Averroes, while the theologians either felt new interpretations were called for or thought Aristotelianism was so thoroughly permeated with errors that it should be totally rejected.

In 1210, French authorities forbade the teaching of Aristotle's metaphysics or commentaries on it under pain of excommunication. Twenty years later, Pope Gregory IX appointed a commission to "correct" the contents of the Aristotelian texts. In 1255, the teaching of all of Aristotle's works was officially permitted at Paris, and eventually a knowledge of them was required of anyone seeking a teaching degree in philosophy.

It is typical of the ironies which result when some people take it upon themselves to determine what other people should and should not think that by the fourteenth century it was forbidden at the University of Paris to teach anything which contradicted Aristotelianism, and that in 1624 the penalty set by the French parliament for teaching anything opposed to Aristotle was death.

Chapter 7

ALBERT AND THOMAS

ALBERT of Cologne was probably the most learned man of his era; certainly he was one of the most highly regarded.

Not only did his contemporaries quote him by name (an unheard-of honor in the thirteenth century, when the phenomenon of the instant authority had not yet been invented), but even during his lifetime they bestowed on him— and on him alone—the epithet "Great." Roger Bacon referred to him as the most famous teacher in Christendom; Ulric of Strassburg, one of his students, called him "the wonder and the miracle of our age."

Albert was born near Ulm, in Southern Germany, around 1200. He studied liberal arts at the University of Padua; there he met Jordan of Saxony, St. Dominic's successor as head of the newly founded Order of Preachers, who was looking for recruits. Albert was interested. There was considerable opposition to the idea from his family—as the eldest son of a wealthy nobleman, more was expected from him than a life of itinerant preaching—but eventually Albert became a Dominican and continued his studies in both Italy and Germany. He then spent several years lecturing on theology, a subject for which he showed such aptitude that the Dominicans decided to send him to Paris for further training.

He arrived sometime in the 1240s, just as Latin translations of Aristotle's works and the Arabian commentaries were becoming available. Although he completed the requirements for becoming a master of theology and was awarded a chair in that subject, Albert was less interested in lecturing on traditional theological topics than in exploring the possibilities opened up by the rediscovery of Aristotelianism.

This was a task of almost overwhelming magnitude. It involved nothing less than presenting to the Latin-speaking world the sum total of all previous knowledge: logic, rhetoric, geography, mathematics, psychology, astronomy, ethics, politics, economics, and all the natural sciences. No one in Europe had done anything like it in fifteen hundred years; it took him two decades to complete. Albert was the only medieval philosopher to write commentaries on all the known works of Aristotle.

Hand in hand with a passionate devotion to the study of Aristotelianism went an interest in the natural sciences which was truly remarkable for his time. Albert has been credited with establishing the study of nature as a legitimate field of inquiry within the Christian intellectual tradition. So unusual was the attention Albert paid to science that even during his lifetime it was rumored that he was a wizard or magician with mysterious powers.

More important than his interest was the attitude Albert took toward the study of nature: he insisted on the necessity of observation rather than mere speculation. In an essay on botany he insisted that experimentation is the only safe guide when investigating nature, and in a geological work he pointed out that the aim of the natural sciences is to identify the causes that produce natural phenomena, not simply to repeat the opinions of others.

Contrary to the attitude of the late Middle Ages, when the authority of Aristotle was unquestioned even when it was flatly contradicted by experience, Albert called Aristotle to task on a number of points where his writings disagreed with Albert's own observations. It was in recognition of his role in reintroducing the study of nature to Europe that, in 1941, he was named the patron saint of scientists.

In 1248, Albert moved to Cologne to open a Dominican house of studies, and six years later he was chosen to administer the Dominican province of Germany. In 1259, contrary to his wishes, he was named Bishop of Regensburg by Pope Alexander IV, but when Alexander died two years later Albert resigned his see and resumed teaching in Cologne, where he resided for most of the rest of his life.

In 1274, Albert attended the Council of Lyons—the same council during which Bonaventure died—and three years later, at the age of nearly eighty, he made the arduous journey from Cologne to Paris, as we shall shortly see, to try to clear the reputation of an old friend who was unable to defend himself.

Albert the Great died on November 15, 1280, and was buried in the Dominican church in Cologne. He is often called the Universal Doctor because of the tremendous range of his interests, and he might well be regarded today as one of the greatest philosophers of the middle ages except for the fact that, like Socrates, he was almost completely overshadowed by one of his students.

Thomas of Aquino, like Albert, was born into the nobility. Unlike Albert, however, he was the youngest son in his family, not the oldest, and his parents not only did not oppose his entrance into religious life, they did everything possible to encourage it. They just wanted him to become something more respectable than a Dominican.

Thomas was born around 1225 in his family's castle at Roccasecca, near Naples. His father was Landolfo, Count of Aquino; his mother, Landolfo's second wife, was named Teodora. It was fortunate that the family had plenty of living space: Thomas had five sisters, three brothers, and at least three half-brothers.

His family had plans for Thomas—at the age of about six he was placed in the nearby Benedictine abbey of Monte Cassino with the hope that he would one day become abbot.

This was no small ambition, for the Benedictines at the

time were perhaps the most wealthy and powerful force in Christendom. One of their abbeys in Paris, to cite but a single example, owned 42,000 acres of land. The abbot of Monte Cassino, ruler of the first and most famous Benedictine community, was one of the most important men in Europe. Still, young Thomas did have an inside track to the job: the incumbent abbot, one Landolfo of Sinnibaldo, was a relative of his.

Thomas stayed at Monte Cassino until he was about fourteen. It was here that he learned to read and write, and for seven centuries scholars have cursed the unknown monk who taught—or failed to teach—young Aquinas penmanship. No medieval manuscripts are particularly easy to read, but Thomas's writing looks like a cross between Arabic and cuneiform.

In 1239 he was sent to the University of Naples, where he discovered Aristotle and the Order of Preachers at about the same time. Thomas was attracted to them both, and in 1244 he joined the Dominicans. His superiors, having had enough experience by this time with the nobility to realize that Thomas's parents would not be pleased by his career choice, had no intention of letting them interfere with his decision. They immediately sent him to Rome for safekeeping.

Thomas's mother was more than not pleased. She was outraged. For a young nobleman to join a mendicant order in those days was something like a Rockefeller heir becoming a Hare Krishna. The distraught woman hurried to Naples to rescue her son, and from Naples to Rome, but Thomas was already on the road north to Bologna.

At this point Teodora resorted to a tactic that parents in similar situations sometimes use today: she had her son kidnapped and brought back home by force. In an era before professional deprogrammers, Teodora used a mother's most potent weapon, tears and supplications; but even after months of this treatment Thomas remained adamant. Finally

Teodora gave in. Thomas returned to the Dominicans in Naples, and shortly afterward was sent to Paris.

It is not certain exactly where or when Thomas met Albert the Great, but when Albert set up the Dominican house of studies in Cologne in 1248, he chose Thomas as his assistant. Four years later, when he was asked to recommend someone to study for the doctorate in theology at Paris, Thomas was the one he picked.

Aquinas arrived in Paris just as the conflict between the mendicants and the regular professors was reaching its crescendo. He assumed the normal duties of a graduate student and lectured on the *Sentences* of Peter Lombard, a compilation of citations from the church Fathers and other accepted authorities which every advanced student in theology had to comment on as part of the requirements for recognition as a master teacher.

In 1254 his career was briefly interrupted: a delegation of regular professors persuaded Pope Innocent IV to suspend all teaching privileges for members of the mendicant orders. The ban did not last long—Innocent died two weeks after issuing it, and soon afterward his successor, Alexander IV, restored the mendicants' privileges—but feelings of hostility against the newcomers persisted.

Alexander had to order the university to grant Aquinas a "license" (as it was called then, and is still called in European universities) to teach. Bonaventure received his license at about the same time. It took another papal command to force the university to let Thomas give his inaugural lecture, the symbol of his acceptance as a master in the teachers' guild; and there was so much opposition to that action that soldiers had to be called in to guard the lecture hall.

Thomas taught as a master in Paris from 1256 to 1259, following the traditional academic routine of lectures and disputations.

Lectures (the Latin word was *lectio,* which means "a
reading") were something like an early version of a Great
Books program; they were held in the mornings. The idea was
that a student should begin his education by mastering the
classic works of the past—Euclid for geometry, for example,
and Cicero for rhetoric. In theology, the "Great Book" was
the bible.

Since books were scarce, the only way students could study
these works was for the master to read them aloud. But lectures were more than verbatim readings. The master was expected to explain the author's key ideas, present and evaluate
all arguments both for and against them, summarize the
opinion of leading commentators, and resolve conflicting
opinions and apparent contradictions. The students took
notes.

All of this was aimed at producing a full understanding of
the passage under consideration. These lectures, obviously,
could be deadly dull with an unimaginative or lazy master.
Aquinas quickly earned a reputation for raising original issues
and suggesting new approaches to traditional problems.

Regular disputations, the *quaestiones disputatae,* were held
in the afternoons; they were discussions of questions arising
from the morning lectures. There was a set format. The position to be discussed was stated by the master, then students
proposed objections, which were answered by the *bacca-
larius,* or graduate assistant. Then the master summarized the
discussion, expounded his own position, and gave his own
answers to the students' objections. We will encounter this
method of examining issues again: it is precisely the literary
form Thomas used in the *Summa Theologiae.*

The other form of disputation, the *disputationes de quo-
libet,* were held only during Lent and Advent. These were
open to the public and were less rigidly structured. Here a
master of theology undertook to answer questions posed by

anyone in the audience on any theological subject at all. Twelve such disputations by Aquinas have been recorded.

From 1259 to 1268 Thomas taught in Italy, either at or near the papal court, and continued his systematic recasting of the Christian faith in Aristotelian terms. In part this meant working on the *Summa Contra Gentiles,* a book he had started in Paris primarily to aid in the conversion of Jews and Mohammedans in Spain. He also wrote at least the first part of his masterpiece, the *Summa Theologiae,* a textbook so different from those then in use that commentators believe it originally must have been intended for students in the Dominicans' own seminaries because it would never have been accepted by the authorities in Paris. In his spare time, at the request of Pope Urban IV, Thomas wrote the mass and office for the feast of Corpus Christi, including the hymns *Pange Lingua* and *O Salutaris Hostia.*

In 1269 Aquinas returned to Paris. Again he arrived in the middle of a controversy. At issue was the propriety of using the Aristotelian worldview in theological writing, as Albert and Thomas had done. Bonaventure, no longer a professor but still influential in Paris through his preaching, practically led the opposition to Aristotle.

In part this was an issue which the church has had to face every time a new way of looking at things became popular— the theory of evolution, for example, or geological evidence that the earth is actually millions of years old. Since the Christian tradition has always rejected the idea that faith and reason can be in conflict, a new way of looking at things generally provokes a crisis.

The initial reaction is usually that if the new theory is in conflict with faith (and some people will always find it to be so), then it cannot possibly be true. An equally valid reaction, but one which occurs to people much less frequently, is that if the new theory is true, it cannot possibly be in conflict with faith.

At the same time it is undeniably true that Aristotle held some beliefs which seemed directly contrary to Christian teachings. One of these had to do with the origin of the world. Like most of the Greek philosophers, Aristotle held that the universe had always existed. According to Genesis, however, the heavens and the earth were created by God. Aristotelianism therefore contradicted the Bible. Or did it? Opponents of Aristoteliansim seized on the creation issue more than any other to bolster their arguments that the "new learning," as it was sometimes called, was pernicious and incompatible with orthodoxy. Thomas might have responded to this by conceding that Aristotle had been wrong on this point but that the basic principles of his metaphysics were still compatible with the teachings of faith. It is not clear why he did not choose this strategy—perhaps he felt that such an admission would only strengthen the position of the anti-Aristotelian forces. He decided, instead, to argue that Aristotle's position was not really contrary to scripture.

In theory there was a way to do this: God might have created the world from all eternity. Thomas, by identifying Aristotle's Prime Mover with the Christian God, suggested that Aristotle could be interpreted in this way. This kind of reasoning drove Bonaventure into a near-frenzy. Eternal creation out of nothing, he retorted, "is so contrary to reason that I cannot believe that any philosopher, no matter how deficient in reasoning ability, could uphold it." Besides, Genesis states quite clearly that there was a time when the world did not exist.

This was a dilemma, but medieval philosophers knew precisely how to handle such a situation. So automatic was their response that it was even formalized in a Latin slogan: *solvitur distinguendo* (solve the problem by making a distinction). Thomas made a distinction which in the opinion of some people brought him dangerously close to teaching that something can be true in philosophy and false in theology. We know from revelation, he said, that the world had a beginning in time, but the eternity of the world cannot be disproven by reason alone, either by Aristotle or by anyone else. This is not a contradiction but only an example of the limitations of reason, just as human reason can lead us to a belief in the existence of God but cannot, without the aid of revelation, arrive at knowledge of the Trinity. Other people found this a strange answer indeed: what kind of metaphysics is it which cannot even answer the question of whether the world had a beginning?

But the most powerful opposition to Aristotelianism was not rooted in a generalized hostility to new ways of thinking or in specific positions Aristotle had adopted. It originated instead in the fact that when Aristotle's writings were made accessible again to European scholars, they were accompanied by a substantial body of Arabian interpretation and commentary. This represented the consensus of a tradition which had been studying Aristotle for several centuries on what his writings meant and what they implied.

The interpreter most respected by medieval Aristotelians was Averroes—even Aquinas referred to him as "the Commentator," as though only one person were worthy of that title—and it was some of the interpretations of Averroes which caused the most vehement opposition to Aristotelianism. Chief among these was his contention that there is only one passive and active intellect for all people.

This is equivalent to saying that the individual person does not have a spiritual intelligence—that as individuals we can receive and process sensations but cannot really think. The main problem with this was that the Christian tradition identified spiritual intelligence with the human soul. In effect, Averroes was saying that there is only one soul for everyone, and this means that there can be no personal immortality.

Of course this is contrary to basic Christian doctrine, but the so-called Latin Averroists (a group which was strongly opposed by Aquinas) dealt with that inconvenience by making a distinction even more subtle than that made by Thomas. Faith is known by supernatural revelation, they said; philosophy only by the power of human reason. Thus a position contrary to theology may still be necessarily true in philosophy, because reason is less certain than faith.

Making distinctions is a bit like slicing salami: eventually you can slice so thin that nothing is left. To many people, the Latin Averroists' position was really no different from saying that reason can contradict faith. That was going too far—and when the reaction came, church authorities turned out to be not nearly so good at making distinctions as the Aristotelians had been.

In December of 1270, the Bishop of Paris condemned as heretical eighteen propositions then being taught at the university by Aristotelian professors. Two concerned the eternity of the world, and several others had to do with the theory that there is but one human intellect for all persons.

Aquinas came within a hair's breadth of being condemned himself: no position which he had specifically upheld was included in the final declaration, but two of his teachings had originally been included and were removed for one reason or another before the list was published. (One was his contention that the human soul is the only human substantial form —this caused technical difficulties in explaining some of the details of the Resurrection—and the other was related to his argument that pure spirits are forms without matter.) He would not be so lucky the next time.

About eighteen months later Thomas left Paris to establish a Dominican house of studies in Naples. It was here, in the midst of his work on the third part of the *Summa,* that he had an experience while saying mass which caused him to abandon his writing and teaching. He told an associate that he could not bear to continue working, since everything he had written seemed worthless compared with what had been revealed to him. It is not clear what the nature of his experience was: the *Catholic Encyclopedia* suggests that he may have suffered a breakdown of some sort.

Meanwhile, the controversy over his writings continued to grow. In 1277, in what is somewhat euphemistically known to history as "the Great Condemnation," the Bishop of Paris drew up a new list of 219 propositions, including at least fifteen which Aquinas had taught, and excommunicated those who held them. This decision was ratified several weeks later by Pope John XXI.

It was in an attempt to forestall this action against his former student that Albert the Great made his last journey from Cologne to Paris. Thomas was unable to defend his teachings himself: he had died three years earlier, on his way to the same Council of Lyons which Albert and Bonaventure attended. He was less than fifty years old. The condemnation against him was not removed until half a century after his death.

Aquinas left behind a body of work impressive both for its quantity and for the closely reasoned, almost relentlessly methodical character of its exposition.

"Summa Theologiae" is not so much the title of a particular work as it is the name of a literary form: many masters of theology wrote *summae theologiae,* or summaries of theology. (Not everyone was impressed by this trend. Roger Bacon complained that the first such *summa,* that of Alexander of Hales, weighed enough to stagger a horse.)

The *Summa* of Thomas consists of three main parts, the first dealing in general with God and other celestial beings, the second with man, and the third with Christ. To make things a bit more confusing, the second part is itself divided

into two parts, one treating human acts in general and the
other treating them in particular. In Thomistic commentaries
these are often referred to as I-II and II-II, or *Prima Secundae* and *Secunda Secundae:* the First Part of the Second Part
and the Second Part of the Second Part. Each of these four
sections is divided into Questions—a total of 521—and each
Question is divided into Articles, an average of perhaps eight
or nine per Question.

Among the subjects treated are the Trinity, creation,
angels, nonrational creatures, the natural and supernatural
human ends, natural vices and virtues, natural and supernatural law, grace, the theological virtues, the different states
of life, the incarnation, the sacraments, death, and resurrection and judgment.

The articles follow the pattern of a medieval disputation.
Each begins with the formula "It seems that . . . ," introducing a series of objections to the proposition Thomas is trying to establish, followed by an argument favorable to his
side. Then comes his own resolution of the problem, introduced by the formula "I, however, reply that . . . " and an
answer to each objection.

Typical articles deal with such problems as "Whether the
Five Exterior Senses Are Properly Distinguished," "Whether
the Will Moves the Intellect," "How God May Be Seen in
His Essence," "Whether the Mean of Moral Virtue Is a Real
Mean or a Mean of Reason," and "Whether of Those Who
See the Essence of God, One Sees More Perfectly Than
Another."

The *Summa Contra Gentiles,* because of its relatively more
fluid style and the fact that it was aimed at an audience unfamiliar with Catholic doctrine, is perhaps the most accessible of Thomas's writings for the modern reader. Bertrand
Russell, for one, considered it his greatest work.

Among Thomas's many other writings are a number of

volumes of *Quaestiones Disputatae,* dealing with such subjects as truth, the nature of evil, the soul, the virtues, and the
power of God. There are also several volumes of scriptural
interpretation, numerous commentaries on Aristotle, various
polemical writings (directed mainly at the Latin Averroists,
critics of the mendicant orders, and those who held that creation of the world in time could be proved by reason alone)
and a great deal more.

But a mere listing of his works hardly does justice to the
man, and we have yet to consider the two most important
questions concerning Aquinas. What did he really have to
say? And what difference did it make?

Chapter 8
THOMAS AQUINAS

THE great north window of the cathedral of Chartres, the Rose of France, glitters with fragments of frozen color locked into serene harmony. Invisibly connecting its glowing reds, blues and golds is an intricate set of mathematical patterns— twelve groups of spirals based on a progression in which each number equals the sum of the preceding two, all this superimposed on a grid of interrelated squares and triangles within a circle. The north window of Chartes is geometry crystalized in glass and stone—mathematics in the service of faith. It was constructed about the time Thomas Aquinas began his philosophical studies.

This may not have been entirely coincidental. If the rose windows of medieval cathedrals personify the union of geometry with theology, the work of Aquinas personifies the union of theology with systematic metaphysics. The *Summas* of Thomas are something like the Rose of France in verbal form: all-encompassing in scope and almost geometric in the consistency of their logic. As intellectual accomplishments, they are the most perfect examples of their kind.

What Thomas did was to reconstruct Catholic theology on a foundation of Aristotelian metaphysics—to weld church doctrine so firmly to Aristotle, in fact, that no one has yet really succeeded in separating it. He was the first one to completely formulate Christian belief on a rigorously consistent metaphysical basis; for this he has been credited with founding theology as a science. Almost every topic he treats, from God to the sacraments to moral good and evil, Aquinas discusses in Aristotelian terms: matter and form, potency and act, essence and existence, efficient and final causality.

Probably the best known passage in the *Summa Theologiae*

100

is Part I, Question 2, which discusses the existence of God. It is the only part of Aquinas that most people have actually read (provided, of course, that they have read any at all). This is unfortunate, because I, 2 is quite possibly the least impressive portion of all Thomas's writings. His heart obviously is not in it.

There is an excellent reason for this. The existence of God was not seriously questioned in the thirteenth century, and had not been since at least the fall of Rome. There had not even been any pagans to speak of, let alone complete atheists, for perhaps five hundred years. Even the unorthodox elements in Europe—Arabs, Jews, and heretics of various descriptions—all believed in the same God as did the pope in Rome. Thomas even felt obliged to construct arguments against the very real objection that it is neither necessary nor possible to prove God's existence, because it is self-evident. To prove God's existence in the thirteenth century was almost a formal exercise, something like proving that the earth is round would be today. It simply was not a task to which the best minds devoted much effort.

The key to understanding Aquinas's basic approach to the existence of God is the same as the key to understanding Aristotle's basic approach to metaphysics the concept of potentiality. The general thrust of his first three proofs, which in reality are three different forms of the same argument, is that we know from experience that the existence of some things is contingent: they come into existence and go out of existence, so it is clear that they do not exist necessarily. But if nothing exists necessarily, then everything receives its existence from something else.

But this casual chain cannot stretch on to infinity, or else there would be no beginning cause to activate things. So there must be some necessary being, something which is the cause of its own existence. And this being—Thomas calls it a "first mover" in the first proof, a "first efficient cause" in the second, and a "being having its own necessity in itself" in the third—is what we call God.

This argument is often grossly distorted in philosophy and religion classes. Thomas is presented as arguing that no causal chain can be infinitely long, so the world must have had a beginning and there must therefore be a creator. In view of Aquinas's repeated and unequivocal insistence, at no small risk to his reputation, that it is impossible to prove by reason alone that the world is not eternal, this interpretation is simply outrageous. It is the exact opposite of what Thomas explicitly taught.

The kind of causal chain Aquinas was referring to was not a sequence of events in time, but rather the hierarchy of causality existing at any given moment. The distinction between the two is quite clear in principle, but it is a bit difficult to conceptualize without an illustration.

Imagine people standing in line, one behind the other. Eventually they get tired of standing, and each person says to the one in front of him, "I'll step out of line, but only if you do." Now imagine that the line ahead is infinitely long. If each person does no more than agree to move if the one in front of him does, no one will ever move. A mere willingness to act is not sufficient.

Someone actually has to step out of line—someone whose decision is not contingent on the decision of someone else— or the long series of potential moves will never be realized. Nothing will ever actually happen. It is this kind of sequence —an infinite series of contingent relationships, of events which can happen only if something else does—that Aquinas was talking about. It has nothing to do with temporal duration: even if communication in the line was instantaneous, and everyone agreed to move at the same time, nothing could happen until one person agreed to move whether or not the person in front of him did.

Once one person actually does move, the effect will be transmitted back through the line. If these effects are transmitted one after the other, the fact that the line is infinitely long does mean that it may be a very long time indeed until the effect reaches some people in the line, but if you have eternity to work in this is no great problem.

The point is that you cannot have an infinite series where no effect can take place unless the one in front of it does, not that you cannot have an infinite series of effects moving backward. God might have created the universe from all eternity, had he so desired, but someone did have to get the ball rolling.

What Aquinas was really addressing in his first three proofs is a question which has no scientific answer: Why is there anything, rather than nothing? A thing does not happen simply because it is possible; something has to actualize that possibility. If everything were merely contingent, it would be impossible to explain why any of it actually exists. Nothing could really be understood. And it was one of Aquinas's most basic suppositions—one he shared with Aristotle, but not with a number of modern philosophers—that everything in the natural world is capable of being understood. The idea of an absurd universe was, for the medievals, literally unthinkable.

Thomas's fourth and fifth proofs are little more than afterthoughts to his main argument. The fourth is really an application of Plato's concept of ideal forms.

Aquinas argues that the existence of gradations of perfection in created things (more or less good, more or less true, etc.) points to the existence of a maximum of each perfection, a maximum which causes the greater or lesser degree of the perfection in individual things. The sum total of these max-

104

William A. Herr

imum perfections is what gives all things their perfections, and this is God. For a variety of reasons, this argument does not hold water: the conclusion does not even follow from the premise. The "fourth way" is something of an embarrassment even to dedicated Thomists; one of them once described it as pure sophism. It may be the single worst paragraph Aquinas ever wrote.

The fifth proof leans heavily on Aristotle's notion of final causality. Thomas argues that even beings without intelligence, even inanimate objects, seem to act in a purposeful way. They seem directed toward the accomplishment of harmonious results. But since they lack the intelligence to achieve these results deliberately, their actions must be directed by an intelligent being, who is God. This is a better argument than the last one, but it still rests on a presupposition which is demonstrably false. It assumes that if the harmony in question could not result from mere chance, then it must have been established by God. But in fact these are not the only two possibilities, as astronomers and evolutionists were eventually able to show.

But assume that the existence of a supreme being has been established—what kind of being is it? Thomas, as might be expected, gives this question an Aristotelian answer.

In every contingent being we can distinguish the kind of being it is (its essence) from the fact that it is (its existence). These things receive existence, they possess it—and then eventually they no longer possess existence and are no more. But this is not true of God: God does not possess existence—one might even say that God does not exist—because God *is* existence. In God alone of all beings there is no distinction between essence and existence: to be God and to be are exactly the same thing. Existence is the definition of God, in the same sense that "rational animal" is the definition of a human being. This is why

Aquinas says that the most fitting name for God is the name he gave to Moses: "I am 'He who is.' "

As we saw, for Aristotle a person is not a soul trapped inside an animal body but a union of body and soul, form and matter. To be united in this way is a soul's natural state and is beneficial to it, not unnatural and harmful. But to anyone who believes in personal immortality—as Aristotle did not —this creates problems. How can forms whose purpose is to animate bodies survive after the bodies disintegrate, any more than the shape of a sugar lump exists after the lump dissolves? And if they did survive, how could they be distinguished from one another—that is, how could your soul be any different from mine if it is matter which distinguishes different manifestations of a given form?

Aquinas solved these difficulties quite ingeniously. First he reaffirmed, in opposition to Plato and Augustine, that to be united to a body is not a punishment or a form of exile for the soul; it is the soul's natural state. But then is not the soul in an unnatural state after death? And is not an unnatural state a kind of contradiction, which eventually must be resolved in some way? Precisely, replied Aquinas. It must indeed be resolved. And the only way it can be resolved is for the body and soul to be reunited.

By a neat twist of Aristotelian metaphysics, Aquinas developed as persuasive a philosophical argument as anyone has ever come up with for the resurrection of the body (a concept which would have made Aristotle himself cringe). And it is this inclination to be reunited with a body—not just any body, but its own body—which distinguishes one soul from another after their bodies' death. What will make your soul different from my soul after we die is that your soul will have a natural tendency to be reunited with your body, and my soul with mine.

There is another aspect of Aquinas's conception of the soul which today causes considerable embarrassment to authorities of the Catholic Church, because it tends to contradict their teaching on abortion.

Plato and Aristotle both distinguished three kinds of souls, corresponding to the three main types of activity which living beings perform: the nutritive or vegetative soul, which is the principle of such activities as nutrition and reproduction; the sensitive or animal soul, the principle of sensation and independent motion; and the rational or human soul. Since human beings are capable of all three kinds of activity, the question arises whether we have three different souls to perform them or whether in us the rational soul is the principle of all these activities. Plato taught that the three are separate; Aristotle's position was ambiguous.

Thomas insisted that we have only one soul, the rational soul, through which we perform all three types of operations. But the human embryo is capable only of growth and nutrition in the early stages of its development, of independent motion only later, and only much later yet of fully human activities. How can this be explained, if it has the same kind of soul all this time?

Thomas's answer was that the embryo at first has a vegetative or nutritive soul. At a later state in its development, this is removed and replaced by a sensitive or animal soul. At a still later stage, this animal soul is removed and replaced by a rational soul (see the *Summa Theologiae*, Part I, Question 76, Article 3 and Question 118, Article 2).

But since it is the union of a rational soul with a body which constitutes a human being, this means that Aquinas held that the fetus is not a human being at the time of conception—in fact, that it does not become a human being until a fairly late state in its development. This is in complete conformity with Aristotle's teaching that the fetus is an animal before it is human.

At the same time, once a fetus has reached this stage— once a rational soul has been joined to a body—the resulting composite is always human, no matter how monstrously deformed or hopelessly retarded. Aristotle and Aquinas agreed that abnormalities result from deficiencies in the matter: there is never a deficiency in the rational soul which is its form.

Now angels are a different question entirely. As pure spirits, they are forms without matter. And Aristotle taught that different forms establish different species and that it is matter which distinguishes the different manifestations of a given form. So there are only two possibilities: either all angels have the same form, or they have different forms. But if all have the same form, they will all be identical—which would mean there is really only one angel—and this is unacceptable.

On the other hand, if they have different forms, and different forms establish different species, then each angel must belong to a different species. This means that two archangels —Michael and Gabriel, let us say—are as different from each other as a lion and a panther, while an archangel and an angel might be as different as a lion and a crocodile. This position caused quite a bit of controversy—Bonaventure, in particular, was upset by it—but Thomas insisted that it must be so. It is an inescapable conclusion of Aristotelian metaphysics.

The matter / form way of looking at things—and the distinction between substance and accidents, which is related to it—was also ideally suited to explaining such doctrines as the Eucharist. And it was during the Council of Trent, when many of these doctrines were formally defined, that Thomism really triumphed over other philosophical traditions within the church. But that is getting ahead of our story.

Aristotle begins his metaphysics with the observation that all people naturally desire knowledge. Thinking is the activity which most clearly distinguishes us from other animals, and the pleasure which comes from knowing—the joy of discovering and understanding things—is the characteristically human form of happiness. For better or worse, Aquinas accepted this belief that we are, above all else, intellectual beings. It had a substantial impact on his conception of our relationship with God.

As we have seen, Aristotle held that all beings naturally tend toward some final state, toward their fulfillment. For us, the final state toward which we naturally tend is happiness. And when it came to the question of what can give us the greatest happiness, Aristotle reasoned that it must involve the application of our highest and most noble activity (rational thinking) to the highest and most noble object (the most supreme of the Unmoved Movers), supplemented by such lesser pleasures as friendship, honor, and worldly possessions. For Aristotle, perfect earthly happiness (the only kind he was interested in) consisted in being something like a cross between Albert Einstein and Carl Sagan.

Aquinas accepted all of this except the final step. Like Aristotle, he believed that perfect happiness consists of intellectual contemplation of the most perfect object. But he had a more perfect object than Aristotle's in mind.

Since all agents act for a good, for the acquisition of something beneficial which they lack, and since God is the supreme good, it followed for Thomas that God is the final end toward which all creatures, from archangels to centipedes, naturally tend, each species in its own proper fasion. Since we are intellectual beings, our proper manner of tending toward God is by knowing him; not, as with Augustine and Bonaventure, by loving him.

He presents several excellent arguments—intellectual arguments, of course—to support this. Love, or desire, cannot be the distinguishing feature of human beings, for desire is found in all living things. And it is only fitting that our ultimate happiness be realized through our most characteristic trait, our intellect. Also, to love something is different from possessing it (it is possible to love what you are still seeking), but our final happiness should come from something we actually possess. Finally, love is an act of the will; but the will, which is automatically attracted to every apparent good, cannot distinguish true happiness from false—only the intellect can do that.

So our innate desire for complete and permanent happiness must come through knowledge of God. But what kind of knowledge? Not that of ordinary popular opinion, for this is incomplete and mixed with error. Not the knowledge which comes from logical proofs, for these do not present God as he really is. Not even the knowledge of faith, for faith comes through an act of the will, and it has already been shown that true happiness cannot come about through an act of the will. In fact, contrary to Aristotle, we are not able to satisfy our natural desire for perfect happiness in this life at all.

The Latin term which means "in vain" is *frustra,* and it was a basic tenet of Aristotelian and Thomistic metaphysics that nature never acts in vain. No being has a natural desire which cannot be satisfied. Neither Aristotle nor Thomas could believe that nature could be so diabolically sadistic as to condemn any species to a literally frustrated existence. A malevolent cosmos, for them, would have been a contradiction.

Since we have a natural desire for perfect happiness, then, and since this desire cannot be satisfied in this life, Aquinas concluded that it must be capable of being satisfied after death. This means that we must be capable of knowing God

after we die. It also means that God must be capable of being
known. Even granting the immortality of the soul, both of
these raise serious difficulties.

Thomas's basic answer, in opposition to an extremely well-
entrenched Christian tradition, was that since God is pure
being and being is intrinsically knowable, God is actually in
himself the most knowable of all things. But we cannot
achieve this knowledge without help: God's essence is like an
unlimited form which after death he presents to us in a manner that our intellects, which are capable of comprehending
forms, can grasp it.

The details of how all this occurs are rather technical, and
we need not go into them. The important thing is the end result, the achievement of our greatest natural desire: knowledge
of God "face to face," the highest possible fulfillment of our
highest faculty, forever. It is a kind of eternal intellectual
ecstasy—the beatific ("happiness-causing") vision.

This approach to eternal bliss is decidedly intellectualist,
but then so is Thomas' approach to God generally. He ends
each of his five proofs for the existence of a philosophically
necessary being with an almost casual comment to the effect
that this being is what everyone calls God. But in fact no one
but a metaphysician, and only a miserably small-souled
metaphysician at that, could call such a being God, if by
"God" one means an object of adoration and love.

The God of Abraham and Isaac was not an Unmoved
Mover. It was not the son of a first efficient cause who became incarnate and was crucified. Even Aquinas never
prayed to a "being having its own necessity in itself," any
more than Aristotle ever worshipped the movers of his
celestial spheres. Of course, Aquinas realized this. But then it
may simply be impossible to construct an intellectual argument for the existence of an object of love. This does not
mean that Thomas's arguments are invalid as metaphysical

demonstrations, merely that there may be limits to what logical reasoning can accomplish.

Why is Thomas Aquinas important? Primarily because he was able to establish Christian belief on a more solid foundation, or at least a more objective one, than either Augustine or Bonaventure had been able to do. Although his worldview may seem unfamiliar—even alien—to us today, it is immeasurably closer to our way of thinking than even that of his contemporary Bonaventure. The main difference was in his use of Aristotle.

As appealing as Platonism in many respects is, the fact remains that for Plato—and thus for Augustine (and, to a lesser extent, for Bonaventure)—this world was essentially an illusion. Its significance, at the very most, was to point toward and prepare the way for a higher reality. It is a worldview very congenial to mysticism, self-abnegation, and total unconcern—even contempt—for the physical aspects of human existence. Aquinas, following Aristotle, took what we today would consider a much more moderate and realistic attitude toward the physical world.

He also placed a much greater reliance on human reason than either Augustine or Bonaventure—even declaring, as we have seen, that the innermost nature of God himself can be grasped by the human intellect (even if we do need divine assistance to do so). In a sense, Aquinas did with metaphysics in the theological realm what Newton did with physics in the astronomical realm: he insisted that the same basic explanatory principles apply to all reality. In the thirteenth century, many considered this to be heretical reationalism, utterly pernicious to faith.

Thomism, born of a union of logic and metaphysics, developed and hardened in the dialectical give-and-take of medieval lecture halls, proved to be a much more potent

112 William A. Herr

weapon in theological debates than the highly subjective worldviews of Augustine and Bonaventure.

And yet, as always, there was a price to pay. Theology is not religion, and the spirit does not live by explanations alone. It would not be true to say that Aquinas took love and mystery out of Christian belief, but he did provide an instrument which tended to have that effect. It may not be impossible for a logician also to be a poet, but it must be unusually difficult. The Thomistic synthesis is so impressive in its scope and its logical consistency that it tends to encourage the delusion among some people that Thomism contains within itself the essence of Christianity—that the most important aspect of religion is knowing the right answers. One could never make that mistake with the writings of Augustine and Bonaventure.

It is important to remember what Aquinas did—and what he did not do. He was not a follower of any philosophical school. He did not blindly follow any human authority, even Augustine or Aristotle. What he did was to take the soundest philosophical system available—a controversial, highly suspect one—and the most enlightened scientific ideas of his time and use them to explain the contents and implications of faith. That is what Augustine had done; that is what every great theologian does. That is what Thomas would be doing were he alive today—to the utter consternation, no doubt, of many Thomists.

Thomism is basically a way of looking at things, in many respects an extremely useful way. But at best it is a help to understanding, one help among many, and not an end in itself. Its usefulness, like the usefulness of all tools, depends on the skill of the one who uses it, and this includes an ability to recognize its limitations.

Like the Rose of France, Thomism can transmit no light unless there is light shining through it.

Chapter 9
DUNS SCOTUS

TO the extent that scholasticism was characterized by detailed metaphysical analysis, reconciliation of different traditions, and the resolution of problems by making distinctions, *John Duns of Scotland*—better known as Duns Scotus—was probably the most typically scholastic of the great scholastic thinkers. Thanks in part to some of the implications of his own work, he was also the last.

Whereas Aquinas so completely and harmoniously developed the possibilities of his worldview that, at least for a time, his followers could do little more than defend and comment on his teachings, Scotus carried his analyses and distinctions so far that they helped prepare the path for a completely different way of treating philosophical and theological problems.

The life of Duns Scotus, like that of Aquinas, was short and relatively uneventful. He was born in southeastern Scotland in 1265 or 1266, about eight years before the death of Aquinas; his family name derived from Duns, the chief town of county Berwick, which may have been his birthplace. He entered the Franciscan order at age fifteen, and about ten years later was sent to study at Oxford. Several years thereafter, following his ordination, he went to Paris to study for a doctorate in theology.

Scotus left Paris without completing the degree requirements, however, and lectured for several years at Oxford on the *Sentences* of Peter Lombard. The notes of these lectures, which he frequently revised, constitute the most important of his writings. He may also have lectured at Cambridge. In 1302 he returned to Paris to complete his studies, but this time he became embroiled in a controversy between the pope and the French king over taxation of the clergy and was forced to leave the country with his work still unfinished. Scotus might be considered the unofficial patron of those who have trouble completing their doctoral dissertations.

He finally received his doctorate in 1305, when he was nearly forty and had only three more years to live. He taught in Paris for two years; then he was sent to Cologne, where he died in 1307. Despite the best efforts of the Franciscans, Scotus was never canonized, although he is venerated as a saint in the diocese of Cologne.

We saw earlier that the basic difference between Plato and Aristotle was one of viewpoint, of looking at the same problems and the same facts from different perspectives. To a large extent this was also true of Aquinas and Scotus. They lived at about the same time and wrote in the same intellectual environment, and both founded their thinking on Aristotelian metaphysics.

But there was a difference in emphasis in their views of human nature: Aquinas stressed the intellect, while Scotus—perhaps because of his Franciscan training—stressed the will. All through his writings, Aquinas emphasized knowledge. Scotus, like Augustine and Bonaventure, emphasized love. His work can be seen as an attempt to reconcile Aristotle and Augustine. In a sense, this meant reconciling Aristotle and Plato.

Probably Scotus's main reason for focusing on the will was that he viewed it primarily as the faculty of choice, not merely of desire. Aquinas taught that the will is blindly attracted to goodness, so that it automatically chooses whatever the intellect presents to it as being the greatest good. Scotus replied that the will can govern the intellect by causing it to focus on a particular side of an issue or to consider one object rather than another. So highly did Scotus esteem the will's freedom that he insisted that even the saints in heaven love God freely, rather than necessarily as Aquinas had taught. In theory this implied that their wills could turn away even from God, the greatest good, and that they could choose to sin, although Scotus was convinced that in fact this could never happen.

Also, he argued, the will must be superior to the intellect since corruption of the will is worse than corruption of the intellect: to hate God, for example, is worse than to deny him. In addition, it is not a sin to know something evil, but it is a sin to will evil.

Whereas Thomas, following the book of Exodus, had characterized God as that being whose essence is existence, Scotus took his inspiration from the Gospel of John: God is the infinite being who is Love. It is out of the fullness of this love, and as a manifestation of it, that God willed the incarnation. The more common explanation, that God became human in order to atone for our sins, was abhorent to Scotus: How could the greatest of all goods have been brought by sin? Scotus taught that Jesus would have been born even if Adam had not fallen, but in that case he would have come simply as an expression of divine love, not as a redeemer.

Love also formed the foundation of Scotus's ethical system. The first moral principle, for him, was that God must be loved above everything else, and he went so far as to say that no act can have positive moral goodness unless the agent refers the act to the love of God. If it is merely consistent with love of God, but not performed with some relation to this love, it is morally neutral.

One of the classic debates in Christian ethics concerns whether an act is wrong because God forbids it, or whether God forbids it because it is wrong. Scotus's answer to this problem had far-ranging and probably unforeseen consequences.

Take the case of lying. A Thomist would argue that lying is intrinsically sinful because it is a misuse of the power of speech and thus a violation of the eternal natural law. God forbade it from all eternity because it is wrong. Subtle here as always, Scotus differentiated between the content of divine law and the obligation it imposes. In a sense, he distinguished between ethics and morality.

Scotus agreed that reason, by examining human nature, can determine an objective standard of right and wrong. It can determine, for example, that lying is destructive of the human society on which we all depend and harmful to the person who does it. A wise and prudent person, therefore, will not tell lies, and whoever does so will suffer the natural consequences.

But Scotus added that while a rational study of human nature can establish an objective standard of behavior, it cannot establish a moral obligation to follow that standard. As far as human reason is concerned, to tell the truth is simply good practical advice. Lying may be an action which will hinder the accomplishment of what we naturally desire, but it is not a moral offense and it does not create guilt. In a similar sense we might say that there is an objective standard which tells us that one should not head toward Miami if one wishes to get to Seattle; but one who does so commits no sin, he simply will not arrive in Seattle. At this point we have ethics as Plato and Aristotle understood it.

Then where does moral obligation arise? It originates, says Scotus, in the free will of God: something becomes morally evil because God has chosen to forbid it. God chose to forbid lying, and thereby made it an offense against authority, a crime meriting punishment. Otherwise it would merely be unwise behavior.

But Scotus was quick to add that this decision of God, although free, cannot be capricious. God is an eminently rational being. He need not have chosen to impose any obligations on us, but once he decided to do so, then it was necessary that these obligations be rationally related to our natures. Thus the content of the moral law is objectively based on the nature of things, but our moral obligation to obey it results from a free decision by God to impose this obligation on us.

If moral obligation derives from a free act of God's will, could God dispense us from the obligation of obeying the ten commandments? Thomists said no, since the commandments merely express the eternal natural law. Scotus, characteristically, made a distinction.

As a rational being, he declared, God cannot violate the natures of things, including his own. He could not, for example, command us to worship trees instead of him, for the moral obligation of a creature to honor its creator is inherent in the nature of their relationship. Some of the commandments—the first two and possibly the third—are of this type, and God cannot dispense us from these. The others, however, are morally obligatory only because God has chosen to make them so; and, if he so wished, he could dispense us from the obligation of obeying them.

In its general orientation, the ethical theory of Scotus is quite modern. Considerable effort in recent years has gone into arguing that no analysis of objective facts can establish the existence of a moral obligation. One cannot validly deduce, for example, from an examination of human nature that one must or must not do anything; one can merely point to the consequences of doing it or not doing it. As the argument is often summarized, you cannot deduce an "ought" from an "is." Scotus would have agreed wholeheartedly: human nature does not establish moral obligations, God does.

Even in his own time, this position had important consequences. Although such an idea was undoubtedly the furthest thing from Scotus's mind, the fact remains that it was only a short step or two from his teaching that moral obligation derives from a free act of God's will to declaring that the moral law is entirely arbitrary, that there is no objective distinction between moral good and evil—just a choice of God, with no foundation in the nature of things, to command one thing and forbid another. The ten commandments, in other words, could be no more than capricious whims.

And if this is true of divine law, it is a short step indeed to arguing that it is also true of civil law: that law is simply whatever the ruler wishes it to be, and that there are no objective standards by which one can contend that a given law is unjust. But that is getting ahead of our story.

There are styles of thinking just as there are styles of writing or painting, and the style of Scotus was characterized in part by extraordinarily intricate metaphysical analysis. He seemed unwilling to get along with just one distinction in an argument if there was a way to work in three or four. When he had used up all the standard distinctions, Scotus found new ones.

He was not content, for example, to prove the existence of God by arguing from the existence of material things to the existence of a necessary first cause, as Aquinas and others had done, since the existence of the physical world itself is only contingent. That is, it is true that the world exists, but it does not have to exist. How can one arrive at a necessarily true conclusion about God unless one starts from a necessarily true premise?

But Scotus found necessity underlying the contingency. If the world exists, he reasoned, even only contingently, then the possibility of its existence is absolutely and necessarily true. In other words, if something exists, it may not have to exist, but it does have to be able to exist. He then proceeded to construct an argument for the existence of a necessary first cause very similar to the argument of Aquinas—but an argument based on the possibility of the existence of the physical world, not on its actual existence. This was a clever technical twist, although it seems unlikely that anyone not convinced by Aquinas's argument would be swayed by that of Scotus.

Scotus also rejected the unmoved mover proof Aquinas had adopted from Aristotle, contending that it is merely an argument about physical causality and does not demonstrate the existence of an infinite—and therefore divine—being. (Aristotle certainly would have agreed.) On the other hand, Scotus thought highly enough of Anselm's proof to spend considerable energy turning what had been a relatively straightforward argument into one of the most complicated demonstrations of God's existence ever constructed.

Previous philosophers had spoken of real distinctions (existing between things which can be physically separated, at least by God) and virtual or mental distinctions (cases where the mind can make a distinction, but there is no corresponding actual difference in the object). There is a real distinction, for example, between shape and color, or even between matter and form, but only a mental distinction between being a father and being a male parent. In the latter case, separation is not only actually impossible, it would be a contradiction.

These two were not sufficient for Scotus, who introduced the formal distinction: the case where two things cannot actually be separated, but where such a separation would not be contradictory. There is an actual, objective difference, for example, between the pope and the bishop of Rome: the two terms do not mean the same thing. To physically separate the pope and the bishop of Rome would not be a logical contradiction; it is just not possible in fact.

All this would have remained an obscure footnote in philosophical history except that once Scotus had discovered this new distinction, he proceeded to use it. And one place he used it was on the problem of universals. Scotus disagreed with those who, like Aquinas, considered essence and existence to be two different things. Consider the concept "to be a horse." From one point of view, it is composed of two separate elements, a noun and a verb: the verb can be combined with other nouns, the noun with other verbs. The essense ("horse") and the existence ("to be") appear to be separable.

In fact, insisted Scotus, this is not the case. You cannot separate existence from horseness; there are not, nor can there be, any horses which do not exist. Granted that existence and horseness do not mean the same thing; still, not even God and all his angels can separate the two. As in the case of the pope and the bishop of Rome, there is a formal distinction between them but not a real one.

Then what is the relation between a universal and an individual—between being human, let us say, and being Socrates? A human being is a union of matter and form. But Socrates is a union of *this* matter and *this* form, and so is every other person. To be human, therefore, means to possess not merely matter and form, but a certain *thisness.* (Scotus called it *haecceitas,* a made-up Latin word which literally means "thisness.") Thisness (Socratesness, for example) is not exactly the same as humanness, but to be Socrates and to be human cannot be physically separated. They are, again, formally but not really distinct.

Since humanness is inseparable from thisness, humanness in itself is not universal. And since it is not the same as Socratesness, or any other example of thisness, it is not particular. If humanness were universal, then being human would not mean being a specific individual; and if it were particular, then there would be no justification for general statements about people. Scotus taught that this same sort of relation, a formal and not a real distinction, holds in every case between the general and the individual.

Whereas Aquinas held that it is prime matter which individuates a form, Scotus objected that if prime matter differentiated specific individuals, then in cases of substantial change (such as food's being turned into flesh and blood), the old and the new substance would have to be identical, since the prime matter is identical. But that is the same as denying the reality of substantial change. Again, it is absurd to call prime matter the principle of determination and at the same time to say that it is completely indeterminate. How can anything confer a quality which it does not possess?

The true principle of individuation, according to Scotus, is the individual entity itself, the concrete composite of matter and form. And what really individuates is thisness, which is conferred through the form but is something distinct from it.

Scotus also insisted, in opposition to Aristotle and Aquinas, that we have real knowledge of individual things, not merely of essences. This position he supported with an argument typical of him: it is individuals that we love, not essences, and since love presupposes knowledge (no one can love something of which he or she has no knowledge), then we must have real knowledge of individuals. Besides, the fact of inductive reasoning, in which we arrive at a general truth by examining many specific cases, cannot be explained in any other way.

These conclusions were an open invitation to a far more radical position: if there is no real distinction between universals and individuals, and if we have a real knowledge of individual things, why postulate the existence of universals? What facts are there which cannot be explained without them?

And what, precisely, is "thisness"? Even Scotus found that a difficult question to answer. "Thisness" is a classic example of a philosophical dead end: an explanation which explains nothing. It can neither be proved or disproved, which is one of the signs of a poor explanation.

But even this was, in a sense, a positive accomplishment. A dead end in philosophy, as in physics or astronomy or most other disciplines, is usually indicative of a basic unresolved problem. And calling attention to the existence of a problem is a first step toward its solution. Such was the case here. "Thisness" was a symptom of the fact that the scholastic tradition had failed to adequately solve the problem of universals. As we said earlier, one of the best things to do in this situation is to examine one's presuppositions, and eventually this is exactly what happened.

Scotus agreed with Aquinas on a number of specific issues, such as the impossibility of disproving the eternity of the world (he parted company with Bonaventure on this point to side with Aquinas), but they differed on many more.

Scotus could not, for example, accept Aquinas's argument that the existence of a natural desire for complete happiness proves the soul's immortality. It is begging the question, he contended, to conclude anything from a presumed natural desire for perfect happiness when the possibility of such happiness has not yet been established. In fact, Scotus was convinced that unaided human reason is incapable of proving the soul's immortality.

He also did not think much of Thomas's theory that souls after death are differentiated by their relations to the bodies they previously informed. Such a teaching, he declared, implies that the soul exists for the sake of the body. Besides, there cannot be a relation of one soul rather than another with a particular body unless there is some distinction between the souls—which is precisely the point at issue.

Whereas Aquinas had taught that the soul is united to the body for the sake of the soul, Scotus believed that it is for the good of the composite itself, the actual person, that the union exists. At the same time he argued, in opposition to Aquinas, that the rational soul cannot be the only form of the body. After all, he pointed out, a person's body remains in existence, at least for a time, after the rational soul has departed, and this would not be possible unless it had a form of its own. Also, the body of Jesus lay three days in a tomb after his death: how could it truly have been the body of Jesus before, during and after this period unless it was united to the same form all that time, even when the rational soul was not informing it?

There is, taught Scotus, a form of corporeity, which unites with prime matter to constitute the body. This form of corporeity is transmitted at conception, and God subsequently infuses the rational soul. It is worth noting that Scotus was writing after the condemnation of 1277, when Aquinas's position that the rational soul is the only form of the body had been declared heretical.

Another issue on which Scotus differed with Aquinas—and with most of his other predecessors—was the Immaculate Conception. Thomas, along with Origen, Bernard of Clairvaux, and most other theologians in the Western church up to the time of Scotus, had held that such a thing was impossible. Scripture teaches that Christ is the redeemer of all people. This would not be true if one person, by never having been subject to original sin, had not needed redemption.

If anyone could find a distinction to resolve this difficulty, it was Scotus. If Mary had been preserved from original sin, he wrote, this could have come about only through the merits of her son. Christ was therefore her redeemer as much as anyone else's, in the sense of shielding her from the effects of sin, and so the universality of Christ's redemptive role presents no obstacle to believing that Mary was at no time subject to original sin.

With this simple argument, Scotus single-handedly removed the major theological stumbling block to the eventual definition of the Immaculate Conception as an article of faith.

Right after the scholastic tradition produced Thomas

Aquinas, Duns Scotus, quite unintentionally, broke the mold. He broke it by stretching it too far, and he broke it in several places.

By inviting a critical examination of the reality of universals and by separating moral obligation from the natural order of things, he opened the door to an attack on the common metaphysical foundation from which the entire scholastic tradition drew its sustenance. By insisting that the immortality of the soul and similar beliefs cannot be proven by reason, he weakened the harmonious synthesis of philosophy and theology so characteristic of the medieval worldview. And by his tendency to draw elaborate distinctions and to postulate such mysterious entities as "thisness," he contributed to the degeneration of the entire scholastic way of thinking. But the main fault, especially on this last point, was not his.

It is possible that no major thinker in history was less well served by his followers than was Scotus; eventually they were responsible for turning his very name into a term of reproach.

Rather than building on the original and constructive elements in his work, they tended to concentrate on developing more and more intricate arguments and more and more subtle distinctions for use in debates over issues which made no real difference one way or the other. For them, cleverness became an end in itself. This was a pitiful caricature of the vigorous academic disputations which had originally given rise to the scholastic synthesis. It was scholasticism, deprived of its vital principle, decomposing into its constituent elements. This is the stereotype which the very mention of medieval philosophy still conjures up for many people.

The followers of Duns Scotus were known, naturally enough, as Duns men. It was not the fault of Scotus, a brilliant and innovative thinker, that these people eventually acquired such a reputation for useless quibbling that this phrase became the origin of the English word "dunce."

Thinking itself was being suffocated. Someone had to cut through this jungle of extraneous verbiage. And just at this point there appeared a man with one of the sharpest knives in the entire history of philosophy, and he began cutting with a vengeance.

Chapter 10
WILLIAM OF OCKHAM

WE have an almost irresistible tendency, it seems, to assume that there is an object of some sort corresponding to every noun in our language. As a result, we often accept without question explanations which explain nothing.

Ask someone why an unsupported rock falls to the ground, for example, and he or she will probably say it happens because of gravity, as though gravity were a special force that makes things move downward. Actually, gravity does not make anything move, because "gravity" is no more than a word—a word used to refer to the fact that every physical object in the universe is attracted to every other, and that, if nothing keeps them from doing so, they will move toward each other. The word "gravity" (which literally means no more than "heaviness") does not make it easier to understand what happens when a rock falls; it makes it more difficult. Or, to take a different sort of example, is "truth" really anything more than a word referring to the fact that some statements have been or can be verified?

These kinds of questions, and this type of analysis of the meanings and uses of words, characterize one of the most important currents in contemporary philosophy. They were also a major concern of the Franciscan logician and theologian whose work marks the start of the transition between medieval and modern thought. If Duns Scotus broke the mold of scholasticism, William of Ockham scattered the pieces so widely that no one was ever able to put them back together.

Bonaventure and Scotus may have had short academic careers, but Ockham hardly had any at all. He was born in southeastern England around 1290, entered the Franciscan order, and studied theology at Oxford. But Ockham was too far ahead of his time. Even before being certified as a master theologian, he was denounced as a heretic on the basis of his commentary on the *Sentences* of Peter Lombard and was summoned to the papal court at Avignon. One thing led to another, and Ockham spent the remaining 25 years of his life either under house arrest or as an excommunicated fugitive.

Right from the start, things went badly at Avignon. A six-member commission was appointed to investigate the heresy charges; one of the six was the man who had originally denounced him. A list of more than fifty of his allegedly heretical teachings was drawn up for condemnation. The case dragged on for years, and Ockham was forbidden by the pope to leave Avignon until a final decision was reached. Unpleasant as all of this must have been, however, Ockham did not start learning the real meaning of trouble until the Minister General of the Franciscans, Michael of Cesena, arrived in town.

Michael was in an even worse fix than Ockham was. The debate on evangelical poverty in the Franciscan order which Bonaventure had tried to solve was still raging. Spiritual Franciscans, as they were called—those who advocated absolute poverty—insisted that they be allowed to follow the original Rule of St. Francis in all its strictness, even though many in the order, with the support of several popes, had adopted a less rigorous interpretation of their vow.

The dispute became considerably more acrimonious in 1317 when the Spirituals sent a delegation to the newly crowned pope, John XXII, to plead their case. John had the petitioners thrown into prison and turned 25 of them over to the Inquisition; four were burned at the stake. Then he commanded Michael of Cesena, who had sided with the Spirituals, to report to Avignon and submit to an examination of his own orthodoxy.

By this time, a rational discussion of the issues was nearly impossible. When Michael arrived in Avignon and found Ockham there—the greatest thinker of his age, and a fellow Franciscan as well—he urged him to get involved in the dispute. Ockham probably did not need much urging. Like Abelard, he seems to have had a penchant for getting into trouble. (This may be an occupational hazard of logicians: perhaps the nature of their work tends to make them argumentative. Specialists in such fields as aesthetics, on the other hand, tend to be a relatively placid lot.)

Ockham examined John XXII's pronouncements on the poverty issue and decided that the pope himself had fallen into heresy and should be deposed. Avignon not being an auspicious place in which to announce these findings, he and Michael fled the city—for which act of disobedience they were excommunicated and expelled from the Franciscan order—and took refuge with the only one in Europe who was willing and able to protect them from the pope: Ludwig of Bavaria, the Holy Roman Emperor and John XXII's bitter enemy. The following year Ludwig had a Franciscan Spiritual crowned as the antipope Nicholas V.

Circumstances now cast Ockham in the role of antipapal polemicist in the emperor's service. And John XXII, by a remarkably ill-considered action, obligingly gave him plenty of ammunition.

In 1331 and 1332 the pope preached a series of sermons in which he expressed his personal belief that the blessed in heaven do not yet enjoy the beatific vision and will not do so until after the last judgment. He had a cogent philosophical reason for this position—the beatific vision is a reward for the whole person; but the whole person is a union of body and soul, and the body will not be reunited with the soul until after the last judgment—but this teaching was rejected by most of the theologians of Europe, and John was forced to retract it.

This permitted Ockham to argue that since the pope could err in doctrinal matters—and had, in fact, just done so—the possibility of appeal to a higher authority, a general council of the whole church, was necessary to prevent a pope from leading the faithful into error. The argument that a council is superior to the pope found a ready audience, especially among bishops who resented papal interference and kings who opposed the growing burden of papal taxation; and Ockham's writings contributed substantially to the growth of the Conciliar Movement in the fourteenth and fifteenth centuries. In 1339, he wrote a treatise defending the right to England's Edward III to tax church property, and he was a vociferous critic of the pope's temporal power.

After John's death Ockham continued the battle against his successor, Benedict XII, and then against Clement VI. But it was a a lost cause. Michael of Cesena died, and then Ludwig of Bavaria died, and finally Ockham died in 1347 and was buried in the choir of the Franciscan church in Munich.

It is as true in philosophy and theology as in any other type of endeavor that where you choose to start goes a long way toward determining where you will end up. This was particularly true of Ockham. Many of the most characteristic elements of his thinking had their origin in one basic theological insight: God is absolutely all-powerful and absolutely free.

Ockham certainly was not the first one to describe God as omnipotent. But usually we begin to qualify—and therefore to deny—this description almost as soon as we make it. Yes, we say, God is almighty, but he is also all-wise and all-just and thus cannot do anything unjust or foolish. To all intents and purposes the scholastics, implicitly at least, invented a new attribute: God as all-rational.

Perhaps we do this because we cannot bear to think about

what omnipotence really implies. Part of Ockham's originality lay in drawing out and accepting these implications.

For Ockham, divine omnipotence meant precisely what it
said: God is totally unlimited, totally unrestricted; God can
literally do absolutely anything. And just as Scotus had
focused on the human will rather than the intellect, so
Ockham focused on the divine will. God can do whatever he
pleases; he is not bound by such human concepts as wisdom
or rationality.

If God wishes to be what we might call capricious, there is
nothing whatsoever to stop him. God can make water flow
uphill, or people's ears turn green, or a cow give birth to a
kitten. God can make us see things which are not there.

This means that everything is totally, radically contingent.
Everything depends on God's absolutely free will from each
instant to the next. And there is simply no way of telling what
God might do, or when. There is no necessary connection between past and future; anything and everything can change at
a moment's notice. There is no necessity and therefore there
is no certainty about anything, except through faith.

This kind of uncertainty could make a person who dwells
on it afraid to get out of bed in the morning. And when it
comes to metaphysics, its implications are devastating.

In order for absolutely anything to be possible at any moment—for any event to be able to follow any other event—
each event and each object in the universe must be totally
separate. To see why this is true, consider a pile of children's
blocks. If all the blocks are separate from each other, one can
combine them in any way one chooses. But if someone were
to glue some of the blocks together, then certain combina-
tions would no longer be possible. The necessary connections
between certain blocks would be a limitation on what a person could and could not do in combining them.

If God is really omnipotent, there can be no intrinsic or

necessary relations between things—between fire and heat, for example, or sugar and sweetness, or any cause and any effect—and this means that metaphysics as most people understand it is impossible.

No fact about any object in the universe can be used to prove anything for certain about any other object. Since God can produce any effect without the intermediary of its customary cause, and can prevent any cause from producing its customary effect, no causal argument can prove anything conclusively. (One implication of this is that any proof of God's existence based on causal reasoning, as most of them are, is invalid.) Nothing follows necessarily from anything else.

But if everything is completely distinct from everything else, what does it mean to say that Socrates and Plato are both human beings? The scholastics would have said that they both have the same nature: that this nature existed as an idea in the mind of God from all eternity and was the model, so to speak, which God followed in creating people. To Ockham, these eternal models implied a limitation on God—they suggested that God was obliged to create things in a certain way and not in some other way. So he denied their existence.

There is no such thing as human nature, said Ockham: Socrates has a nature, and Plato has a nature, but "human" is simply the word we use to express the fact that these two natures are similar in many respects. It does not stand for anything except individuals, because there is nothing but individuals.

The so-called universals are merely words which can be used to refer to more than one individual at a time; they are the verbal mechanisms we use when generalizing about similar objects. The similarity on which this generalization is based is real, but its only importance is that it helps us to group individuals.

The point is that we must not be misled into thinking that

the general word refers to something else than those particular individuals. That would be like someone's assuming that if, in the middle of a conversation about three of my friends, I should use the word "they," this word would refer to some sort of mysterious common entity distinct from the three individual friends.

This was really an attack on the whole tradition of classical Greek philosophy, and Ockham intended it as such. In his eyes, the Greek concept of essences or universals was fundamentally anti-Christian; it was an affront to the Christian conception of God.

There is also, according to Ockham, no reality corresponding to many of the words we use to express relationships. The reality lies in the concrete objects involved rather than in the supposed relation. There is no such thing as priority, for example; there are simply some things which happen at one time and other things which happen at another. Nor is there such a thing as motion: "motion" is simply a word referring to the fact that an object is first in one place, and then in another.

Again, it is valid to use these words to generalize—to refer to the fact that, for example, there are many objects which are first in one place and then in another—so long as we do not make the mistake of assuming that the word refers to some reality distinct from the objects.

Not content to do away with the essences and relations, Ockham went on to formulate a general methodological principle with which his name has been associated ever since. Basically what he said was that when a simpler explanation suffices to account for something, one should not choose a more complicated one. In practice this means that the number of factors used to explain things should be held to a minimum. Or, put another way, if you can account for all the phenomena without recourse to a given factor, do not include that factor in your explanation. This is sometimes called the principle of economy of thought or the principle of parsimony, but it is more familiarly known as Ockham's Razor.

We take this principle so much for granted that it comes as something of a surprise to realize that there is no way to prove that simple explanations explain any better than complicated ones. From a logical point of view, it is basically a matter of aesthetic preference. We have chosen to accept unnecessary ornamentation in architecture and to reject it in science; another culture might well have chosen the opposite.

Simple explanations do, however, have at least two important advantages. First, they tend to prevent the problem Ockham was primarily concerned with: the simpler explanations are, the less chance there is of using as explanatory principles entities which do not really exist. Second, the desire to explain as much as possible with as few principles as possible has been the driving force behind the best scientific theorizing. But this has been true, not because simple explanations are intrinsically better than complicated ones, but because (at least if nuclear physicists are to be believed), beneath the apparent diversity and complexity of nature, reality is actually quite simple. This is something Ockham could not have known.

Using his Razor, Ockham began slicing away at the explanations of his predecessors. Scotus's *haecceitas,* predictably, was an early casualty: it is simply not needed to explain anything, particularly if the existence of universals is denied. The active and passive intellects Aquinas had posited met the same fate—it is possible to explain all the phenomena with the hypothesis that there is only one intellect. And on and on and on.

Given his theological orientation and that of his age, Ockham probably could not have forseen what target his principle would most frequently be aimed at, but it is not difficult to guess which traditional explanatory factor a more secular mentality would tend to find least necessary. When Napoleon remarked to the French scientist Laplace that one of his theories made no mention of God, Laplace replied that he had "not found a need for that hypothesis." The words were Laplace's own, but the spirit behind them was that of Ockham's Razor.

Ockham's way of thinking may have been a body blow to traditional philosophy, but it was the breath of life to empirical science. If one cannot reason out a thing's intrinsic relations and how it "ought" to behave by considering the logical implications of its nature, and if one cannot prove with certainty that a causal connection exists between any two things, then one must obtain knowledge about the world not by logical analysis but by painstakingly observing thousands of separate entities. The method of science, in other words, becomes inductive, not deductive.

This knowledge is only probably and contingently true, not absolutely and necessarily true, but that is the only kind of knowledge about the world which acceptance of God's omnipotence permits us to have. The primary focus of scientific inquiry shifted from trying to understand the innermost natures of things to predicting their behavior under various conditions, and this is generally where it has remained.

A classic example is Galileo's experimentation with the velocity of falling bodies. It still seems like no more than plain common sense, just as it did in his day, that a five-pound weight should fall five times as fast as a one-pound weight. That seems like the kind of thing a child could reason out, the kind of thing it would be a waste of time to investigate empirically. And yet it turns out not to be true. Reliance on deductive reasoning is not only inconsistent with belief in God's omnipotence, it is also a poor way to find out the truth about the physical world.

All of this seems obvious enough today, but it is well to remember that nothing is obvious until someone makes it obvious. It is also well to remember that it is easier to recognize someone else's shortcomings than it is one's own. The medievals may appear simple-minded to us for attempting to deduce a things's behavior from an analysis of its nature, but in fact we do something similar all the time. We do it, for example, whenever we appeal to "human nature" as an explanation for something.

We would laugh at someone who said that stones fall to earth because that is the nature of stones; but if someone says that people cheat on their incomes taxes because that is the nature of people, we seem to feel, for some reason, that he has made a meaningful statement. One need not be a William of Ockham to see that saying that people act in a certain way because of human nature is the same as saying that people act in a certain way because that is the way people act.

Ockham's insistence on God's absolute omnipotence and his emphasis on the freedom of the divine will also had important implications in the ethical realm. He agreed with Scotus that an action is morally good or evil because God has chosen to command or forbid it, but he did not agree that the content of what God chooses to command or forbid must be in rational conformity with human nature (or, as he would have preferred to put it, with people's individual natures). For Ockham, as we have seen, God is not restricted by our concept of rationality. Morality is entirely arbitrary, in the sense that it can be whatever God chooses to make it at any given moment, and we depend on revelation to know what God has chosen it to be.

Nor is God bound by such concepts as fairness or justice. God can choose to forgive an unrepentant sinner, or refuse to forgive a repentant one. Salvation is not earned; it is a free gift whose granting or withholding need follow no human logic and need not be related to the merits of the individuals concerned. This is very close—perhaps identical—to salvation by faith alone, which is why Luther was to call himself a follower of Ockham.

Even in the Middle Ages the approach of Ockham was known, prophetically, as "the modern way." It fourished in spite of official disapproval, much as Aristotelianism had a century earlier, and with a comparable effect on succeeding generations.

Ockham's attack on the foundations of metaphysical reasoning meant that many religious beliefs which scholastics had thought could be proved by reason alone—such as the existence of God and the immortality of the soul—could in fact be known with certainty only by faith. This effectively destroyed the synthesis of reason and faith upon which scholasticism had been based.

On the one hand, philosophy, deprived of the hope of reaching certain conclusions, turned toward the realm of the merely probably and concerned itself less with absolute truth and more with predictability. As we have seen, this tendency led to the rise of empirical, experimental science. On the other hand, faith separated from reason turned toward mysticism. (In fact it is impossible to determine how much of this tendency can be attributed to purely intellectual factors. People usually turn away from reason and toward pure faith when times are bad, and before long times got very bad indeed.)

Another effect took longer to manifest itself. The tendency to attribute more and more of what had been the common province of reason and faith to faith alone was not catastrophic so long as that faith remained unshaken. When later events called faith itself into question, however, the natural result was skepticism about the possibility of attaining certain truth about anything.

But it takes more inner strength to live without certainty than most people—perhaps anyone at all— can muster. In time, an attempt was made to establish certainty on the basis of reason alone, in effect reversing the trend Ockham had started. That attempt was the beginning of modern philosophy.

As faith developed in one direction and reason in another, scholasticism, the child of their union, languished. What had been a vigorous and innovative tradition gradually ossified into various "schools"—followers of Aquinas, Scotus, Bonaventure, and so on—who often put loyalty to their patron above the pursuit of truth. Thus the Dominicans felt obliged for several centuries to deny the Immaculate Conception, despite its almost universal acceptance by the rest of the church, for little better reason than that Aquinas had denied it. Even before the Reformation, Catholic thought was acquiring a defensive mentality.

It is tempting to speculate on what might have happened if someone had been able to synthesize Ockham's philosophy with church doctrine, as Aquinas had done with Aristotle— the effect might have been to narrow or even prevent the rift between faith and reason. But this never happened, in part because in the middle of the fourteenth century intellectual life came to a virtual stop. Like Augustine, Ockham was followed by chaos.

The thirteenth century had been a good time to live; the fourteenth was a good time to die. It was a period when almost everything went wrong.

The fourteenth was the century of the Hundred Years' War, which ravaged the land and people of France literally for generations; it was the century of the Great Schism, when two men, then three, claimed to be the lawful pope. Religious upheavals broke out in such widely separated places as England (John Wycliffe) and Bohemia (Jan Hus).

Peasants rose up against their landlords in country after

country—the Jacquerie in France (1358) and Wat Tyler's rebellion in England (1381) were but two examples—and were savagely repressed. In 1348, an earthquake centered near Naples caused destruction as far north as Germany.

But all of this was merely a backdrop to the greatest disaster in the recorded history of Europe.

It is impossible for anyone to imagine the suffering and devastation caused by the Black Death: a full-scale nuclear war might not equal it. No one knows how many millions died. The best modern estimates are that half the population of Paris and Siena, two-thirds that of Vienna, three-quarters that of Florence, and perhaps one-third of the total inhabitants of Europe perished. Nothing could stop the disease; victims often took sick and died in less than a day. People thought it was the end of the world.

It was, in fact, the beginning of the end of the medieval world. There is symbolism of a sort in the fact that Ockham, the last of the great medieval philosophers, was killed by the Black Death. It is clear in retrospect that by the time he died, things were already beginning to fall apart.

Chapter 11
ERASMUS AND THOMAS MORE

OUT of the carnage and destruction of the fourteenth century, like fresh foliage emerging from a burned-out landscape, like the start of a new revolution in the cycle of life and death, blossomed the Renaissance.

Renaissance: literally, a rebirth. But a rebirth of what? There was, first, a rebirth of prosperity, of commerce, of peace and order. A smaller population meant that both farmers and artisans could command more for their labor. The social disruptions of the fourteenth century led to a loosening of the rigid bonds of feudalism. Peasants headed toward the cities and many prospered there; some degree of upward mobility developed. Trade and industry flourished.

Wealth made leisure possible, and leisure made possible a revival of culture. In Italy particularly, where this process first occurred, the revival took the form of a rebirth of interest in classical art and literature. Greek and Roman authors enjoyed a popularity unknown since the fall of Rome. Also reborn was a worldview centered on human reason, human needs, and the human person generally.

But all of this might have remained an eccentric preoccupation of a few antiquarians had it not been for one of history's most revolutionary inventions. The printing press was the technological underpinning of the Renaissance, just as the steam engine was the technological underpinning of the Industrial Revolution. Suddenly ideas, old and new, could be disseminated across the continent with breathtaking speed. Learning, suddenly, was no longer the exclusive province of the church and the universities.

As the Renaissance spread northward from Italy, humanists throughout Europe dreamed of establishing a new golden

139

age. It was a time of optimism, of confidence. At the start of
the sixteenth century, as at the start of the twentieth, people
thought they were entering an era of unparalleled peace and
progress.

And in both cases it turned out that, for a few years, they
were.

Desiderius Erasmus of Rotterdam personified the northern
Renaissance just as Voltaire was to personify the Enlighten-
ment. Like Voltaire, he was the preeminent literary figure of
his time; like Voltaire, he used his fine-honed wit to mock the
foibles of church and society. Unlike Voltaire, however,
Erasmus was also a major religious figure in an age which
took religion very seriously indeed. It was his fate to be the
conscience of Europe at the time of Europe's most traumatic
crisis of conscience.

Erasmus was born in 1466, or eleven years after the printing of Gutenberg's first bible. At about the age of nine he
came under the influence of the Brethren of the Common
Life, a religious society centered in the Netherlands, who
trained him in what was known as the "modern devotion."
This approach to spirituality, a reaction against both scholastic speculation and the mysticism of the late fourteenth century, aimed at the development of a Christ-related daily life
of asceticism, solitude, meditation, and devotional reading.
Its classic expression was *The Imitation of Christ* by Thomas
a Kempis, probably the society's most famous member.
Erasmus was educated by the Brethren of the Common Life
for twelve years, and their ideals greatly influenced his later
life. (Martin Luther briefly attended a school run by the same
society in Germany.)

On the advice of a guardian (both his parents died when he
was seventeen), Erasmus entered an Augustinian monastery
near Delft. Here he began the serious study of classical and

religious literature; here he was ordained. And here he discovered, belatedly, that he was not cut out for community life.

But it was not easy in those days to leave a monastic order.
His opportunity finally came in 1494, when the Bishop of
Cambrai asked the young scholar to become his secretary. On
the strength of this invitation, Erasmus obtained a dispensation to leave his monastery. In less than a year he was enrolled at the University of Paris, and the bishop was looking
for a new secretary.

Like many other young people serious about learning,
Erasmus found the university courses, mostly lectures on
scholastic philosophy and theology, a disappointment. Instead he devoted his energies to literature, and helped to
support himself by tutoring some of his fellow students in
Latin. In 1499, at the invitation of one of these pupils, he
went to England.

Erasmus was now thirty-three, and this trip was a turning
point in his life. Like many present-day visitors to Britain he
detested English weather and English beer (Erasmus had
spent too much time in Holland not to remember what beer
was supposed to taste like), but the intellectual climate he
found quite congenial indeed. He met and befriended the
humanist theologian John Colet, as well as the future Archbishop of Canterbury, William Warham, and the future
Bishop of Rochester, John Fisher. He also struck up a warm
friendship with Thomas More, then twenty-two years old and
just beginning his legal career.

It was during this period, and partly under the influence of
such men as Colet and More, that Erasmus began to conceive
the project which would become his life's work, a project
which perfectly suited both his religious outlook and his
literary gifts.

The Italian Renaissance, through the rediscovery and
dissemination of Greek and Roman literature, had encour-

aged a glorification of Greek and Roman—that is to say,
pagan—morality. But what if one could apply the same edi-
torial and critical techniques to the great masterpieces of
Christian literature, especially to the works of the Fathers
and to the bible itself? Might not that encourage a revival of
genuine Christian morality and a return to a piety based on
the teachings of Christ?

To accomplish his task Erasmus needed two tools then in
short supply in northern Europe: a thorough knowledge of
Greek and a mastery of the principles of textual criticism.
Greek he picked up where he could, but fortune intervened to
give him a head start in learning how to work with texts. In a
Belgian monastery he came across a manuscript by the Italian
classicist and philologist Lorenzo Valla which criticized the
accuracy of St. Jerome's Latin translation of the Bible (for
nearly a thousand years the standard version across Europe)
and set forth the methodological principles upon which a new
translation should be based. Erasmus determined to make
Valla's program his own.

For the rest of his years Erasmus lived a life which bore
about the same relation to the academic careers of the university professors of his time that the mendicant way of life had
borne to monasticism: he was a wandering scholar, traveling
wherever his studies led him—France, Italy, Switzerland,
Germany, England, the Netherlands—sharing what he had
learned as he went, living from the proceeds of his writings
and gifts from benefactors.

He published two immensely popular books: The *Adages,*
a collection of more than three thousand proverbs culled
from the works of classical authors, and a booklet entitled
Handbook of a Christian Knight, whose principal theme was
that spiritual perfection is achieved not through outward
religious observances but by prayer and cultivation of the
inward life of the soul—in short, by the very elements em-

bodied in the "modern devotion" he had learned as a child.

In 1509 Erasmus returned to England. There, while living in Thomas More's house and waiting for his books to arrive from the continent, he wrote in one week what is today his most famous work: *The Praise of Folly,* a playful essay filled with classical references, elaborate figures of speech, and homey Netherlandish proverbs, which begins by arguing that foolishness, not wisdom, is the source of all that is good in life and ends with a bitter attack on dissolute clergy and ostentatious church officials. (Clerical immorality was a favorite target of Erasmus' caustic wit. This may have been related to the fact that he and his older brother were illegitimate sons of a priest.) He also taught Greek for three years at Cambridge at the invitation of Bishop Fisher; the rooms he occupied can still be visited at Queen's College.

In 1516 Erasmus's revolutionary New Testament, the product of careful comparison of different Greek manuscripts and the readings of various commentators, was published in Switzerland. This was the first Greek text of the New Testament ever published (Erasmus's own Latin translation ran alongside), and it opened a new age in critical biblical scholarship.

In his preface Erasmus expressed the wish that the Bible might be translated into every language, so that its verses could become familiar even to illiterate farmers and peddlers. That wish also had been part of the program of the Brethren of the Common Life, and it was fulfilled: Erasmus's text became the source for many of the Reformation era vernacular translations, including that of Luther.

The Greek New Testament was followed by critical editions of the works of Jerome, Cyprian, Iranaeus, Ambrose, Augustine, Chrysostom, Origen and other church fathers. From 1517 to 1521 Erasmus taught at the University of Louvain in Belgium, where he helped to establish a school dedicated to the study of Latin, Greek and Hebrew. Also during this period he began publishing his long series of *Colloquies,* witty dialogues commenting on the popular issues of the day. He kept up a steady correspondence with religious, political and academic leaders throughout Europe; several thousand of these letters still exist.

Erasmus was now the leading intellectual authority of his time, a widely read social commentator, and a well-known critic of church corruption. All of this put him in a most difficult position when the Reformation began. The reformers, many of whom were echoing Erasmus's own criticisms of ecclesiastical abuses, naturally appealed to him for support (Luther twice asked him to intervene on his behalf), while Catholic leaders insisted that he devote his immense prestige to the cause of preserving Christian unity.

It was one of those cases where both sides were right and both sides were wrong; and Erasmus, who had close friends in both camps, tried to steer his own middle course between them. So even-handed was his public stance that at one point he was credited with being the real author both of a Lutheran treatise and of Henry VIII's reply to it.

But he had become too important a person to be allowed the luxury of neutrality. Too many people looked to him for leadership. Erasmus managed to keep his head when all about him were losing theirs; sure enough, both sides blamed it on him. He was savagely attacked by Catholic polemicists as having been the real instigator of the Reformation and "worse than Martin Luther"; Luther's followers denounced him as a traitor to the cause of reform, too cowardly to act on his convictions when the time for action came.

Erasmus's dilemma was a common one—familiar, for example, to anyone who remembers the bitter arguments over protests against the Vietnam war. He agreed with the reformers' aims, but was afraid of what their methods might lead to. As the situation in Germany degenerated into social revolution, Erasmus finally made his choice. He wrote a pamphlet against Luther's doctrine on free will; predictably, it satisfied neither side. An exchange of polemical works followed.

Erasmus died in 1536 in Switzerland, in the house of his publisher. Although he professed himself to the very end to be a faithful Catholic, he was buried in the cathedral of Basel, which by that time had become a Protestant church. And although Pope Paul III had offered to make him a cardinal, the Council of Trent, thirty years after his death, saw fit to put his works on its new Index of Forbidden Books.

The drama surrounding Thomas More's death has tended to overshadow the accomplishments of his life. This is ironic, for few martyrs ever fought as tenaciously as he did to stay alive —but then few ever had as much as he had to stay alive for.

The eldest son of a successful London lawyer and judge, More learned early the advantages of wealth and privilege. He was educated in the best elementary school in the city, and at the age of twelve he became a page in the household of John Morton, who was both Archbishop of Canterbury and Lord Chancellor of England. The boy thus had as his mentor not only the highest ecclesiastical and highest administrative personage in the kingdom, but also a master in the art of power politics: Morton had been instrumental in overthrowing Richard III and bringing Henry Tudor, Henry VII, to the throne.

At Morton's urging More went to Oxford in 1492; there he studied Latin, logic and literature and made the acquaintance of leading English humanists. But Sir John More had definite plans for his son's future, and an academic career did not figure in them. Obediently but reluctantly, More returned to London to study law, and was admitted to the bar in 1501.

But now another element of his rich and complex personality rose to the surface. Suspecting that he might have a religious vocation, he lived for four years in the Carthusian community in London, sharing as much of the monks' daily life as possible while continuing to practice law.

Deciding at last—after no little persuasion by his father— that he was not meant for the religious life, More threw himself whole-heartedly into establishing a family. Within five years of leaving the monastery, he had married and fathered four children. When his first wife died less than seven years after their marriage, More quickly wed again.

Law is a profession which rewards intelligence and a willingness to work hard; and More, who in addition to these qualities possessed an engaging personality (an acquaintance once described him as "born for friendship") and an honesty which astounded both colleagues and clients, found himself well rewarded. Success followed upon success, honor upon honor.

More frequently represented the great guild corporations of London in both foreign and domestic negotiations. He became undersheriff of London and won renown for helping stop a riot of the city's apprentices against competition by foreign workers, after which he intervened with the king on the apprentices' behalf. He published a biography of Richard III which is considered a milestone in English historical writing and which strongly influenced Shakespeare's dramatic portrait of that monarch. He was elected several times to Parliament.

Such a series of accomplishments inevitably attracted the attention of the new king, Henry VIII. Henry appointed More, now a seasoned veteran of international trade negotiations, to a commission charged with revising a commercial treaty between England and Flanders. The talks dragged on for six months, during which More began his most famous work, the *Utopia*. He entrusted the finished manuscript to Erasmus; it was published at Louvain in 1516, the year before Luther nailed his 95 theses to the church door in Wittenberg.

Renaissance humanists were reformers in the social as well as the religious sense, and *Utopia* is perhaps the greatest example of humanist reform literature. (The word "utopia" itself is one of More's gifts to the English language. Although it is now used to refer to an ideal society or condition, it is actually a made-up Greek word meaning "nowhere.")

The book opens with an impassioned denunciation of the greed of English landowners who were evicting peasants from their farms in order to increase the pasturage available to graze sheep for the increasingly profitable wool trade. This, More argued, not only inflicted suffering and starvation on thousands of innocent peasants—English sheep, he remarks ruefully, have become so ferocious that they now devour people—but also created a large class of dispossessed vagrants, driven by hunger to theft and other crimes, as well as disrupting the entire economic and monetary system of the country.

More then proceeds to describe the imaginary island of Utopia, somewhere in the New World. (As the great voyages of discovery were then bringing home stories of exotic civilizations in newly found lands, "the New World" was a favorite setting for make-believe communities.) Utopia is More's vision of a rationally organized society.

All material possessions in Utopia are owned in common, thus eliminating the basis for envy and greed. (The Utopians, anticipating an idea of Lenin's, use gold to make chamberpots.) Since tastes are simple and everyone does productive work—there are no servants or beggars, and an absolute minimum of government functionaries and priests, while women work on an equal basis with men as far as their strength allows—six hours of toil per day suffice to satisfy everyone's needs. War, which More describes as a crime committed by rulers against their subjects, is avoided whenever possible.

Religious diversity is not only tolerated, it is institutionalized: public services utilize only prayers which all citizens can recite without offending their own beliefs, while the rites peculiar to different sects are performed by each family in its own house.

More's Utopia bears more than a passing resemblance to B. F. Skinner's *Walden Two,* although without the advantages (or disadvantages) of modern technology and operant conditioning techniques. Both envision essentially communistic societies in which simplification of needs and an equitable apportionment of work allow everyone ample time for cultural and artistic pursuits. Both propose an economic system which aims not at producing the greatest possible amount of wealth but at minimizing the hours citizens spend in burdensome toil.

Many others have shared this vision. Subsequent writers described dozens of similar ideal societies, and so highly was *Utopia* esteemed by nineteenth-century socialists that Thomas More's name is listed in Red Square in Moscow as one of the heroes of the Workers' Revolution.

No one person can establish a perfect society, but one person can at least make a beginning in his own home. Erasmus once described More's household as a Christian version of Plato's Academy, and More himself called it his school; it was unquestionably the center of his life. Eventually the community grew to include children and stepchildren, their spouses, grandchildren, tutors, and houseguests. Permanent quarters were provided for Erasmus.

What Erasmus accomplished as an individual—a life which combined learning, humor and piety—More and his family managed to realize together.

As in Utopia, idleness and gambling were not allowed, and everyone was expected to do some manual labor. Equal education was provided for both sexes; children were taught by tutors and by each other. Prayers were said in common. Visitors remarked on the frequency with which laughter was heard in the More household.

Approximately two years after the publication of *Utopia,* in which he had described in great detail the dangers and frustrations which await the well-intentioned person who dares to advise kings to govern with justice and wisdom, More agreed to enter the service of Henry VIII. He now had a larger stage upon which to display his talents—and, as he had predicted, a more precarious one.

In 1520 More accompanied Henry VIII to his historic meeting with the French king Francis I at a place near Calais known to history as the Field of the Cloth of Gold; the same year he negotiated an agreement with the Holy Roman Emperor, Charles V. The following year he established a treaty with the Hanseatic merchants, and the year after that he was knighted. More was chosen speaker of Parliament and high steward of Oxford and Cambridge. Henry appointed him chancellor of Lancaster, which made him the chief judge and administrator of a large part of northern England. He represented Henry at negotiations leading to the Peace of Cambrai in 1529.

More became the king's personal humanist, the court intellectual. He made official speeches, drafted treaties, received and entertained foreign ambassadors. Even the Reformation served to enhance his stature. More became—with the approval of the king, who had no sympathy with Luther's teachings—the unofficial champion of the Catholic cause in England, publishing seven volumes of anti-Lutheran writings. By assisting the king in the writing of his *Defense of the*

Seven Sacraments, he was instrumental in Henry's receiving from the pope the title Defender of the Faith, which English sovereigns still claim.

Almost everything was going More's way. There was only one small storm cloud, low at first on the horizon, which eventually grew to overshadow everything else. King Henry had no son, and he needed one badly.

It was a situation which would never have arisen in the first place but for a long series of historical accidents. If Arthur, Henry's older brother, had lived, Henry would never have become king at all. If it had not seemed necessary, in order to help cement an alliance with Spain against France, that Arthur's widow, Catherine of Aragon (the daughter of Ferdinand and Isabella of Spain), marry the new heir to the throne in spite of an express prohibition against such a marriage, the controversial dispensation would never have been requested.

If Henry VIII and Ferdinand had not had a diplomatic falling-out, the second marriage would probably have taken place years earlier, and Catherine might well have borne a son. If England had not just emerged from a disastrous civil war, and if it had been certain that a woman would be acknowledged as the legitimate ruler, the lack of a male heir would not have been so crucial. And, finally, if the Holy Roman Emperor, Charles V, had not been Catherine's nephew, and if he had not had Clement VII effectively under his thumb (in 1527, the year Henry began pressing for an annulment, Charles's army had invaded and pillaged Rome, keeping the pope prisoner for several months), Henry's request for annulment might have been granted, and that would have been the end of the whole affair.

But things were not destined to work out that way. Henry entrusted his chancellor, Cardinal Wolsey, with the task of obtaining an annulment. In 1529, when it became obvious that Wolsey had failed, the king stripped him of power and selected as his new chancellor Thomas More, the first layman ever to hold that office.

More had now risen as high as it was possible to go. With the example of Wolsey fresh before his eyes, he could not have failed to realize what would be expected of him if he wished to stay there. In 1531, he promulgated the opinions of Oxford and Cambridge favorable to Henry's cause, but not long afterward he tried to resign. The following year, on the day that the clergy of England promised not to meet or to legislate without the king's permission—thus in effect placing the church under royal control—More finally did resign.

He hoped, no doubt, to protect himself and his family by retiring from the center of controversy, but that was impossible. Like Erasmus, Thomas More was an international celebrity, too important a figure to be left alone. While he did not speak out against the king's divorce and remarriage, the fact that he obviously did not approve of them made him an embarrassment which had to be removed.

But More was a difficult person to attack. He was probably the most respected man in England, and several attempts to charge with bribery while in office a man whose name had become synonymous with judicial integrity collapsed of their own weight. His name was added to a bill of attainder accusing a number of persons of conspiring against the king, but the House of Lords refused to pass the bill until More's name was removed. Finally he was charged with treason for refusing to sign an act of Parliament which denied the pope's supremacy over the church.

Like a cornered animal, More used every legal argument, every rhetorical trick, every logical twist and turn to acquit himself of the charge. He did everything possible to save his life except to sign the act. Convicted on perjured evidence, More was beheaded in 1535. His severed head was displayed on London Bridge; it took the place of the head of Bishop

Fisher, who had been executed on the same charge two weeks earlier. His body was buried in the chapel of St. Peter in the Tower of London.

It was Erasmus who wrote More's true epitaph. In the dedication of *The Praise of Folly,* he applied to his friend the phrase by which he is still known today: *omnium horarum homo,* a Man for All Seasons.

By the last year of Erasmus's life, the great dream of a golden age of learning and literature was in shambles. The unity of the church in Europe had been shattered, perhaps forever. Germany was being devastated by savage civil wars. Thomas More and Bishop Fisher had been executed. The calm voice of reason, in which Erasmus, More, and the other humanists had placed such confidence, was drowned out by sectarian hysteria.

Chapter 12
CAJETAN AND SUAREZ
DOMINICANS VS. JESUITS
THE COUNTER-REFORMATION

AS the church prepared to meet the challenge of the Reformation, its intellectual life came even more under the influence of the religious orders than it had been before. Like everything else in the world, this had both good and bad effects.

On the plus side, the orders provided the continuity and resources necessary for particular schools of philosophy and theology to flourish; on the minus side, the natural interest of the orders in promoting themselves and their members encouraged parochialism and a tendency to concentrate on following a particular order's established tradition rather than engaging in independent inquiry. For better or for worse, two religious orders—the Dominicans and the newly founded Society of Jesus—dominated Catholic thinking in the post-Reformation years.

Around the turn of the sixteenth century there lived two Italian religious leaders, both with the unlikely name of Cajetan, contemporaneous with each other and with Martin Luther. One of them, the son of a count, helped found the religious order of Theatines, was active in the Catholic Reformation, was canonized, and is of no importance to our story. But the other one is.

Giacomo de Vio was born in 1469. At the age of sixteen he entered the Dominican order and took the religious name of Tommaso, but since he came from the town of Gaeta, north of Naples, he became known as Gaietanus (Cajetan in English).

Cajetan studied at Naples and Bologna; then he began an academic career which included the writing of over 150 books and treatises. From 1493 to 1507 he taught at Padua, Pavia and Rome and wrote philosophical works, including commentaries on Aristotle and Aquinas and an important discussion of the nature of analogical reasoning.

In 1508, on the eve of the Reformation, he was appointed master-general of the Dominican order and spent the next sixteen years engaged in constant theological and political controversy. He was an ardent advocate of reform, both within his own order and at the Fifth Lateran Council. He wrote a commentary on the *Sentences* of Peter Lombard and an extremely influential commentary on the *Summa Theologiae* of Aquinas, as well as treatises on the sacraments, social issues, and the religious life. He was made Bishop of Gaeta and a cardinal.

In his spare time Cajetan played a major role in international politics, being instrumental in the election of Charles V as Holy Roman Emperor and in the election as pope of Charles's former tutor, the Dutchman Adrian VI, the last non-Italian pope before John Paul II.

He negotiated with Luther on behalf of the pope during the Diet of Augsburg, and was sent as a papal legate to Germany, Hungary, Poland, and Bohemia to promote a crusade against the Turks. (As though Europe were not having troubles enough of its own, Turkish armies, having captured Istanbul, were advancing steadily westward. By 1529, twelve years after the posting of Luther's theses, they were besieging Vienna and appeared to be unstoppable.)

For the last ten years before his death in 1534, Cajetan devoted himself mainly to exegetical writing. His primary tool was Erasmus's Greek text of the bible. (In the face of considerable opposition, Cajetan contended that St. Jerome's Latin translation was not an adequate instrument for serious scriptural studies.) His commentaries were not timid: Cajetan doubted the literal interpretation of the Book of Canticles and the Apocalypse, and questioned the authenticity of several New Testament books including the Epistle to the Hebrews.

Nor did his philosophical writings lack originality. Although thought of today primarily as an interpreter of the Thomistic tradition—Cajetan was the first theologian to use Aquinas's *Summa* as a textbook rather than the *Sentences* of Peter Lombard, and his commentary on the *Summa* acquired such semi-official status that two popes ordered it published along with major editions of the original text—he was no slavish follower of Thomas. He argued, for example, that the existence of a divine creator and the fact of personal immortality cannot be proved by reason alone. On many points, he followed Aristotle much more closely than Aquinas had.

Perhaps Cajetan's most influential original work was his study of analogy and the conditions under which human language may legitimately be applied to God. This issue, obviously, is a crucial one: it calls into question the very possibility of Christian theology.

When we speak about God we must do so using terms which derive their meaning in some way from the objects of our everyday experience. And yet the full reality of God, by definition, transcends our experience. When we use the same word to refer to God and to an object of experience—for example, to call both God and our male parent "father"— what is the relation between the two uses of the word?

There are two easy answers, both unacceptable. One is that the two uses of the word have an identical meaning (that is, they are univocal). This is unacceptable because it implies that God can be understood in the same way that a human being can, which is contrary to scripture. The other is that the two uses have completely different meanings (they are equivocal). This is unacceptable because it would make use of the same word in both cases meaningless.

But there is a middle ground. Two uses of the same word can be similar in some respects and different in other respects. That is, the meanings can be analogous to each other. When we say, to take the same example, that God is the father of us all, we mean that his relation to us is in some respects the same as the relation between a human father and his children and in some respects it is different. It is only through such analogical reasoning, Cajetan taught, that we can achieve real knowledge of God.

But there are different varieties of analogy. One form of analogical reasoning often applied to God is the analogy of attribution: if a person is in a healthy state, and if vitamins contribute to that state, then both the person and the vitamins can be called "healthy." Or, more to the point, since God is responsible for all of the qualities which created beings display, these qualities can in some way be attributed to God as well.

The kind of analogy which Cajetan favored, however, was the analogy of proportionality. That is to say, goodness in God bears the same relation to God's nature that goodness in humans does to human nature. This is the concept which was adopted by many subsequent Thomists, and it is frequently still taught today.

Several areas of Europe were relatively unaffected by the intellectual upheavals of the Renaissance and the Reformation. One such area was the Iberian peninsula, somewhat isolated geographically from the rest of the continent and, thanks to the diligence of the Inquisition, almost untouched by innovative religious ideas.

In this artificially sheltered environment there occurred, in the fifteenth and sixteenth centuries, a remarkably fruitful revival of scholastic philosophy and theology. Here also occurred perhaps the most outstanding example of the kind of unproductive quibbling which was so largely responsible for the degeneration of scholasticism and which drained away much of the creative energy of Catholic thinkers just when it was most needed.

Chief among the promoters of the scholastic revival was a Spanish Jesuit named Francisco Suarez, who today is generally recognized as the greatest scholastic writer after Aquinas. Born in Granada in 1548, Suarez joined the Society of Jesus at the age of eighteen. After a difficult and unpromising introduction to academic studies he began a lifetime of philosophical and theological work, teaching at Avila, Segovia, Valladolid, Alcala, Rome, Salamanca, and Coimbra and producing more than twenty volumes of writings before his death in Lisbon in 1617.

Suarez's metaphysical disputations represented a landmark in the history of Western philosophy: it was the first attempt to develop a systematic scholastic metaphysics, not simply a series of commentaries on Aristotle. The work was an immediate success, going through eighteen editions in less than a hundred years and being widely used in both Catholic and Protestant universities for the next two centuries. Descartes, Leibnitz, and Schopenhauer, among others, valued it highly.

Suarez insisted that Aristotle's argument from the phenomenon of movement to the existence of an Unmoved Mover—an argument which, as we have seen, Aquinas adopted—is insufficient to prove the existence of God. He advanced several reasons for holding this, but his most basic and most interesting argument was that the supposed proof rests on a basic fallacy: it is simply not necessarily true that whatever is moved is moved by another. Some things may move by themselves; indeed, some things appear to do precisely that.

What is required, according to Suarez, is not a proof based on physics but one based on metaphysics. Whatever is produced (comes into being) is produced by another, for it is self-evident that nothing can make itself. This line of reasoning leads not to an Unmoved Mover but to an Uncreated Creator, which of course is really the kind of being whose existence a theist is interested in establishing in the first place.

Suarez also maintained, in opposition to Aquinas, that prime matter is not the principle of individuation and that there is only a mental distinction, not a real one, between a thing's essence and its existence, although this mental distinction does have an objective foundation because the mind abstracts essences from actually existing things. He agreed with the nominalists that there are as many essences as there are individuals.

Perhaps his most original and most important contributions were in the field of political and legal theory, topics which were receiving particular attention in the sixteenth century because of the rise of unified nation-states and the extravagant claims of divine-right monarchs.

He founded his political philosophy on the belief that civil government in some form is required by human nature—it is not, as Augustine had held, a consequence of Adam's fall. Suarez taught that political society is necessitated by people's fundamental social needs, and that there would have been some form of civil government in Eden had Adam not sinned, although it would not have been, as ours is, coercive in nature. Its existence also does not depend on an arbitrary social contract which people were free either to make or not to make, although the particular form of civil government is indeed to be determined by common consent.

Suarez insisted that neither God nor nature has directly

given any person the right to rule over another. Everyone is born free, and although it is true that all authority comes from God, the authority to govern is given directly to the people of each community, who determine which form of government they wish and then transfer that authority to a sovereign.

Political power obtained without consent or by unjust force does not confer legitimate authority (unless the people subsequently acquiesce), and tyrants and usurpers may be deposed. Indeed, Suarez went so far as to approve of regicide in some cases. On the other hand, once authority has been freely transferred from the whole people to a ruler, that ruler becomes the vicar of God and the natural law demands obedience to him.

While this may seem a bit reactionary today, at the time it was a substantial advance over the theory of divine-right monarchy, which held that sovereigns received their power and authority directly from God—that God willed, in other words, that a particular person occupy a particular throne. The notion that a sovereign received his authority directly from the people and not directly from God and that it could be withdrawn if the sovereign overstepped certain boundaries infuriated divine-right monarchs. James I of England was so upset that he had the book in which Suarez expounded this theory publicly burned by his hangman.

By his insistence on the initial equality of all people, Suarez provided a theoretical foundation for the development of a Catholic theory of democracy. He also devoted considerable attention to the concept of "natural rights," a topic hardly considered by Aquinas but one which became central to the thinking of such later writers as John Locke. And by arguing that political society arises from and is required by human nature itself, he encouraged subsequent theorizing on the nature of political justice.

As long as one believes, with Augustine, that living under

civil government is simply part of the curse we bear for Adam's sin, there is not much point in worrying about how to construct a just society. For Augustine that would have been a contradiction: civil society is intrinsically unjust. One might as well speculate about how to make slavery equitable. With Suarez came the transition to modern political theory.

When it came to the relation between the spiritual and the secular orders, Suarez argued against the view that the pope holds supreme temporal as well as supreme spiritual power— that is, the civil rulers are merely the pope's representatives, ruling in his name—and he insisted that church and state are independent societies, each with its own end.

But he was not content to stop there. Since, he continued, the spiritual order is superior to the temporal, the pope does have the right, even the duty, to insist that temporal rulers use their power to promote the spiritual good of their subjects. If they fail to heed his instructions on how best to do this, the pope has the right to depose them.

This position is really only a logical extension of Augustine's theory of the Two Cities, but it had a substantial effect on the development of a Catholic position on the relation between church and state and provided ammunition for many years to those who claimed that Catholicism is a politically subversive religion.

Along with his near-contemporary Hugo Grotius, Suarez was also a major contributor to the theory of international law. For him the existence of such a standard of conduct, established not by written legislation but by customs which transcend national boundaries, is made possible by and is a manifestation of the basic unity of the human race—not mere biological unity, but unity in a moral sense. It is somewhat analogous to the common law, based on immemorial customs and accepted usages; it is like an expression of the collective human conscience.

As is the case with political society, international law rises out of a natural need. Just as no person is self-sufficient but must establish social relationships in order to survive, so also no nation is self-sufficient. States as well as people must establish relations with each other. In both cases, a system of law is required to protect and regulate these relationships, for nations also constitute a kind of society.

International law is not deducible from natural law. It does not simply identify actions which are already intrinsically wrong in the way that natural law does; rather, like civil law, it makes acts morally evil by forbidding them or morally obligatory by commanding them. There is nothing in the natural law, for example, which stipulates that international conflicts should be settled by war. Custom has, however, established war as one means for resolving such conflicts, and has further established a number of limitations on how, when, and why war may legitimately be waged. Once accepted by common consent, such provisions are morally binding on participants.

Cajetan and Suarez represent perhaps the best original Catholic thinking to come out of the Reformation era. Unfortunately, not all efforts were being directed toward such constructive ends. It is a disconcerting fact that at the end of the sixteenth century, when followers of Luther and Calvin were steadily increasing their influence at the expense of the church of Rome, the most bitter theological confrontations were taking place not between Catholics and Protestants but between Dominicans and Jesuits.

These squabbles, which dragged on for twenty-five years, absorbing the time and energy of the highest levels of the hierarchy and many of the church's top theologians, give some indication of how many of the best minds in the Catholic church were occupying themselves in the crucial years following the Council of Trent.

At issue was the problem of how to reconcile free will, God's foreknowledge of future events, and the manner in which grace influences human actions. Since the relation between grace and free will had been one of the cornerstones of Luther's theology, and since the Council of Trent, which had clarified many other doctrinal issues, had failed to formulate a definitive position on the question, the problem was a natural one for theologians to turn their attention to. Unfortunately, what started as an exercise in theological speculation soon got completely out of hand.

Three basic beliefs shared by all parties to the dispute established the limits within which the problem was argued: human actions are, in some sense, free; God is all-knowing, with nothing—past, present, or future—escaping his cognizance; and God's grace is both a necessary and a sufficient aid for the performance of every virtuous act. It is possible that any two of these three could be squared with each other without undue difficulty, but trying to construct a theory which would satisfactorily harmonize all three was well-nigh impossible.

If God's grace is always sufficient for the performance of good, why do people sometimes do good and other times do evil? According to the prevailing theory of the day, held by Aquinas and succeeding generations of Dominicans, the answer is that there are two kinds of grace. Both are sufficient, but one becomes effective only if the will cooperates with it, whereas the other produces its effect through the nature of grace itself.

In 1582, a Spanish Jesuit named Prudentio de Montmayor attacked this theory as tantamount to predestination and a denial of human free will. The Dominicans complained, and the Spanish Grand Inquisitor—the operation of the Inquisition was generally controlled by the Dominican order—

prohibited the teaching of Montmayor's position. Round One to the Dominicans.

Enter, several years later, Luis de Molina, a Jesuit teaching in Portugal, who wrote a book proposing that in fact there are not two different kinds of grace but only one. All grace is of itself sufficient for the performance of a virtuous act, but it becomes actually efficacious only if the free human will cooperates with it.

Molina's position, as it was developed eventually by the two greatest theologians in the Jesuit order at the time, Suarez and Robert Bellarmine, was that whether or not this cooperation occurs depends on whether the grace is suited to the particular circumstances a person finds himself in at the time. If it is not suited to those circumstances, it will not elicit the free consent of the person's will, even though the grace is perfectly sufficient in itself. This might be compared to the seed of the parable, some of which fell on rocky and some on fertile ground. The seed itself was not deficient in any respect, but in one case circumstances were not suited to its reception.

But then, if the effectiveness of grace depends on the disposition of man's free will, how is it possible for God to know our future actions? According to Molina, what God actually knows is how each person would react to each grace in all possible circumstances. In 1588, publication of Molina's book was suspended because of suspicion that it contained the forbidden theories of Prudencio de Montmayor. The Portuguese Grand Inquisitor investigated, and allowed publication to continue. Round Two to the Jesuits.

At this point the Dominicans, led by one Domingo Banez, counterattacked. God's knowledge and God's power, declared Banez, are absolute; they are not limited by acts of the human will. Thus the power of grace cannot depend on an act of the will. It produces its effects, just as Aquinas taught, through its own power. And God knows not merely what would happen in a variety of different circumstances but people's actual future acts; indeed, God moves them to act as they do. But this does not conflict with human freedom, for God moves nonfree beings to act in a nonfree manner and free beings to act in a free manner.

In 1593, Molina discovered that all of his writings were being scrutinized for possible inclusion in the Index of Forbidden Books. Rather than waiting for that to happen, he wrote directly to the Spanish Grand Inquisitor. Banez's theories, he complained, effectively destroyed human freedom. Besides, by making God responsible for all human actions without regard for the operation of each person's will, was not Banez in effect saying that God cooperates in sin? And then, just for good measure, Molina denounced Banez as a crypto-Lutheran.

At this point Dominicans and Jesuits of all descriptions started jumping into the fight, and Pope Clement VIII decided that the matter should be referred to Rome for resolution. Call Round Three a draw.

In retrospect it is easy to see what was happening. The two sides were approaching the problem for opposite directions, so naturally they were reaching opposite conclusions. Ironically, they were both following the same procedural principle, the classic scholastic dictum that one should start with what is more certain and reason toward what is less certain.

To the Jesuits, freedom of the will was more certain because we experience it; starting from there, one must explain God's foreknowledge. To the Dominicans, God's foreknowledge was more certain because it could be proved by indisputable metaphysical principles; starting from there, one must explain free will. The possibility that they might be dealing with a problem to which there simply is no adequate rational solution apparently did not occur to anyone. Humility seems to have been in short supply among the theologians of the day.

And so Round Four, in its own good time, opened in Rome. Three universities, thirteen bishops and eight doctors of theology were asked for their opinions on the matter, and the Jesuits submitted seven treatises defending Molina. A commission of two cardinals, three bishops, and five theologians was set up; it voted to condemn Molina. Then new documents arrived from Spain, and Clement ordered the commission to reconsider. It did reconsider, and reached the same conclusion.

Rather than acting on this recommendation, Clement decided, somewhat belatedly, to attempt a reconciliation. The two sides were brought together four times to settle their differences. They failed. In 1600, Clement asked the commission to shorten its list of Molina's theses which should be condemned. At this point—on the same day, as a matter of fact—Molina managed to excuse himself from further involvement in the proceedings by the simple though drastic expedient of dying.

But the case dragged on. Fifteen sessions of oral debates were conducted on the orthodoxy of Molina's position. Ten additional sessions were required to reach a decision, and again Molina lost. Rounds Four, Five and Six to the Dominicans.

But a number of influential people, including the king of Spain, intervened on Molina's behalf. And Clement, who would easily have outscored Hamlet on an indecisiveness test, came up with a new way to avoid having to make a decision: he decided to have both sides debate the issues in his presence.

This took four years, with 85 sessions and 47 debates, with another year required to reach a decision. Molina lost on all counts. During this period of time Clement died, Leo XI was elected to succeed him and also died, and Paul V was elected.

In 1607, the new pope took an eminently sensible and long overdue step: he declared that, for the time being, both orders were to be allowed to teach their own theories, and each was solemnly warned not to call the other nasty names. Everyone was told to wait for a final decision from Rome. As of this writing, no such decision has been announced, but for all anyone knows there may still be a committee somewhere in the Vatican diligently working away on it.

What relation all of this arguing had to do with the Gospel message or the living of a good Christian life is not clear, and one has to wonder whether that question ever even crossed any of the participants' minds. And while cardinals and bishops were busying themselves with esoteric metaphysical disputations in Rome, the intellectual world was rapidly passing them by.

Chapter 13
TERESA OF AVILA

NOT far from the Israeli city of Haifa lie the holy mountains of Carmel. The prophet Elias chose that spot for his contest with the priests of Baal; the Roman general Vespasian, soon to become emperor, offered sacrifice there. And some time in the early centuries of the Christian era, hermits established themselves on Carmel to practice prayer and mortification after the example of Elias.

In the thirteenth century these hermits became a religious order, following a life of solitude, silence, fasting, and perpetual abstinence from meat. The Brothers of the Blessed Virgin Mary of Mount Carmel, as they were called, devoted themselves completely to prayer, to the closest possible union with God.

This peaceful existence was shattered when the Saracens conquered Palestine. In 1291, following the fall of the crusader fortress of Acre, the Carmelites were expelled from their holy mountain and sought refuge in Europe. This led to drastic changes in their way of life.

Now they had to support themselves by preaching, teaching and normal pastoral work. Their Rule was modified to allow a community of Carmelites to live in the same building, to move into cities, to eat and pray together. They established houses of study, including one in Paris. All of this inevitably meant less time for prayer and contemplation. In 1432, the eating of meat was permitted, and later the rigor of their fasting was moderated. By the time of the Reformation, little remained to distinguish the Carmelites from other orders of monks and nuns.

But the memory of the holy mountain of antiquity, and of the austerities practiced by the followers of the prophet Elias, remained in the collective subconscious of the Carmelite order. One day a woman, with the help of a lyric poet, re-awakened that memory.

Teresa de Cepeda y Ahumada was twenty when she entered the Carmelite convent of the Incarnation in Avila. That was in 1535, the year Thomas More was beheaded.

Her career as a nun began quite pleasantly—too pleasantly, in fact. Like many other Spanish convents of the day, the Incarnation resembled a finishing school more than a religious community. It was a sheltered environment where young ladies could lead respectable lives without having to trouble themselves unduly about the conditions of their souls. Younger nuns visited with friends in the convent parlor much as they might have done in their own homes; gentlemen callers were not infrequent.

Under these conditions Teresa found it difficult to make much spiritual progress. Later she wrote that during this period she would have preferred to undergo the most extreme forms of penance rather than engage in mental prayer. But she persisted, despite occasional lapses and discouragements, and eventually strange things started to happen: she began to have visions and hear voices. Unsure of what these might mean, she sought advice.

She was told that the visions came from God, that they came from the devil; that she should resist them, that she should not resist them. Everyone she consulted seemed to have different advice. And although Teresa pleaded with her advisors to keep her mystical experiences confidential, word of them leaked out, making her something of a spiritual celebrity. She found this acutely embarrassing. Not only did her most intimate secrets become a prime topic of convent gossip, but she was also ridiculed and calumnied by people who chose to believe that she was making the whole thing up.

This pattern of frustration and uncertainty continued for some eighteen years.

At about the age of forty Teresa underwent a kind of spiritual conversion, an intense awareness of God's presence; thereafter she was able to achieve the most extraordinary forms of mystical union. She had visions of Christ. She levitated. She saw an angel thrust a golden spear again and again into her heart, filling her with a burning love of God and a pain so intense that it made her cry aloud. Eventually she would experience the sensation of dwelling permanently within God—like a sponge, as she expressed it, completely saturated with water.

Teresa was reaching the ultimate heights of spiritual ecstasy. Only one thing was missing: a place where she could concentrate on spiritual perfection. A life of prayer, she would later write, requires peace of soul; and the Incarnation convent, filled with the constant chatter of 140 nuns, was not conducive to peace of soul.

Her intention was simply to establish a small community where she and a few other nuns could live according to the ancient Carmelite ideals. At a time when the Council of Trent had stirred up interest in internal church reform, this was not a particularly radical idea. But while Teresa's Dominican, Franciscan and Jesuit advisors all supported the idea (one of the few things which all three of those orders are on record as having agreed to), the local Carmelite authorities were solidly opposed.

Teresa did not let that technicality stand in her way. She had one of her married sisters secretly prepare a house in Avila to meet her needs, while Peter of Alcantara, one of her Franciscan advisors who had friends in high places in Rome, obtained a letter from Pope Pius IV authorizing the founding of the new convent. Armed with this letter, Teresa and her confidants managed to persuade the bishop of Avila to approve the opening of St. Joseph's, as they called their new home.

In 1562, she and four other nuns moved from the Incarnation into St. Joseph's, and huddled together to await the explosion.

It was not long in coming. The prioress of the Incarnation was furious. The Carmelite provincial was livid. Not only had Teresa not bothered to tell him that she was intending to found a new convent, but she and her friends had arranged things so that St. Joseph's was not even under his supervision, but directly under the jurisdiction of the Bishop of Avila.

Had Teresa been a soldier, she undoubtedly would have been shot. As it was, she thought she might be thrown into prison. (As we shall see later, this was not a totally unfounded fear.) And even after she managed to mollify her religious superiors, she still had to face the anger of the townspeople of Avila.

Everyone thought it was a wonderfully edifying gesture for Teresa to start her new convent without an endowment, so that it would have to depend entirely on charity for its support; but the leading citizens of Avila had no doubts about whom she would come to for money once it opened. For them, the establishment of an unendowed convent had about the same effect as an increase in taxes. And people were no more enthusiastic about taxes then than they are now. A meeting was held to discuss the matter; the mayor and the town council wanted the building torn down.

The only one to defend Teresa publicly was someone who had not yet met her, a Dominican priest named Banez. (Yes, this was the same Domingo Banez who would later cross swords with Molina over the issue of free will and grace. He had just arrived in Avila to teach theology and became

Teresa's confessor and spiritual director from then until her death. When Teresa was denounced to the Inquisition some years later, Banez successfully supported her cause.)

Eventually St. Joseph's was saved the same way it had been founded, by going directly to the top: a lawsuit was filed in the royal court in Madrid, and the new community was placed under the king's protection. And the leading citizens of Avila resigned themselves to their fate.

St. Joseph's was designed to reproduce the living conditions of the monks on Mount Carmel, although the nuns lived in community rather than individually, in conformity with the decrees of the Council of Trent. The community was small—only thirteen nuns—and there was almost total silence. Nuns were strictly cloistered and devoted their lives to spiritual perfection, especially mental prayer. The eating of meat was totally forbidden, and the nuns fasted six months of the year.

Finally, to symbolize their commitment to poverty, the nuns wore sandals rather than shoes, just as the Franciscan followers of Peter of Alcantara did. This last detail, probably the least important thing distinguishing the new community from other Carmelites, is what eventually gave Teresa's followers their name. Originally called Contemplative Carmelites, in time they became known as Discalced Carmelites (literally, "unshoed," from *calx,* the Latin word for "heel").

Teresa was now in her late forties. Having finally obtained living conditions suited to her spiritual needs, she now had everything she wanted. Had she accomplished nothing more in her life, she would be remembered as one of the greatest of Christian mystics. But she was able to enjoy her hard-won solitude at St. Joseph's for only five years. Then, just as she was entering her most intense period of private mystical experiences, she was called to begin a public career as one of the leading figures of the Counter-Reformation.

In a sense, Teresa was the victim of her own success. When the head of the Carmelite order, Giovanni Rossi, visited St. Joseph's in 1567, he could not help but be impressed with what he saw. Rossi had already taken some steps of his own to reform the Carmelites, and now he had found an energetic field general to help him. Choosing to overlook the unorthodox manner in which the Discalced convent had been founded, he directed Teresa to establish more.

As with everything else she did, Teresa threw herself into this task wholeheartedly. Undeterred by the fact that her total resources at the time totaled about ten dollars, she is reported to have remarked that Teresa and ten dollars could not accomplish anything, but that Teresa, ten dollars and God would be quite sufficient.

She decided to open her second convent at Medina del Campo, southwest of Valladolid. It turned out to be a fateful choice.

On rare occasions, two people who perfectly complement each other actually manage to find each other; when they do, extraordinary things often happen. In Medina was a young monk who was a perfect match for Teresa. His name was John.

Gonzalo de Yepes had married for love. The son of a wealthy merchant, he defied his family to marry a girl who worked as a weaver. Social differences of that magnitude were taken very seriously in sixteenth-century Spain, and Gonzalo was disowned. He died in poverty and his third son, John, was sent to a school for indigent children in Medina.

At the age of twenty-one John became a Carmelite, and studied liberal arts and theology at the University of Salamanca. He excelled at academic work, but his heart was elsewhere. John was not a scholar; he was a poet and a mystic. Unable, like Teresa, to find an environment conducive to contemplation within the Carmelites, he was considering leaving the order and becoming a Carthusian.

Then he met Teresa and—as usual wherever she was involved—things started happening very quickly.

John became the first Carmelite monk to accept Teresa's reforms; as a symbol of his commitment to the more austere Discalced life he changed his religious name from John of Santo Matia to John of the Cross. Teresa bought land at Durelo, halfway between Avila and Salamanca, and John and two other Carmelite priests established a Discalced monastery there.

Now there were two reform-minded mystics in Spain. They made an unlikely combination. John, the twenty-five-year-old priest, was writing poetry; Teresa, the fifty-two-year-old contemplative nun, was rushing from one end of Spain to the other, founding Discalced communities at the truly astonishing rate of better than one a year—Malagon and Valladolid in 1568, Toledo and Pastrana (near Madrid) in 1569, Salamanca in 1570, and Alba de Tormes (near Salamanca) in 1571.

From 1571 to 1574 her time was fully occupied by an ironic special assignment: she was appointed to reform—of all places—the convent of the Incarnation in Avila. This was not a popular decision. Teresa was not enthusiastic about interrupting her work and returning to the very convent whose lax practices had prompted her to begin the Discalced movement in the first place; the sisters of the Incarnation were outraged that a nun who had found their convent wanting and had gone on to establish an awesome reputation for austerity and self-denial had now been given authority over them. Besides, the Incarnation was not even a Discalced convent.

The following three years saw perhaps the most remarkable accomplishment of Teresa's remarkable life. Taking charge of a convent ten times as large as the ones she had founded, whose nuns followed a different Rule than the one she practiced and who greeted her with anger, fear and resentment, Teresa—through gentle persuasion, a sense of humor, force of example, and pure contagious love—restored both discipline and religious fervor to the Incarnation.

So completely did she win the hearts of those under her charge that three years later they voted for her to serve another term as prioress, and persisted in their choice despite a threat of excommunication—but that is getting ahead of our story.

After her work at Incarnation, Teresa continued establishing Discalced convents: Segovia in 1574, Beas de Segura (northeast of Granada) in 1575, and Seville in 1576. At that point a hiatus was imposed by some particularly nasty Carmelite infighting; then the foundings continued: Villanueva de la Jara (near Toledo) in 1580, Burgos in 1582. Not long after the establishment of Burgos, Teresa died; otherwise there might not be a village in Spain today without a Discalced convent.

Simply traveling between these points was no small accomplishment. The terrain is some of the most forbidding in Europe, and Teresa crossed it in everything from carriages to mule carts, making her way along mountain roads that are no easy trip today and must have been excruciatingly tedious then.

When she finally reached her destinations she had to obtain the necessary civil and ecclesiastical permissions, raise money, buy land, and oversee construction of the convents, not to mention recruiting members, supervising their training, and establishing a community life strong enough that the new convents could function without her. Then she rushed off to begin the process again.

It may have been during this period that Teresa allegedly complained to God of all the suffering she was undergoing in his service, whereupon God appeared and reminded her that

that is the way he treats his friends. "Yes," Teresa is supposed to have replied, "that's why you have so few of them."

It was near the end of her career that Teresa again became the victim of her own success. Many Carmelites, alarmed at the speed with which the Discalced movement was growing, began to worry that unless something were done, they—heaven forbid—might be forced to reform themselves. Eventually, as the result of some jurisdictional confusion within the order, they found a way to put an end to Teresa's meddling. Or so they thought.

After a great deal of maneuvering and bickering, the Carmelite general chapter of 1575 ordered the Discalced faction to close some of its communities; Teresa was told to choose one of her convents and stay there. John of the Cross, whom Teresa had appointed confessor at Incarnation, was ordered by his provincial to return to Medina. When he refused, a group of Carmelite priests kidnapped him, took him to Toledo, and declared him a rebel against the Carmelite rule. This was no trivial matter in those days. John was beaten and imprisoned in a six-foot by ten-foot cell until he managed to escape, nine months later.

Teresa meanwhile had returned to Avila, where the nuns of Incarnation elected her to a second term as prioress. Then the anti-Discalced faction went a step too far: they invalidated the election and ordered the nuns to vote again. They did so, and again elected Teresa, for which impertinence they were excommunicated.

At this point Teresa again went to the top: she had her friends complain to King Philip II. That settled matters. Philip—ruler of the most powerful country in Europe and relentless opponent of the Reformation—was not a man whom the church, let alone a few obscure Carmelite functionaries, could afford to antagonize. The Discalced priests and nuns were established as a province of their own within the Carmelite organization; not long afterward they became a totally separate religious order. As for Teresa, she went back to opening convents.

John of the Cross is best known today for his three great mystical poems—"The Dark Night of the Soul," "The Living Flame of Love," and "Spiritual Canticle"—each accompanied by a detailed commentary. "Spiritual Canticle," the longest lyric poem ever written in Spanish, is also generally considered to be the most beautiful. John died in 1591 and was buried in Segovia.

John of the Cross wrote because he was a poet; Teresa wrote because other people insisted that she do so. It was natural, for example, for Teresa's spiritual advisors to want to find out as much as possible about her, just as doctors want to learn all they can about the lives of people with rare medical conditions. She provided a unique opportunity for them to study in depth some extremely rare mystical phenomena. So they asked her to write her life story. She agreed with great reluctance—writing took up valuable time, she complained, time which could better be spent on more important tasks, like spinning—and completed the first draft shortly before moving into St. Joseph's.

Like most people with no formal education, she wrote the same way she spoke—a simple narrative in conversational Castilian, with no punctuation or separation of paragraphs and numerous repetitions. Her natural exuberance showed itself here as in everything else she did. Those who saw her write reported that she worked quickly, never stopping to cross out a word or think about what to say next. Indeed, she once said she wished she could write with both hands, because ideas came into her head faster than she could put them on paper.

She wrote *The Way of Perfection,* an instruction on the forms and methods of prayer, at the request of the nuns of

St. Joseph's, while her *Book of Foundations* recounts the establishment of the other fourteen Discalced convents she founded. She may also have written as many as 15,000 letters of which about 440 still exist.

But Teresa's great masterpiece is *The Interior Castle,* a guide to spiritual perfection written in two months during the hectic days of the intra-Carmelite controversy.

In this work Teresa envisions the human soul as a castle containing seven concentric dwelling places, the innermost of which is inhabited by God. Progress in the spiritual life involves passage through the various intermediate stages to the center.

The first three dwelling places are attainable by a person's own efforts. The outermost is the domain of those who have turned away from the most serious sins and engage in some prayer, but are still almost totally absorbed in their possessions and business affairs. The second stage is characterized by more intense prayer and a greater receptivity to the edifying effects of such exterior influences as spiritual books and sermons.

The third dwelling place is reached by those who guard even against venial sin, engage in recollection and some degree of asceticism, and practice the virtue of charity. The spiritual life is more important to these people than their possessions, although they are still attached to material things: they lead what would generally be considered good Christian lives.

The fourth dwelling place is the beginning of the domain of passive prayer. This prayer begins with passive recollections, a drawing inward of the soul's faculties; here, says Teresa, the important thing is not to think much, but to love much. At this stage the will finds rest, but the intellect is still restless and distracted. This should not trouble one, Teresa insists, for it is unavoidable. One should simply surrender to love.

Next comes the domain of the prayer of union, in which the soul becomes completely silent. Like a caterpillar crawling into a cocoon, Teresa writes, the soul enters into God and dies to itself and to its attachments; then, like the butterfly, it is reborn.

In the sixth dwelling place the soul enters into a courtship, as it were, with God, and experiences the same kinds of mental ecstasies and agonies one usually associates with courtship. One must endure the opposition and misunderstandings of others, including one's own spiritual advisors; one must deal with anxiety and self-doubt, the fear that one may be deceived or rejected by God, the inner conflicts and ambivalence which the uncertainties of love induce.

At the same time the soul experiences ecstatic unions with God, and sometimes an understanding of divine mysteries. The soul's desire for divine love constantly increases; this yearning, combined with the anxieties and fears, produces an agony which Teresa describes as prepatory purification.

In the final, innermost dwelling place the soul is joined with God, not in a blind ecstasy, but as the object of the soul's own faculties (rather like the union of the beatific vision, as Aquinas describes it). This is the level of "spiritual marriage," in which the soul is inseparably united with God like the water of a river—to use Teresa's imagery—which flows into the sea; entrance to this state comes about through a permanent intellectual perception of the Trinity.

These spiritual experiences, according to Teresa, have a practical purpose: by giving a person greater inner claim, they allow him or her to endure greater exterior turmoil, and thus to serve others better. This may be so. It is unquestionably true that the realization that one is loved gives a person a certain immunity to the tribulations of life; one can only imagine the kind of inner strength that must come from a constant knowledge that one is intimately and specially loved by God.

At the end of the journey which Teresa describes, a person has reached both God and the center of his or her own soul. One is united not only with God, but with oneself.

Teresa's writings are important primarily because of their remarkably analytical examination of the ways God interacts with the human soul. By reflecting on her own experiences she was able to penetrate depths of mystical theology beyond the reach of the most learned scholars.

And yet all her works are clearly and simply written, accessible to every reader. She addressed herself particularly to those whose minds, as she put it, are not methodical but which run from one thing to another uncontrollably, like wild horses—and that surely includes most of us. Teresa insisted that mental prayer and contemplation are not the calling of a special few but are essential elements of every truly Christian life, that whoever fails to achieve intimacy with God will never understand or fulfill the purpose of life. Her ability both to encourage the beginner and to challenge the most advanced is a mark of her greatness as a teacher.

Teresa of Avila died on October 4, 1582, and was buried at Alba de Tormes. The following day, as it happened, the Gregorian calendar reform went into effect, and ten days were simply skipped over. That made the day after death October 15, which became her feast day.

Fate held one final irony for this nun who had been so skillful at getting what she wanted by appealing to higher authorities. Three years after her death, in accordance with a decision of a provincial chapter of the Discalced Carmelites, her body was moved to Avila. Whereupon the Duke of Alba stole a page from Teresa's own book of tricks and obtained a decree from Rome that the body should be returned to Alba, where it rests today.

Philip II, perhaps concerned that Teresa's writings might be shuttled around the country in a similar fashion, had her manuscripts collected and brought to his palace. There he kept them in a special bookcase, whose key he always carried with him.

Teresa was canonized in 1622 along with two of her countrymen, Ignatius Loyola and Francis Xavier, and in 1970 was declared the first woman doctor of the church. John of the Cross was canonized in 1726, and made a doctor of the church in 1926.

Chapter 14
DESCARTES AND PASCAL

BY the beginning of the seventeenth century, the unity of Christian culture—which, in Western Europe at least, had practically been equivalent to civilization itself—had been destroyed. Beliefs and values which had been accepted without question for centuries by the great mass of people were now openly debated, denied and denounced.

Religious warfare had become practically an accepted way of life. In 1567 Spanish troops under the Duke of Alba invaded the Netherlands and imposed an infamous reign of terror. Five years later, on St. Bartholomew's Day, thousands of French Protestants were slaughtered. In 1618 began the Thirty Years War, or series of wars, involving most of the countries of continental Europe. For decades, mercenary armies plundered, raped, burned, destroyed. When it was all over, a third of the entire population of Germany was dead, and the devastation was so complete that recovery took a hundred years. In the wake of these catastrophes inevitably followed skepticism, cynicism and despair.

At about the same time, men such as Copernicus, Kepler, Galileo, Boyle and Harvey were initiating the Scientific Revolution, founding the modern sciences of astronomy, chemistry, medicine and physics, and radically changing the way people looked at themselves and at the world around them. Again, the effect was to challenge ideas which had been firmly held for hundreds of years.

Whatever was considered certain today, it seemed, might be overthrown without warning tomorrow. People naturally wondered what there was left to believe in. The intellectual mood of the age was perhaps best reflected in the pervasive

181

skepticism of Montaigne's *Essays*. Free thinking and agnosticism became the fashion of the day.

Eventually there was a reaction, an attempt to reestablish a basis for certainty, and two of the greatest geniuses in the history of the French nation appeared almost simultaneously to lead the effort.

The circumstances of their lives were remarkably similar. Both lost their mothers at an early age; both were brilliant mathematicians; both were highly religious men whose writings were condemned by the church. Neither married. One's life was guided by a series of three dreams, the other's by a mystical experience. Both were driven by a desire for certainty, but one placed his reliance on reason while the other championed the certainty of faith; both based their worldviews on a conception of the human person, but one focused on the workings of the individual mind and the other on the concrete human condition.

We have observed that where a person starts goes a long way toward determining where he or she will end up, and that the nature of the questions one chooses to ask greatly influences the nature of the answers one receives. Nowhere is this better demonstrated than with Rene Descartes, whose initial question not only shaped his own worldview but also all subsequent philosophy down to our own day. So great was the impact of that first question, and its inescapable answer, that Descartes could justifiably be described as the most influential philosopher, for better or for worse, since Plato.

He was born in 1596 near Tours, in central France, and at the age of eight was sent to a Jesuit-run boarding school. Right from the start he was attracted to things of which he could be absolutely sure, and he felt disappointed and frustrated because almost everything he was taught was a matter of dispute and therefore of doubt. Finally he found the certainty for which he hungered in the same place Plato and many others had found it—in mathematics. And, like Plato and many others, he began to wonder why it was not possible to achieve that same certainty in other fields.

Upon completing his formal education Descartes resolved to study from "the great book of the world," as he put it; and he commenced a nomadic life which included service in two armies and a two-year stay in Paris before he finally settled in Holland, where he wrote his major works. (Even then, "settled" does not adequately describe Descartes' life. In the twenty years he spent in Holland, he changed his residence eighteen times.) He never married, although a Dutch servant girl did bear him a daughter.

What Descartes set out to do was nothing less than to develop a system for logically deducing all possible knowledge in every field—philosophy, theology, physical sciences, and all other forms of inquiry—in such a way that the results would be absolutely certain and beyond dispute. He wanted, in other words, to establish a science of knowing, from which a knowledge of everything else would naturally follow. As he imagined it, once a solid, indisputable foundation had been laid, steady progress could be made toward achieving a universal science; and the results would be as self-evident and unquestionable as the propositions of Euclid's geometry.

At a time when people were killing each other by the thousands over differences in belief, the prospect of developing a means whereby controversial issues could be settled as conclusively and peacefully as problems in arithmetic must have appeared irresistible. And three dreams which he had on the night of November 10, 1619, while serving in the army of Maximillian of Bavaria, convinced him to devote his life to that task.

By 1633, after fourteen years of effort, he had almost completed the draft of a comprehensive work called, appropriately enough, *The World*. But before it could be published,

Galileo was condemned by the Inquisition for advocating many of the same ideas contained in Descartes' manuscript. Whether out of prudence or out of loyalty to his Catholic faith, Descartes halted publication of *The World* and undertook first to demonstrate that his theories had a sound philosophical foundation and were compatible with the teachings of the church.

Toward this end he published in 1637 the *Discourse on Method,* which consisted of essays on meteorology, optics, and geometry, along with a rather informal autobiographical introduction which explained how he had approached the problem of deducing absolutely certain truths about the world utilizing reason alone. This introduction, since it explained Descartes' methodology in a remarkably clear and accessible way, eventually became his most famous work. Four years later he reformulated his basic ideas in a more formal manner in a booklet called *Meditations on First Philosophy.*

Descartes was also active in the mathematical realm, most importantly as the discoverer of analytic geometry, in which an algebraic equation can be expressed as a curve on a graph and geometric problems can be solved by equations. This was particularly significant because it showed that the Aristotelians were wrong in holding that it is impossible to establish a geometric proposition with an arithmetic proof. It showed that there was a single foundation underlying two distinct sciences (geometry and algebra), and thus that is might be possible to find a single foundation underlying all sciences.

In 1644 he published his *Principles of Philosophy,* and in 1649 he published *The Passions of the Soul* (which, despite its racy-sounding title, was not a torrid romance but a treatise on one of the issues with which Descartes' name is most frequently associated, the relation between mind and body).

By this time Descartes' writings had made his name famous throughout Europe, with what proved to be fatal consequences. The twenty-four-year-old Queen Christina of Sweden, having read several of his books, decided to have him personally instruct her in the intricacies of his new philosophy. She would not take no for an answer, as queens are wont not to do, and Descartes reluctantly made the journey to Stockholm. After only a few months' exposure to the Swedish winter he contracted pneumonia, and in February of 1650 he died. If the efforts which cost Descartes his life had any effect on Christina's mind, the improvement was not noticed by her contemporaries.

As a Catholic in a resolutely Protestant land, Descartes—the most renowned philosopher of his age—was buried in Stockholm's cemetery for unbaptized children.

Descartes' basic presupposition, which seems reasonable enough at first glance, was that since it is the nature of the mind to know things, it will automatically arrive at truth when it functions according to its own natural mode of operation. It must not allow itself to become confused by such external factors as prejudice or education, for example, and it must not attempt to understand matters which exceed its capacity. The trick is simply to remove the obstacles which prevent the mind from functioning properly, to proceed according to a method which conforms to the mind's own natural operation. Thus we must think in an orderly way, accept as true only what cannot be doubted, and divide complex issues into many parts to make sure everything has been adequately considered.

Now all Descartes needed was a starting point, and his fateful first question was, "What is there which absolutely cannot be doubted?"

This is not so simple a question as it might seem, for it is possible to doubt almost everything. All my ideas may be false, my sensations may deceive me, God may not exist, and the entire universe, from my own body to the stars in the heavens, may be figments of my imagination. But Descartes finally found his starting point in the fact that it is logically impossible to doubt one's own existence, for one's existence is verified by the very act of doubting.

Augustine had used essentially the same argument more than a thousand years earlier to refute skepticism by demonstrating that there is at least one certain truth: even if I am wrong in everything I think, I am still certain that I am, and thus I am sure that knowledge is possible. But Augustine, perhaps wisely, had dropped that line of reasoning after he had proved his point against the skeptics. Descartes used it as the basis of his whole worldview, with momentous consequences.

For what is this "I" whose existence Descartes has just demonstrated? Since all we know about it for certain is that it thinks, it must be a thinking being, a being whose nature is to think. Since I can doubt the existence of my body, but cannot doubt my own existence, my existence must be independent of the existence of my body. At this point, Descartes shattered the Aristotelian and scholastic conception of human nature.

If a person is a mind (or, if one wishes, a soul), then we are back to Plato's conception of a human being as a soul existing inside the body of an animal. This was not an accident. Despite the philosophical and theological problems which accompany this conception, this is precisely what Descartes was trying to do. He was trying to do it because he wanted to demonstrate as convincingly as he could the possibility of the immortality of the soul. And for him this meant showing that the existence of the soul does not depend in any way on the existence of the body.

For the same reason Descartes considered it essential to deny that animals have sentient "souls." For Aristotle and Aquinas, as we have seen, the soul is the form of the body, for animals as well as for people, and it is the union of matter and form which makes the individual being. But for Descartes this opened this door to the objection that if the souls of chickens and dogs are not immortal, why should we believe that human souls are?

In fact, said Descartes, bodies—whether of cows or of kings—are matter, and matter is completely governed by the laws of physics. From a scientific point of view—or at least from the viewpoint of the science of Descartes' day—an animal is merely matter in motion. In effect, it is a machine made of flesh and bone rather than of metal but as completely determined by physical laws as is a clock.

One fundamental difficulty in Descartes' approach may already have suggested itself. If I can doubt everything except my own existence, how can I ever come to certain knowledge about anything else—about the external world, for example, or even about my own sensations? If I start with the conception of myself as a disembodied intelligence who cannot trust any of his own thoughts or ideas, how can I ever progress beyond this? Descartes' solution was to do what philosophers have done for centuries when faced with insurmountable problems. He sought divine assistance.

Descartes' excursion into natural theology was not a digression. He needed to prove the existence of God and the fact that God is all good and thus not a deceiver in order to be able to argue that our minds are constructed in such a way as to arrive at truth when allowed to operate normally. The existence of God was Descartes' means of establishing the reality of the universe.

Starting, as his methodology forced him to do, from the contents of his own mind, Descartes constructed two proofs for the existence of God. One of these argues from the existence of a clear and distinct idea of an infinite, omnipotent, omniscient, immutable substance to the necessary cause of such an idea, which must be God himself. The other is similar

to Anselm's argument. Whatever cannot be imagined apart
from something else without contradiction—such as a tri-
angle without the longest side being opposite the largest
angle, or two mountains without a valley—must really be
inseparable from it. But it is impossible to imagine without
contradiction an infinite, almighty, all-perfect being who
lacks the perfection of existence. It follows that existence is in
fact inseparable from God, and thus that God exists.

Descartes' worldview—not so much his conclusions as his
starting point and his methodology—had an immediate and
wide-ranging impact.

First, he almost single-handedly shifted the entire emphasis
of philosophy from where it had been in ancient and medieval
times to where it remains today, not on God and the cosmos
but on humanity—and not just humanity in general, but the
individual person. Descartes, probably unintentionally, made
the "I" the center of the universe, and this "I" was a soli-
tary, brooding, disembodied intelligence.

Second, he focused on what subsequently became perhaps
the single most important issue in philosophical investigation
—the nature of the mind as an instrument of inquiry. If I
know things only through my mind, then the way my mind
works determines what I am able to know and in what form I
am able to know it—a line of inquiry which led from
Descartes to Hume and eventually to Kant and beyond.

In addition, his radical separation of soul and body had,
in many cases, exactly the opposite effect of what he had intended. Descartes was the first one to provide a thoroughly
mechanistic explanation of the workings of the human body.
As we saw, he did this in order to safeguard belief in the
immortality of the soul. But if the body is only an organic
machine, and if all its motions and operations can be explained by the laws of physics, what need is there to postulate
the existence of a soul? Ultimately Descartes' arguments

served to weaken people's faith in the very belief he was trying to support.

Something similar happened in another area as well. Despite Descartes' best efforts, the fact is that his proofs for God's existence are not very convincing. And by his method of doubting everything, even the existence of the universe, he made most of the other theistic arguments untenable. Obviously one cannot very well prove God's existence from the design and order of the universe, let us say, and then prove that the universe is real because God exists.

In fact, if one starts where he did, it is probably impossible to prove God's existence at all. It must have come as quite a shock to someone as religious as Descartes when the rector of the University of Utrecht accused him of atheism, but there was at least some justification to the charge.

Descartes intended that his new philosophical method be used in Jesuit schools, and to facilitate this he recast his approach into a more traditional scholastic form in his *Principles of Philosophy*. And although the Jesuits never accepted Cartesianism, and although his writings were placed on the Index of Forbidden Books, the Cartesian approach greatly influenced both Catholic and Protestant thinking for centuries. Eventually even many Catholic seminaries were teaching a version of Cartesian rationalism.

By any standards, let alone those of the seventeenth century, Etienne Pascal was a most conscientious father. When his wife died, he resigned his position as tax court judge in Clermont-Ferrand, west of Lyon, to devote himself full-time to the education of his son Blaise, then age three, and his two sisters. Five years later he moved his household to Paris, where the children could profit from living in the intellectual capital of Europe. Blaise Pascal, who had been blessed with truly extraordinary natural gifts (he is said to have discovered by himself the first 32 propositions of Euclid's geometry by the time he was twelve), blossomed quickly.

In 1639, shortly before his sixteenth birthday, he wrote an essay on the characteristics of geometric cones which drew praise even from the celebrated Descartes. Always a helpful sort of person, he decided four years later to make life easier for his father, who had been appointed by Richelieu to assess taxes in Rouen, so he invented the first known mechanical calculator (data was entered through mechanisms resembling telephone dials). This calculator made him famous throughout France. During his lifetime it was considered his greatest achievement.

Moving on to physics, Pascal demonstrated and measured the weight of air and proved the existence of a vacuum (this was widely disputed at the time, especially by Aristotelians, who insisted that even an apparent vacuum must be filled with a rarified matter of some sort). He performed numerous experiments with the newly invented barometer, during the course of which he proved that barometric pressure varies with altitude (this he demonstrated by the admirably straightforward technique of taking a barometer up a mountain) and that it could be used to forecast weather. As a byproduct of these experiments he invented the syringe and the hydraulic press and formulated Pascal's Law of Pressure, the principle behind hydraulic brakes and every other hydraulic device.

His mathematical writings laid the foundation for the development of integral and differential calculus. And, almost as an afterthought, shortly before his death he developed plans for the first metropolitan bus line, willing most of the proceeds from this enterprise to various charities.

These accomplishments would have satisfied any reasonable man, but Pascal was not willing to settle for being merely reasonable. His very life was evidence for the truth of one of his most famous observations—that the most important facts lie outside the province of reason.

When Pascal was 23 he made the acquaintance of several Jansenists, followers of an exaggerated form of Augustinianism developed by the Belgian bishop Cornelius Jansen. Jansenism emphasized the corruption of human nature, denied free will, and accepted the concept of predestination. But it also insisted that true Christianity was not simply a matter of holding certain beliefs but of integrating Christian values into one's life; it strongly opposed the superficial "polite religion" so fashionable at the time and rejected any compromise with worldliness and skepticism. Jansenism was a revelation for Pascal. It filled a need in his life which the empty formalism of the Catholicism he had been taught had never been able to satisfy.

Then, in November of 1654, he had a religious experience which he later referred to as his "Night of Fire" and which changed his life completely—he wrote a short, somewhat incoherent momento of the event which he carried sewn into his clothing until he died eight years later. He entered the religious community of Port-Royal, the stronghold of Jansenist thinking in France, converted his whole family to Jansenism, and never again published under his own name.

Between 1655 and 1657 Pascal wrote a series of eighteen *Provincial Letters* in defense of Antoine Arnauld, the leading Jansenist philosopher and theologian, who had been severely attacked by the Jesuits and whose orthodoxy was being investigated by the theology faculty of the University of Paris. The *Letters* were an enormous success, as much because of their form as because of their content.

Their literary style alone created a sensation. Written with unusual clarity, precision and succinctness and leavened with generous helpings of irony and satire, they are considered the beginning of modern French prose and are still used in French schools as models of composition. In addition, Pascal's castigation of the Jesuits (always a favorite target for abuse in France) for utilizing self-serving and sophistical ethical reasoning and advocating moral laxity found a welcome audience both among freethinkers and among many devout Catholics. The ink was hardly dry in the manuscript before the book was placed on the Index.

Near the end of his life Pascal determined to write a systematic defense of Christianity for unbelievers, not relying on *a priori* logical reasoning but on an analysis of empirical evidence. This project was never accomplished; fragments from it were eventually published as the *Pensees* ("Thoughts"). Pascal died in Paris in 1662 at the age of 39 after suffering excruciating pain from stomach cancer.

Pascal's fundamental criticism of Descartes was that he ignored the only truly necessary thing in life—his rationalistic system made no provision for love of God. Following the lead of Augustine, Pascal insisted that religious knowledge comes not through reason but through love; love, not reason, leads to faith. No merely rational proofs will convince an atheist or agnostic; and, even if they did, they would not lead to knowledge of the personal Christian God but only to deism —belief in a being who is merely the source of order in the universe, the same sort of god in which the pagans had believed.

Since reason cannot reach an adequate conception of God as he is—that is, God as revealed by Christ—reason cannot provide the knowledge we need to achieve our true happiness. Because of this, because reason cannot provide the answers we require, total reliance on reason necessarily leads to skepticism.

But no one can *live* total skepticism, regardless of what he may profess. Our intuition knows better, and even reason itself can show that there are things which surpass it. Hence, Pascal's famous aphorism, "The heart has its reasons, which reason does not know." By "heart," Pascal did not mean the emotions, but an immediate, intuitive apprehension of truth which can provide us with certitude even if we cannot prove that of which we are certain.

Reason alone cannot reveal us to ourselves; it cannot discern the true human condition. And what is that condition? We are glorious and we are wretched—we are a mean between nothing and everything. A person is, in Pascal's phrase, only a frail reed, and yet a reed which thinks; the universe can easily crush us, and yet we are aware of being crushed while the universe knows nothing. Physically the universe encompasses me; mentally I encompass the universe. In fact we are a paradox, a paradox which cannot be understood without revelation because it is explicable only in terms of Adam's sin. Only through the word of God can we make sense out of our existence.

Yet accepting the commitment of faith means making a choice in a situation where reason cannot justify choosing either alternative. This consideration gave rise to the argument which has become known as Pascal's Wager.

Imagine, says Pascal, that you must wager for or against God's existence. Whatever be the amount you wager, it is a finite amount. And imagine that there is only one chance in a hundred million that God exists. Still, there is infinite happiness to be gained if you bet on God and are right, and only a finite amount to be lost if you are wrong. So the best thing to do is to bet on God. And now, adds Pascal, stop imagining. This is precisely the choice you are faced with, and you cannot avoid making the decision because to remain undecided is to choose against God.

The wager argument can easily be misunderstood. Pascal was not trying to imply that religious belief is simply a matter of prudently playing the odds, and he was not trying to give a demonstration of God's existence. Rather, he was addressing himself to people in a state of indecision and trying to convince them that indifference is not a possible option and that commitment is an alternative worth exploring. The wager analogy was not intended to convince anyone, but rather to prepare people's minds, to produce a disposition favorable to belief.

It was quite clear to everyone which way Pascal had wagered.

In Descartes and Pascal was embodied yet again the eternal tension at the very core of the Christian tradition between faith and reason, the head and the heart. It is a tension which probably can never be resolved, for each has its reasons which the other does not know.

Chapter 15
GILSON AND MARITAIN
THE THOMISTIC REVIVAL

WHETHER in art, science, or philosophy, geniuses seem to appear in clusters. The 1880s brought a bumper crop to France. Four of the major characters in our story were born within a few years of each other—Pierre Teilhard de Chardin (1881), Jacques Maritain (1882), Etienne Gilson (1884), and Gabriel Marcel (1889)—and the last three were all born in Paris. Marcel and Teilhard elaborated highly original worldviews of their own; Gilson and Maritain played leading roles in what was probably the most remarkable development in Catholic intellectual life in the first half of the twentieth century, the revival of Thomism.

So dominating did the influence of Aquinas eventually become that it is something of a shock to discover that a hundred and fifty years ago, Thomism was virtually dead as a philosophical school and was generally considered unworthy of serious academic study, except perhaps by antiquarians. There were several reasons for this.

In the centuries following the Council of Trent, while the experimental sciences flourished and philosophers like Descartes, Locke, Hume, Kant, Hegel and Marx dominated intellectual life in Europe, the church was faced with the choice of making use of the new scientific discoveries and philosophical insights, carefully reinterpreting its tradition in their light, or ignoring them as best it could and concentrating its energies on defending and passing on received truth in its received form. Deliberately to some extent and to some extent unwittingly, it chose the second alternative.

This was an understandable mistake, given the high priority placed on maintaining orthodoxy in the wake of the Reformation, but it was a costly one. By closing its eyes to the world around it—by acting as though nothing of consequence were happening, nothing whose implications had to be taken seriously—the church allowed itself to drift into such an intellectual backwater that the closely knit harmony between faith and reason which it had taken so many centuries to develop was seriously threatened.

Religion and science, the spiritual and the intellectual, came to be seen as opposed to each other, much as they had been in the early days of Christianity. At times it seemed almost as though one had to choose between being a thinking person and being a Catholic.

One of the chief casualties of this mentality was, ironically enough, Thomism. In the deeply conservative spirit of the seventeenth and eighteenth centuries, Catholic philosophers and theologians concentrated on producing summaries and commentaries of existing works, particularly for seminaries, rather than on original inquiry and synthesis. Deprived of the opportunity to assimilate new discoveries and to experiment with more modern formulations of its basic insights, Thomism—and traditional philosophy in general—stagnated.

As science and traditional philosophy became increasingly irreconcilable with each other, it became increasingly difficult to maintain a commitment to both. And as it became harder and harder to ignore the discoveries of science, universities— even seminaries—naturally tended to ignore traditional philosophy. It became hard to see what writers from the thirteenth century, let alone those of the pre-Christian era, could teach the modern reader. The worldviews of the Middle Ages lost credibility as serious intellectual alternatives; even in Catholic circles, "medieval" became a synonym for "benighted."

The status of Thomism deteriorated to such a point that when the head of the Jesuit order decided in 1827 to assign an Italian priest to the Roman College to teach logic, the faculty objected so strenuously to the fact that the professor in question was a Thomist that the appointment had to be withdrawn.

It was Pope Leo XIII who took the lead in reversing this trend. In the encyclical *Aeterni Patris* (1879) he called for the revitalization of traditional philosophy and of Thomism in particular as an alternative to the modern philosophical schools, an alternative which would preserve the best elements of traditional Catholic thinking in a form more compatible with the contemporary world.

This call was reinforced by Leo's successors. Suddenly Thomism became the object of zealous (perhaps overzealous) attention, and a determined effort was made to establish the worldview of Aquinas as the quasi-official philosophy of the Catholic Church—something quite different from what Leo had advocated.

Pius X decreed in 1914 that all institutions granting pontifical degrees must use the *Summa Theologiae* as a textbook. The Code of Canon Law promulgated under Benedict XV in 1917 required all instructors of philosophy and theology in Catholic institutions to teach Thomism. Twenty-four propositions extracted from the works of Aquinas were to be taught in all Catholic universities as basic philosophical truths.

(This last requirement aroused opposition from the Jesuits, since all but one of the twenty-four propositions contradicted the teachings of Suarez. Finally a compromise was reached: the propositions in question need only be presented as "safe norms," not as positions which must necessarily be held as true to the exclusion of others.)

To require the teaching of Thomism in all Catholic schools was simple enough; to find a sufficient number of people capable of teaching it in a competent manner was something else entirely. Predictably, the worldview of Aquinas was often poorly taught by instructors who themselves had been poorly taught. This did nothing to enhance students' opinions about its value.

In addition, that worldview was itself still out of touch with the modern world. A stagnant philosophical tradition, resurrected and imposed by papal *fiat,* was still stagnant.

The true revival of Thomism did not come about through legislation. It was a long, painstaking process involving both historical investigation and original creative thinking. Of all those who contributed to this effort, two laymen, Gilson and Maritain, a historian of philosophy and a theoretical philosopher, deserve particular mention.

Few dissertation directors have had as great an impact on the development of a philosophical movement as did Lucien Levy-Bruhl, Etienne Gilson's advisor at the Sorbonne, who suggested that Gilson expand his research on Descartes to include the relations between Cartesianism and the scholastic tradition. This led the young scholar to the study of Aquinas and to the discovery that a great variety of philosophical viewpoints, not one single monolithic system, had been developed during the Middle Ages. It also led him to his life's work.

After finishing his philosophical studies at the Sorbonne, Gilson attended the College de France and then taught philosophy at several schools from 1907 until the start of World War I in 1914. Commissioned an officer in the French army, he was captured during the battle of Verdun in 1916 and remained a prisoner of war in Germany until 1918. In 1921 he was appointed professor of medieval philosophy at the Sorbonne, and eleven years later he accepted a similar post at College de France. In 1929, he was asked to help found the Pontifical Institute of Medieval Studies at Toronto and later became its director, dividing his teaching time between Canada and France. In 1947, he was elected to the French Academy.

All this time he was publishing historical studies at an impressive rate: *Thomism* (1919), *Philosophy in the Middle Ages* (1922), *Studies on the Role of Medieval Thought in the Formation of the Cartesian System* (1930), *The Spirit of Medieval Philosophy* (1936), *The Unity of Philosophical Experience* (1937), and books on Bonaventure, Scotus, Augustine and Dante, to name but a few.

The contribution Gilson made to the Thomistic revival was two-fold. As a preeminent historian of medieval intellectual life, he helped to promote a general reawakening of interest in medieval studies, an appreciation of the fact that the foundations of European culture were laid during the Middle Ages. (This is a lesson that some have still not learned. Even today one can easily get the impression from many books that nothing of importance happened between the fall of Rome and the Renaissance, a period which encompassed fully one-half the Christian era.)

He also argued eloquently in many of his works that traditional philosophy (or "the perennial philosophy," as its proponents often like to call it), and particularly the philosophy of Aquinas, can provide better answers—or at least a better foundation for answers—to the questions which trouble thinking people most deeply than can newer, more fashionable philosophical schools.

In order to be able to present the medieval worldviews as realistic alternatives to modern philosophies, Gilson had to address the problem of the relation between faith and reason, philosophy and theology. Almost all the great thinkers of the Middle Ages were primarily theologians; they made little or no effort to separate religious beliefs from purely rational conclusions in their writings.

In what sense, then, can the medieval worldviews be called truly "philosophical"? Does the term "Christian philosophy" have any real meaning, or does it simply refer to expressions of a religious faith which many people today do not share? Is it desirable, or even legitimate, to construct from the writings of the medievals synthetic, "pure" philosophical systems, free from all dependence on faith and revelation, even if the results would have been completely alien to the minds of those authors themselves?

Gilson faced this issue squarely. Like Augustine, he insisted that revelation is a necessary supplement to reason, that the two can be distinguished from each other but need not and must not be separated. Reason alone can never discover such basic facts as human freedom and the free creation of the universe, and yet any attempt to understand the human condition would be immeasurably impoverished by ignorance of these facts.

It is entirely possible, he held, for a worldview to be both Christian and truly philosophical at the same time. The Christian philosopher engages in precisely the same activity as the unbelieving philosopher. He or she reasons about the ultimate causes of things, the meaning and purpose of human existence, and in general about the nature of reality. But the reality of the Christian is not the same as the reality of the unbeliever, and an understanding of the reality of a Christian requires investigation of, among other things, our relation to God. Why, indeed, should anyone be expected to exclude from his worldview what he believes to be the most important facts about our existence?

Gilson was also quick to point out that the philosophy of Aquinas, as well as that of most of the other medieval writers, was the philosophy of a theologian; its structure and to some extent its content were influenced by theological considerations. This philosophy, therefore, cannot be separated from its theological underpinnings without changing, distorting, falsifying it. For this reason he stoutly rejected all attempts to construct an artificial Thomistic philosophy, with all influences of faith and revelation removed, in order to make the worldview of Aquinas more accessible to those who do not share his religious beliefs. On this point Gilson is probably in the minority today even among Thomists, but probably also closer to the spirit of Thomas himself.

Like Gilson, Jacques Maritain studied first at the Sorbonne and under Henri Bergson at the College de France. He was greatly influenced by Bergson's philosophy of spirit, which contrasted strongly with the then-prevalent attitude that science can solve all human problems. After studying biology at the University of Heidelberg, he began seriously reading the works of Aquinas. In his mid-twenties, Maritain, born a Protestant, was baptized Catholic.

Whereas Gilson was basically a cultural historian, Maritain was more of a creative thinker; he devoted much of his attention to applying the basic insights of Aquinas to contemporary social issues. He was also more willing than Gilson to separate the philosophical positions of Aquinas from their theological contexts, which helped make his work more accessible to those who do not share Thomas's religious orientation.

Maritain taught at the Institut Catholique in Paris, then at Princeton, Chicago, Columbia, the Institute of Medieval Studies in Toronto, and at Notre Dame, where a Jacques Maritain Center was established to carry on his work. From 1945 to 1948, he served as French ambassador to the Vatican. At the time of his death in 1973, Maritain was hailed as the most important contributor to the revival of Thomism; some considered him to have been the greatest Catholic philosopher since Aquinas.

Although his philosophic interests ranged from aesthetics to epistemology to education, Maritain made his most notable contributions in the realm of political and social philosophy, a field to which Aquinas himself paid relatively little attention; and he advocated the development of a new Christian humanism as a further step in the historical evolution of human freedom. For Maritain, freedom meant individual fulfillment. He considered it analogous to the state of those who possess the beatific vision, and it played a central role in his political thinking.

Maritain emphasized that society is necessary not only for the negative reason that each of us is incapable of surviving without assistance, as many other observers have pointed out, but also for the positive reason that each of us desires to share his or her fullness.

Relating twentieth-century political ideologies to different ways of explaining reality in metaphysical terms, he taught that totalitarian societies view people from the viewpoint of what they have in common, and refuse to recognize the importance of the particular characteristics which distinguish them as individuals. This is the political counterpart of metaphysical doctrines, such as Platonism, which concede full reality only to the universal and hold that individuals have importance and value only insofar as they reflect or manifest that universal.

Other types of social organization, on the other hand, such as the extreme forms of capitalism, consider people only as individuals, as particulars, focusing on what separates them and taking little account of the fact that each person is closely related to all others of his or her kind. This is analogous to nominalist metaphysics (that of Ockham, for example), which denies the reality of universals and considers each individual as radically distinct from every other one.

Thomism, according to Maritain, because it is founded on an Aristotelian metaphysics which views each individual object as a union between a universal form and an individualizing principle, can provide the basis for a political and moral philosophy which does justice to the total human person in both his universal and his particular aspects, a social order which both satisfies people's individual needs and respects the fact that they have a destiny which transcends the temporal order.

By the same logic Maritain argued that since ethics is concerned with human actions, the actions of individual people, it cannot simply draw logical conclusions from a universal concept such as abstract human nature. It must take into consideration every source of information which helps us better understand people, sources such as anthropology, psychology, sociology, history—and revelation.

Recognition of our ultimate end is an indispensible precondition for a true appreciation of the dignity of the human person, and thus of the proper relation of the individual to society. The individual has an eternal destiny while every human society will ultimately perish, and in this respect the individual is intrinsically superior to the state. Again, this truth would be difficult or impossible for us to discover without revelation.

While not denying the validity of Aquinas's five proofs for the existence of God, Maritain was convinced of the necessity of exploring more intuitive approaches to God, approaches based not so much on metaphysical reasoning as on analysis of certain types of human experience. An artist, for example, by devoting his life to the appreciation of beauty, is actually (although probably unconsciously) pursuing God, the source of all beauty, while by the process of artistic creation he or she is imitating and carrying on God's creative activity.

Similarly, the person who becomes aware of the reality of love and moral goodness, and who chooses to believe that goodness will triumph over evil and that love is preferable to indifference or hate, has, at least implicitly, made a commitment to God, the source of goodness and love.

Maritain's many books include *Man and the State, True Humanism, Freedom in the Modern World, Philosophy of Nature, Creative Intuition in Art and Poetry, The Person and the Common Good, Science and Wisdom,* and *Moral Philosophy.* The titles give some indication of the breadth of his interests.

Like everything else in the world, the Thomistic revival had both good and bad aspects. And, like everything else in the world, it cannot be understood in isolation from what was going on around it.

Leo XIII did not promote the rehabilitation of Thomism on a mere whim. He had certain specific objectives in mind. One of these objectives was to provide an intellectual alternative to the various worldviews of the nineteenth century which were considered, rightly or wrongly, to be incompatible with traditional Christian teachings. But mature philosophical systems cannot be produced overnight. Especially in view of the deplorable state into which Catholic intellectual life had been permitted to fall, revival of an already existing philosophical tradition of unquestioned orthodoxy was, at the time, the only feasible solution.

Another consideration was Leo's desire, in a period when radical social movements were sweeping both Europe and America, to encourage the development of a nonrevolutionary Christian theory of social justice, a theory which would support the legitimate demands of workers while safeguarding the concept of private property.

It was no coincidence that *Aeterni Patris* was written only thirty-one years after *The Manifesto of the Communist Party.* As Maritain later pointed out, Thomism's metaphysical foundation was ideally suited to serve as the basis for such a theory. And it was in fact the philosophy of Aquinas which inspired the social teaching Leo set forth in encyclicals such as *Rerum Novarum.*

Viewed in terms of these objectives, the Thomistic revival was an unqualified short-term success. It provided Catholics with a knowledge of at least one philosophical system compatible with their faith, a standard with which other worldviews could be compared; it stimulated intellectual life within the church; and it provided the theoretical basis for a Catholic position on social issues which helped to increase the church's appeal to the laboring classes.

The concept of promoting an established philosophical system as a "safe norm" was brilliant so long as it was adhered to; but the attempt to institutionalize a static form of Thomism prevented a good short-term solution from developing into a successful long-term one. The very factor which made Thomism such an ideal instrument for accomplishing Leo XIII's purposes—its close relation to Aristotelian metaphysics—proved, as time went on, to be one of its greatest shortcomings.

Because of this close relation, the establishment of Thomism, at least in the minds of many people, as the church's semi-official philosophy had the effect of making Aristotelianism the church's semi-official metaphysics. This was a mistake. For one thing, the church has no business having a semi-official metaphysics, any more than, at the time of Galileo, it had any business having a semi-official astronomy.

In both cases a fallible, manmade theory, one way among many of organizing and interpreting experience, was practically turned into religious dogma; in both cases denial of the theory came to be seen as tantamount to an attack on the faith.

In point of fact, however, no mention of final causes is made in the Gospels, and belief in prime matter is not a requisite for salvation. It is all well and good to use a particular metaphysical worldview to help elucidate religious beliefs, but to say that a metaphysical theory is wrong because it is in conflict with faith makes no more sense than to say that an astronomical theory is wrong for the same reason. Besides, metaphysical theories, like astronomical ones, tend to be replaced by more satisfactory ones as our knowledge of the physical world increases.

Aristotle's worldview was basically a solution to the problem of how change and real knowledge can both be possible; and it was a marvelously ingenious one, given the state of scientific knowledge at the time. But Aristotle's problem is not considered a critical one today (in part because our concept of knowledge is different from that of the Greeks), and scientific discoveries since his time have created serious problems with some of his basic concepts.

To cite but one example, Aristotle's worldview depended on belief in unchanging forms, and therefore in eternal and unchanging species. It is not often that a scientific discovery invalidates a metaphysical system, but it did happen in this case: biological evolution, particularly the development of new species, is radically inconsistent with Aristotle's metaphysics.

This might not have mattered greatly had there been a greater willingness in the years following *Aeterni Patris* to explore reformulation of Aquinas's basic ideas in ways which did not depend on strict adherence to Aristotelian metaphysics. It was not really necessary to teach generations of students that they had to view the world in the same way that Aristotle did in order to understand the Catholic philosophical heritage. And doing so had the effect of making that heritage virtually incomprehensible.

In more recent years, fortunately, such a reformulation was begun, and "orthodox" Thomists today probably represent a minority of the creative thinkers working within the tradition founded by Aquinas.

The Thomistic revival marks the final step thus far in what can be called traditional Catholic thinking, or systems of thought based on a foundation of Greek philosophy. The second half of the twentieth century has seen a wide variety of attempts to develop Christian worldviews on fundamentally different foundations.

Chapter 16
GABRIEL MARCEL

IT is impossible to imagine the shattering impact that the First World War had on the generations which lived through it. More than any other single event, it marked the end of the old established order of gentility and certainties and ushered in our chaotic modern era.

What made the impact especially shocking was the fact that the bloodiest, most inconceivably destructive war in history up to that time erupted in the middle of a period of seemingly irresistible scientific and technological progress. People were simply too civilized to lapse again into the barbarism of total war—or so they liked to believe, much as people today like to comfort themselves with the thought that we are simply too reasonable and too advanced to permit a nuclear war to occur. Learned men wrote best-selling books proving that a protracted European war was economically and politically impossible.

The outbreak of World War 1 in 1914 had about the same humbling, frightening effect on the intelligentsia of Europe that the sinking of the *Titanic* in 1912 had on its shipbuilders. It demonstrated, with a loss of life more horrible than anyone could have imagined, that, despite its lofty pretensions, the human race was not yet master of its own destiny.

Out of four years of senseless, incomprehensible slaughter, the names of three places in particular stand out. In eastern France, Germans assaulted the fortress city of Verdun in a battle unequaled for sheer savage butchery. The nine-hour opening artillery barrage could be heard 100 miles away. From February 21 to July 11, 1916, approximately 350,000 French soldiers and 337,000 Germans were killed or wounded in this single battle. When the fighting died down, the positions of the two armies were almost exactly where they had been at the start.

On the Somme, to the northwest, the British army chose to attack the strongest portion of the entire German line, positions which the enemy had been fortifying for almost two years. On the first day of the battle alone—July 1, 1916— 57,000 British soldiers were lost, 20,000 of whom were killed. Of the British troops engaged that first day, 40 percent of the enlisted men and 60 percent of the officers were killed or wounded. When the battle finally ground to a halt nearly five months later, the French had suffered 200,000 casualties, the British 420,000, and the Germans 450,000. For this price, the Allies managed to advance their lines roughly six miles.

And then there was the unspeakable morass of Flanders, where it was not uncommon for soldiers and pack animals alike to simply be swallowed up in the bottomless mud. The battle dragged on for about six months in 1917. The cost— perhaps 450,000 British and 270,000 German casualties. The effect on the positions of the two armies—negligible.

During the war as a whole, perhaps 10 million were killed, not counting civilians, and another 21 million wounded. For many years thereafter it was simply called "the Great War," for no one imagined there could ever be another like it.

Like Descartes, Gabriel Marcel was programmed from his early childhood to withdraw into a world of theoretical abstractions. And that is precisely what he did do, just as Descartes had—until reality, inescapable and undeniable, forced his attention back to the facts of everyday life.

He was born in Paris in 1889, the only child of an eminently cultured family. His father, a noted diplomat, later became director of the French National Library and curator of several national museums. His mother died unexpectedly when Gabriel was four; this left him with a deep feeling of loss but also with a strong conviction that the dead woman was still somehow mysteriously present to him. This concept eventually found its way into his mature philosophy.

When Gabriel was eight his father was named ambassador to Sweden, and the child spent a year with him in Stockholm. This, plus frequent foreign vacations, seems to have been the beginning of a lifelong passion for travel, a desire to make himself at home in unfamiliar surroundings. This peripatetic outlook also may have had some effect on his philosophical development. One of Marcel's most famous books was entitled *Homo Viator* ("Man the Wayfarer").

Marcel, again like Descartes, hated school. As happens with many children without brothers or sisters, he did well in his studies but never well enough to satisfy his family. Descartes had found his escape from a rigid educational system in mathematics; Marcel found his in music and drama. At an early age he developed a serious interest in playing and composing, particularly on the piano; and at the age of eight he wrote his first drama. Playwriting, like music, remained one of his chief preoccupations for the rest of his life.

Philosophy was the only academic subject toward which Marcel showed much interest. He studied at the Sorbonne and in 1910 was certified to teach philosophy in secondary schools, although he never completed his doctoral dissertation. As might be expected of someone with his background, he was strongly attracted to idealistic philosophies like those of Hegel and Schelling.

One may speculate, if one wishes, on what might have happened to Gabriel Marcel had a nineteen-year-old boy named Gavrilo Princip not shot Archduke Franz Ferdinand at Sarajevo in 1914. In fact, what happened was that the cultured young Marcel, long in the habit of escaping from everyday concerns into the dream world of his imagination, schooled in highly abstract, intellectual pursuits, was assigned to aid the Red Cross in locating missing French soldiers.

This was the turning point of his life. Like uncounted millions of others, Gabriel Marcel was radically changed by World War I. He was probably one of the few for whom the experience was beneficial.

It was during the war that Marcel discovered the unbridgeable gulf between abstractions and the concrete human reality which they attempt to represent. It did not take him long to realize that the words and numbers neatly written on the little file cards with which he worked were totally inadequate representations of the flesh and blood soldiers for whom they stood. It is possible, even useful for some purposes, to refer in an abstract way to specific human experiences—to speak, for example, of a certain number of amputations, or cases of gangrene, or a certain number of millions of widows and orphans—but one can never, starting from these representations, recapture the human reality which gives events their true significance.

Human reality cannnot adequately be represented by abstractions, because it cannot be separated from the individual persons participating in it without distortion and falsification.

And it did not take Marcel long to conclude that the same principle applied to the abstract, idealistic philosophies whose very remoteness from the physical world had once so attracted him. Abstraction may be a necessary step in the process of human understanding; but human experience, reality as it is lived, can really be understood only as *someone's* experience—from the inside, as it were, and not as an object, something separable from an experiencing subject. This conviction became the cornerstone of his subsequent thinking.

Marcel's approach to philosophy—an approach fully in keeping with his emphasis on concrete, individual experience—concentrated not on systematic explanations but on inquiry, explorations of particular themes. He focused particularly on topics such as faith, trust, fidelity, and despair—subjects which the academic philosophers saw little need to take account of in their lofty systems. The phenomenon of intersubjectivity became his particular field of investigation.

There are no real "conclusions" in philosophy, he held, in the sense of objective results which can be separated from the process of discovery which produced them and handed on to another in the way that mathematical knowledge, for example, can be passed on from one person to another. This means that there can be no absolutely certain results which can serve as the foundation for the kind of systematic progress in philosophy which Descartes had envisioned. It also means that Marcel's thinking is unusually difficult to summarize. The best that can be done is to describe his general approach and give some examples of his most basic beliefs.

The nature of philosophy, for Marcel, is to be exploratory. It requires continual starting again from the beginning. And the personal experience of the person who engages in this process is more important than any particular conclusions which result from it.

After the war, Marcel taught philosophy only occasionally; he earned his living primarily as a writer and editor, and was instrumental in introducing many foreign writers to French readers. In 1927, he published his *Metaphysical Journal,* a kind of intellectual notebook with entries covering the period from 1914 to 1923. This was followed by such books as *Being and Having, The Mystery of Being,* and *Men Against Mass Society.* He also wrote a number of plays.

Although religion had not been a part of Marcel's upbringing—his father, a lapsed Catholic, had professed agnosticism and taught his son that reason and science provide sufficient guidance for the direction of one's life—he eventually concluded that his philosophical convictions demanded acceptance not merely of faith in general but of a specific form of faith. In March of 1929 he was baptized a Catholic, although he always viewed this more as a commitment to Catholicism in the literal sense of a universal faith than as loyalty to an ecclesiastical institution.

Central to Marcel's worldview is a distinction between two ways of dealing with experience. One way to appreciate the difference between the two is to consider those doctors, especially the younger ones, who seem more interested in curing diseases than they are in treating patients.

Each year the nation's medical schools disgorge into our hospitals a new crop of interns, eager to put their hard-won skills to use and delighting in diagnosis. Should someone happen to recover from an undiagnosed malady, an older, more merciful doctor is likely to mumble something about a virus and send the patient home. Younger doctors often seem reluctant to let anyone escape until they have determined what caused the illness, even if it requires the use of every diagnostic test ever invented and even if the answer no longer makes any practical difference. These latter doctors give the impression of being primarily interested in scientific problems, and of viewing the patient merely as a source of puzzles to be solved.

But this way of thinking is not peculiar to the medical profession. Many people—usually those who fit the stereotype of the "intellectual"—tend to treat everything as though it were a theoretical question. Their interest is in understanding things, and they tend to look on people and situations primarily as sources of things for them to understand. Faced with individual cases, they see general issues. A routine romantic disappointment may become for them a metaphysical crisis of cosmic proportions; human tragedies like death and illness they may treat as occasions for speculation on the problem of evil or the nature of divine providence. So involved do they become with this theorizing that the human meaning of what is happening often seems to escape them.

This manner of dealing with experience, the kind of thinking we associate with science and philosophy, Marcel called primary reflection. It abstracts from a concrete situation the data needed to answer a general question, and it seeks answers which are objective in the sense that anyone who considers the same evidence should reach the same conclusion. The only way to accomplish this is for the thinker to separate himself or herself from what he or she is thinking about, to deny or ignore any relation to or involvement with it, to consider the situation as though looking through the eyes of an impartial third person.

Some kinds of questions, those which Marcel calls "problems," are best handled like this. It is a good thing, for example, that engineers try to be objective when they calculate how much stress an airplane wing can tolerate, and that all engineers who use the same data in considering the problem come up with comparable answers. No engineer takes his personal relationship to the wing in question (should he happen, for some strange reason or other, to have one) into consideration. Answers thus arrived at are, in a sense, public property, equally accessible to any qualified observer, and they can be handed on from one person to another. When the curiosity which gives rise to such questions has been satisfied, the questioner loses interest. The problem has been solved.

The difficulty with primary reflection—and thus, by implication, with traditional philosophy—is that, since it does not consider the subjective element in situations, it necessarily misses the human significance of things. And because it requires the thinker to consider what he or she thinks about as something separate from himself or herself, it is a procedure particularly unsuited to trying to understand oneself. In its most extreme form, it leads to things like Cartesianism.

Abstract concepts can certainly help me to understand what

kind of being I am, but to properly understand my nature I must leave the realm of abstraction and begin again, this time grasping the experience of my existence, not as human existence in general but specifically as my own existence.

This experience is not something which must be proved, in the manner of Descartes. It is immediately given. It is lived. And the most basic fact revealed by my experience is that I am incarnated. I do not *have* a body, as one might possess a corpse; in a very real sense I *am* a body. My unity as a person cannot be established through primary reflection, for then I am considering my body as separate from me. And once this separation is made, as Descartes himself found out, the original, experienced unity cannot be recovered. Primary reflection, which focuses on distinctions rather than on relations, necessarily leads to dualism.

This kind of return to experience is the start of what Marcel calls secondary reflection. This term does not refer, as one might expect, to a higher level of abstraction, but to a totally different way of dealing with experience. Whereas primary reflection sees in experience only problems and information to be processed and used to solve them, secondary reflection sees in experience what Marcel calls "mysteries," facts to be accepted and valued for their own sake rather than manipulated for the satisfaction of our curiosity. We make problems ourselves, by the questions which we set ourselves to answer; mysteries reveal themselves to us.

A mystery, as Marcel uses the term, is not something unknowable; it is an immediate given. It is something in which I am necessarily involved, something in which the distinction between what is me and what is not me has no validity. It is the original unity which dualism presupposes. Secondary reflection looks at experience before I withdraw from it, before I turn the mystery into a mere problem, thereby voiding it of its human meaning.

Let us consider two people who love one another. They know their mutual love as something they participate in; it has meaning for them, not because it is love, but because it is their own love. But then suppose that one of the two people decides to look at the matter "philosophically." Not content with accepting the reality as it is given in concrete experience, this person wants to understand what love itself is, what love in general means. This is primary reflection.

Now the person is looking at love not as something he or she is involved in (which is precisely what gives it its true significance), but as something separate from himself or herself—in Marcel's terminology, as an object. He or she will tend to analyze the concept of love, define or explain it in terms of something else, discover "facts" about love which can be passed on to others. He or she may try to understand love in terms of sublimated biological drives or psychoanalytic theories.

But at some point the perceptive person will realize that the concept of love that he or she is trying so hard to analyze and understand is something quite different from the original experience of love shared with one another, that to truly understand love one must stop examining it from the outside and return to the original subjective experience. This is secondary reflection.

Here the emphasis is on considering the lived experience from within, not as a situation separate from the thinker but as a situation in which no complete distinction between the thinker and the experience can be made. Experienced things are seen, not as representatives of certain classes (in the tradition started by Plato and Aristotle and continued by the scholastics), but as unique beings in their own right. The advantages of attempted objectivity are exchanged for the insights made possible by the thinker's privileged position as a participant. Marcel held that abstraction, primary reflection, removes us from lived experience, falsifies it. But reason itself, he argued, can overcome this rational obstacle and restore what abstraction deprives us of.

The same is true for such basic experiences as evil, death and faith. They can be properly treated only as mysteries, not —as philosophy has historically attempted to do—as problems. If I should succeed in "solving" the problem of evil, explaining evil philosophically, what would I really accomplish? I would simply trivialize the problem, destroying its significance.

If there is a solution to evil, then there is no evil. I would have explained evil away, but I still would not have touched the reality of the person who experiences evil, something which can be grasped only from the inside. If I deal with evil by analysis, by reducing it to something other than what it is, I do not really come to grips with the reality at all. I must confront evil as it is encountered in actual situations by actual people, for it exists nowhere else. Again, to adequately deal with freedom, I must accept it as an experience, not grapple with it as a theoretical problem.

But treating experience, not as an object separate from oneself to be used and manipulated as one chooses, but as something which one is necessarily related to, requires an attitude of openness (Marcel used the word *disponibilite,* which means something like "availability" or "accessibility"). It demands an acknowledgement of my involvement (*engagement,* to use Marcel's term) with my surroundings. For although to be "in a situation" is of the essence of being human, we can choose to ignore that fact, refuse to make ourselves accessible, to deny rather than affirm our existence. That choice leads to despair and suicide.

And the most important aspect of experience to which we must remain open, accessible, is other people. Intersubjectivity is intrinsic to being human. Indeed, if we were to choose one basic fact about ourselves to serve as the center of our worldview, that fact would not be a self-subsistent "I am," as with Descartes, but "we are."

It is our intersubjectivity, the nature of our relations with others, which determines the (subjective) world we live in. Although we are in fact necessarily related to others, we can choose to deny this, refuse to make ourselves accessible to others, shut other people out of our lives on every level except the physical. We can make them feel as though they do not exist as people, as subjects, as far as we are concerned. We can, in other words, treat the other person as an object, extrinsic to ourselves, rather than as a "thou" whom we value because of our intimate interrelatedness. We can choose to remain totally absorbed in ourselves.

Just as I must allow a mystery to reveal itself to me, so I must allow the other to be present to me in an intersubjective way. It is through this person-to-person relation, this process of dialogue, that an individual develops in a fully human way.

This is true even of God, the absolute Thou. We are by nature oriented to this absolute Thou, but we must choose to make ourselves accessible to it. We can shut God out of our lives, just as we can shut other people out.

God is not something to be proved. And God is not an object, the solution to a philosophical problem. Religious faith is not belief about something, it is belief in someone. God must be encountered in a unique personal relationship, and the love and joy which we experience in our relations with others point to the possibility that such an encounter can be achieved.

Gabriel Marcel died in 1973. He might be thought of as a cross between Soren Kierkegaard and Martin Buber. Like Kierkegaard he emphasized the validity of faith and the importance of the concrete against rationalism and the abstractions of idealism; like Buber, he made the concept of dialogue a central element in his worldview.

Marcel could also be called a religious existentialist—in fact, the first of the French existentialists—even though he eventually repudiated the term "existentialist" in order to emphasize the distinction between his thinking and that of Jean-Paul Sartre, to which he was radically opposed. It was Marcel who introduced into French philosophy much of the vocabulary which was later adopted by existentialist writers —the term *engagement,* which eventually became inseparably linked with existentialism in the public mind, is a prime example—and two of his last books were entitled *The Philosophy of Existentialism* (1961) and *The Existential Background of Human Dignity* (1963).

His real significance lies not so much in the fact that he pointed out the subjective nature of human experience—that much should be evident to anyone who gives the matter a modicum of thought—as in his insistence that this subjectivity has a legitimate place in philosophy. This is still considered heresy in many quarters, although it was a natural step in a long process of development.

Western philosophy began as speculation about the physical world. Nature played the central role in the worldviews of the ancient Greeks, and nature was seen as objective, existing independently of us. Christian worldviews, at least until recently, were theocentric, God-centered. They still sought to explain the natural world, but now the world was usually considered not as completely objective or independent but as related to God.

It was Descartes who developed the first important anthropocentric, human-centered, worldview—here the fundamental thing to understand was oneself, and everything else, including God, only afterward. Still, Descartes tried as hard as he could to be objective (it was not his fault that this is impossible by definition), and he insisted as resolutely as any laboratory scientist that anyone who followed his procedures would arrive at the same results.

But Descartes also focused attention on the thinking subject, on the fact that nothing has existence for me until I have knowledge of it. Later thinkers, following this lead, concentrated on the relation between the knowing subject and what is known. Some of them—Kant is a notable example—declared that we can never know reality as it exists in itself (that is, independently of our knowledge of it), but only reality in the form that our particular human way of knowing things allows it to appear to us. This meant that knowledge is relative rather than absolute—relative, that is, to our way of knowing things—but still objective in the sense that individual differences between knowing subjects and data accessible only to privileged observers (such as the nature of a love relationship) were excluded from consideration.

Marcel might be thought of as going Descartes—and Kant, for that matter—one step further, taking as the center of his worldview not just the generalized thinking subject (the disembodied intelligence of Descartes) but the lived experience of the individual person. His worldview is, in many ways, the diametric opposite of Plato's—subjective, concrete, practical, inquiring and tentative, rather than objective, abstract, theoretical, systematic, and final.

His worldview was different from Plato's because the data he looked at and the questions he asked were different. Marcel concentrated on those facts which most of us consider to be of primary importance in our lives. His was not a philosophy for philosophers; it was a philosophy for people.

Chapter 17
TEILHARD DE CHARDIN

SCIENTIFIC data will often collect for decades—perhaps even for centuries—until someone is able to construct a general theory to explain the thousands of individual facts. Such was the case with evolution.

By the beginning of the nineteenth century, a mass of evidence had been collected which suggested that species are not permanent and unchanging—as Aristotle, for example, and his followers had assumed. Too many fossils of extinct and intermediate forms had been found. But by themselves these fossils did not explain anything. They awaited someone who could identify the mechanism responsible for producing the changes which differentiate one species from another.

The first one to try was a Frenchman by the name of Jean Baptise Lamarck. In 1801, he proposed that the evolution of different species occurs through the inheritance of characteristics acquired after birth. Animals which live in an area where the only suitable food grows on trees, let us say, will constantly stretch their necks when they feed; hundreds of generations of this sort of thing will produce animals with very long necks. And the same general process produces the other characteristics which distinguish different species.

Lamarck made a number of notable contributions to science —it was he, incidentally, who coined the word "biology"— but his theory of evolution was eventually discredited.

As more became known about genetics and heredity, and as more and more experiments were conducted to test Lamarck's hypothesis, it became increasingly clear that the physical characteristics which an animal acquires during its lifetime are not passed on to its descendants.

220

Approximately sixty years later, Charles Darwin set forth a different theory. In Darwin's view, individual differences arise spontaneously; those which give their possessor an advantage in feeding or breeding are passed on simply because animals which possess them live longer and have more offspring than those which do not. Thus, to return to our previous example, it was not stretching for food which gave giraffes long necks. To oversimplify, those giraffes who happened to have long necks were more likely to survive than those which did not, so more baby giraffes were born with long necks than with short ones.

This theory, which provided a more plausible explanation of the mechanism by which evolution progressed than Lamarck had done, created a sensation. Darwinism became synonymous with evolutionism in the public mind—and sometimes in the minds of scientists themselves—even though there were many non-Darwinist evolutionists.

But although Darwinism took the scientific world by storm, it left several important questions unanswered. For one thing, there is nothing in Darwinism to explain why evolution proceeds in the direction of greater complexity.

Darwinism itself is strictly materialistic—concerned only with anatomical changes and observable causes—but there does not seem to be any purely materialistic reason why simple forms should not stay simple, rather than becoming more specialized. If, as evolutionary theory proposes, our ancestors once lived in the oceans, why were they not content to stay there?

On the other hand, it is not necessary to interpret evolution in purely materialistic terms. Henri Bergson, who was born in 1859, the same year in which *The Origin of Species* was published, insisted that a true understanding of evolution requires a metaphysical analysis of the nature of living beings.

And this analysis, he contended, reveals the existence of an *elan vital,* a life-urge, an innate impulse which is the real driving force behind evolution.

This *elan vital* enters into matter and gives rise to living beings. It seeks to realize all the potentialities of which a being is capable, and evolution is the history of the different forms this striving has assumed. Since the life-urge is not limited to earth but is found throughout the universe, "creative evolution," as Bergson called it, is a cosmic process.

With the appearance of human intelligence, the *elan vital* reached its most complete expression. We are the culmination and *raison d'etre* of terrestrial life. Seen from another perspective, evolution is God's way of producing beings worthy of his love.

From his podium at the College de France, Bergson preached his doctrine of antimaterialistic, "creative" evolution to generations of students. He was enormously influential—in theology, for example, his ideas contributed to the conception of God as perfect and yet incomplete (a contradiction for traditional metaphysics), God as involved with the development of the world.

But by that time Darwinism had become firmly entrenched as a scientific explanation, and Bergson's *elan vital* was perceived by many as nothing more than a shadowy metaphysical entity—or nonentity. Scientists, in other words, did not accept it as an explanatory principle. And most religious leaders, meanwhile, were still vehemently denying the concept of evolution itself.

It is tempting to speculate about what might have happened had Bergson appeared before Darwin rather than after him. Perhaps the traumatic split between religion and evolution, the biological and the spiritual, might not have occurred.

But in fact it did occur. And by the time an attempt was

made to interpret evolution in terms of Catholic theology, neither side was willing to listen.

Pierre Teilhard de Chardin is remembered by one of his former highschool teachers as having been an excellent but unenthusiastic student and "disturbingly" well-behaved. He often seemed lost in a dream world. Like Descartes and Pascal, the young Pierre had an early compulsion to find something solid and permanent. Rather than mathematics, however, he daydreamed about rocks.

Perhaps it was inevitable. Born near Clermont-Ferrand in the rocky, mineral-rich Auvergne region of south-central France and distantly related to both the passionate believer Pascal and the skeptical freethinker Voltaire, Teilhard seems, in retrospect, to have been almost predestined for a career as a religiously oriented, independently minded geologist—on the one hand rigorously scientific and on the other hand almost mystically speculative. And that highly unusual combination is precisely what he became.

In 1899, at the age of eighteen, he entered the Jesuit novitiate at Aix-en-Provence. Three years later, following the passage of some particularly stringent anticlerical laws, French Jesuits transferred all their seminarians out of the country, and Teilhard was sent to the island of Jersey.

This was, in several respects, a foretaste of things to come. It was the first foreign voyage in what would prove to be an extraordinarily travel-filled life, and the first of several times he would find himself exiled because of religious controversy. It was also on Jersey that he published his first geological article.

After teaching physics and chemistry for several years at the Jesuit high school in Cairo, Teilhard went to England to study theology and there was able to continue his scientific work. Destined to participate in two of the most famous anthropological discoveries of all time, he would encounter the first one here. Working with an English archeologist named Dawson, he unearthed one of the teeth of Piltdown Man, a half-human, half-ape creature which created a sensation in a world press fascinated with the search for the "missing link."

(Years later, when Piltdown Man was proved to be a hoax —perpetrated, apparently, by Dawson—Teilhard remarked, with typically Gallic irony, that it had always seemed strange to him that intelligent life should have first appeared in England.)

After his ordination, Teilhard was assigned to begin the serious study of paleontology at the Museum of Natural History in Paris. But the First World War intervened in his life just as it had in Marcel's. At the start of 1915 he was sent to the front as a stretcher bearer.

Teilhard saw his share of death and suffering. In addition to enduring four years' worth of casualties in the trenches of Flanders and along the Meuse, his regiment was chosen to make the final French assault against Fort Douaumont, some of the most savage fighting in the indescribably brutal ten-month battle of Verdun.

And yet his wartime letters reveal a curious detachment from the carnage around him. The realities of death and dismemberment, as we saw, encouraged Marcel to shift his focus from the universal to the individual; Teilhard chose to view them not as personal tragedies but as elements of a necessary process. From his enthusiastic reading of Bergson and his personal interpretation of the Christian message, he had already formed the basic outlines of his worldview. And seen from that view, the war was promoting the realization of humanity's inevitable cosmic destiny.

In 1919 Teilhard returned to his studies in Paris, lectured at the Institut Catholique and received a doctorate in geology from the Sorbonne. Then what he later called "the chance of my life" presented itself.

A French Jesuit working in Mongolia had sent some fossil-bearing bones to Paris for analysis. Teilhard was assigned to study them. Before long he was on his way to China to examine the sites where they had been found. He returned sixteen months later to resume his lectures, but other people had other ideas.

It was apparent now that Teilhard's view of the universe involved certain theological difficulties. This was not remarkable. New scientific ideas cause theological problems because many theological beliefs have been defined in ways that—perhaps unavoidably and almost certainly unintentionally—presuppose a particular scientific (or prescientific) view of the world.

Evolution was one such idea. In addition to whatever problems it caused with the interpretation of Genesis, it also presented a number of difficulties with the concept of original sin. Teilhard's attempts to resolve some of these problems had raised eyebrows in Rome, and his Jesuit superiors thought it best to order him to stop teaching. They then forbade him to publish anything but scientific material. And finally they asked him to leave the country.

Fortunately for Teilhard, who preferred field work to teaching anyway, he now had somewhere to go. In April of 1926 he sailed back to the Orient, landing in Saigon and taking a train northward through Hanoi and into China.

A year later he was appointed supervisor of all research on vertebrate fossils in China by the Carnegie Foundation. He spent the next two decades criss-crossing central Asia, with side trips to such places as Ethiopia, India, and Burma, constantly searching for more evidence to support his unique interpretation of the evolutionary process. In 1928, when the

prehistoric Sinanthropos—Peking Man—was discovered,
Teilhard directed the excavation.

He was establishing a solid reputation as one of the world's
leading paleontologists. Between 1915 and 1945 he published
some 170 scientific articles and technical papers, most of
them dealing with the fossils of Asian mammals or with
various examples of geological stratification.

Side by side with his scientific work went his speculative
writing. He began *The Divine Milieu* shortly after his return
to China, and started *The Phenomenon of Man* in 1937. He
was never allowed to publish these or any of the other works
for which he is best known today.

He also made several trips to the United States, where he
faced the same combination of professional acclaim and ecclesiastical disapproval he had encountered in France. In
1937, he addressed the National Academy of Sciences in
Philadelphia. Not long afterward he arrived at Boston College to receive an honorary degree only to discover that the
award had been withdrawn under pressure from Cardinal
William O'Connell.

Stranded in Peking after the Japanese invasion of China,
Teilhard was unable to return to France until 1946. Shortly
afterward he suffered a heart attack. Professional honors
continued to shower steadily upon him, but ecclesiastical
restrictions closed tighter and tighter.

In 1947, he was told to stay away from philosophical
speculation. The next year he was ordered not to accept a
teaching position at the College de France (a particularly
mean-minded prohibition, it would seem, since he could have
taught for only one year anyway before reaching the man-
datory retirement age). Then he was forbidden to participate
in major intellectual conferences.

Teilhard, plainly, had become an embarrassment to the
Jesuit order. Finally, in 1951, it was agreed that he should go

to New York. He had the foresight, before leaving, to place his letters and manuscripts in trusted hands.

He took up residence in the rectory of a Jesuit parish in Manhattan, but it was a melancholy existence at best. He suffered fits of weeping, and wrote a friend that without meaningful work to occupy his days he felt like a parasite. His official assignment—helping to classify material in New York's Natural History Museum—was little more than a formality. Actually, as he well knew, his real duty in New York was simply to die.

Once upon a time, a Catholic theologian wrote a book containing an extraordinarily dynamic conception of the universe.

He taught that even inert matter can be said to have a goal —to achieve the most advanced state of development of which it is capable, to become as much like God as possible. This striving of matter to reach the divine results in a hierarchy of complexity, from the chemical elements through vegetable and animal life to human intelligence, the greatest perfection of which matter is capable. All matter desires, as it were, to achieve rationality and understanding, and the destiny of rational humanity is eternal union with God.

The theologian, though his ideas were enthusiastically received for a time, was eventually condemned as a heretic. His name was Thomas Aquinas, and the book was the *Summa Contra Gentiles* (see, for example, Book III, Chapter 22).

Teilhard de Chardin's position, once freed from the esoteric vocabulary and sometimes convoluted phrasing in which he expressed it, is remarkably similar. It can be understood as resting on three basic concepts.

First, contrary to one of the most hallowed tenets of Western (but not Eastern) metaphysics, there is no fundamental distinction between matter and spirit. They are like two forms of the same thing. Consciousness has existed as a potentiality in matter from the beginning, and it has gradually emerged from matter. All parts of the universe, from the most simple to the most complex, possess a greater or lesser degree of consciousness.

Second, the universe as a whole is engaged in an irreversible progression toward the complete realization of its total spiritual potentialities. The physical world is not and never has been in a state of equilibrium. Even before the appearance of life it was undergoing evolution. And the path of this evolution—cosmogenesis ("universe-generation"), Teilhard called it—is not random. It proceeds in the direction of increasingly complex structures, culminating in the appearance of human life.

Teilhard was convinced, too, that there was solid evidence that this evolutionary progression toward greater organic complexity has been accompanied by a corresponding increase in consciousness, a progressively greater degree of spiritualization.

He visualized the hierarchy of the universe in terms of concentric circles, each developing out of and depending on the one below it. Most fundamental is the geosphere ("earth-circle"), the realm of inanimate matter; from this evolved the biosphere ("life-circle"), the vegetable and animal kingdoms. With the emergence of human intelligence appeared the noosphere ("mind-circle"), and evolution became aware of itself.

This third sphere, the realm of thought, is the characteristic environment of humanity, distinct from but superimposed on the biosphere, just as the biosphere is distinct from but presupposes the geosphere. The more complex and more highly concentrated physical structures become, the greater self-awareness they display. Physical and spiritual development go hand-in-hand. Biological evolution is not only the precondition but also a cause of human moral and social progress.

Teilhard's noosphere is not a sort of world-soul. It does not exist independently of individual minds any more than the biosphere exists independently of individual living things. It is, in a sense, the interrelation of individual minds, just as the biosphere is a sort of network of interdependent individual beings.

But the evolutionary progression has not ended; we in our present state do not represent its final product. The two-fold process of human development, unification and spiritualization, will inevitably continue. And Tielhard held—this was his third basic concept—that Christianity had the answer to a riddle which no evolutionist had yet solved: What is the purpose of evolution? What is it heading for? Why, in other words, has all this happened?

On one level, he wrote, increasing intellectual and cultural convergence will lead to the unification of the human species. A world culture will emerge, as will a far greater degree of social unity.

At the same time—since greater concentration and complexity of matter leads to greater concentration and complexity of spirit—this unification will lead to the appearance of a hyperpersonal consciousness, a state in which individual persons will retain their own identity but still be joined with each other to form a whole greater than its parts, "the whole group of mankind," as Teilhard put it, "forming a single body and soul in charity."

This will be accomplished by love, which permits unity without loss of personal identity, by the spirit of Christ moving in and through history. It will bring forth the Christosphere ("Christ-circle"), the final goal of evolution and the purpose of creation, the progressive unification of all humanity with the risen Christ, so that at the end of history —at what Teilhard called the "Omega Point"—Christ will truly be, as St. Paul expressed it, "all in all."

The driving force behind evolution for Teilhard was not an impersonal life-urge but the desire for union with an eminently personal God.

On April 10, 1955, Easter Sunday, Teilhard suffered a rupture of his coronary artery and died almost instantly.

The *New York Times* devoted nine paragraphs to his obituary; the Jesuit periodical *America* gave him but one. He was buried at a Jesuit novitiate in upstate New York, an institution which was subsequently sold to a cooking school.

Publication of his nonscientific works began in the year of his death—vows of obedience, fortunately, cannot follow a person beyond the grave.

But vindictiveness can. Some twenty years after his death, a group of militant Catholics petitioned the New York archdiocese to have Teilhard declared a heretic and to "correct" the error by which he had been given a Christian burial.

Why was Teilhard considered so dangerous? What he tried to do, basically, was to reformulate Bergson's interpretation of evolution in theological terms. For him this was not a matter of reconciling conflicting views.

Quite the contrary. He saw the evidence of paleontology as reaffirming one of the oldest concepts of Christianity, an idea which can be traced at least as far back as St. Paul: the return of all things to God.

And yet his attempt to harmonize theology and science pleased neither scientists nor theologians.

On the one hand, Teilhard's speculations went far beyond any scientific evidence available at the time, or any that might conceivably become available. He strayed even further— much further—from the empirical facts than Bergson had. (This is hardly surprising, since he formulated his basic position before even beginning his scientific studies.)

Teilhard's worldview was a sort of meditation on the nature of living things, an appeal to the Christian imagination, and the near-mysticism of his vision embarrassed many other scientists. Even his close friend Julian Huxley, who wrote the Introduction to *The Phenomenon of Man,* confessed that he found the concept of Omega Point incomprehensible.

At the same time, the mere fact that Teilhard accepted the evolutionary hypothesis at all upset many Catholics. In the atmosphere of the time, when for most people evolution meant Darwinism, and Darwinism meant atheism, such a thing seemed tantamount to apostasy.

But that was not the only problem. Teilhard was a poet as well as a scientist, and sometimes the exuberance of his poetic imagination led him to make statements whose theological implications were ambiguous at best. What was one to make, for example, of his anticipation of "the emergence of an even Greater Christ?"

Even more serious was the fact that some of his writings tended to verge on the pantheistic. Nor did Teilhard seem overly concerned about this. He once spoke of the "pantheistic aspirations" which "will always rise in man's heart," and went so far as to call St. Paul "the surest theorist of a sort of Christian pantheism."

It is worth recalling in this regard, however, that Teilhard was never given permission to publish his nonscientific work, and that this had the effect of preventing discussion of his ideas during his lifetime. There is no way of knowing how much he might have rephrased or modified or developed his positions had he been given a chance to expose them to the criticism of his fellow scholars.

Henri Bergson may have been born too late; Teilhard was almost certainly born too soon. It was his misfortune to have lived during one of the most intellectually repressive periods in the church's history. And yet there is more than a little irony in the popular image of Teilhard as a victim of inquisitorial heavy-handedness, for he seems to have had no problem with the idea of censorship before it was applied to him.

In his wartime letters, for example, he spoke of "a high proportion of uninformed or defective minds that will need to be forced into the mold of truth" and "the legitimacy of preventitive measures . . . which go with the privileges of truth and light." Perhaps it is best, in looking back on those days, not to point fingers.

Even if Teilhard did fail to bridge the chasm which separates science and religion, failure—as we have seen before—can lead to quite positive results.

It was precisely the boldness of his attempt, the breadth of his vision, which created such an impact when his major works were finally published. To the generation of the 1960s in particular, impatient both with science which showed no regard for the spirit and with religion which took but little notice of the world around it, Teilhard became something of a folk hero. He may have failed to reconcile science and religion, the spiritual and the empirical, but at least he tried.

Chapter 18
JOHN COURTNEY MURRAY

THE United States is and always has been an experiment unique in history—an attempt to form a nation by throwing open a rich and immeasurably vast wilderness to literally anyone in the world who was willing and able to take possession of it. And sometimes it must have seemed, as floods of humanity surged across both oceans, that everyone in the world had accepted the invitation.

The nature of the experiment was summed up in the new country's motto, *E Pluribus Unum:* to make many peoples into one people, to make immigrants into Americans. But what was an American? And what did it mean to become one? Particularly in the realm of religion, historically a cause of the bitterest and most implacable of human hatreds, what did it mean for people of different cultures to be "one"?

The Catholic Church especially found itself in a new and somewhat confusing situation. In Europe the Vatican was used to dealing with governments; the church's status in many countries was defined by a formal agreement, or Concordat. In 1783, Rome dutifully asked the Continental Congress for permission to establish an American bishopric and was told to do as it pleased, that Congress had no jurisdiction over the matter. Catholicism would be granted no recognized status—no restrictions, but also no privileges.

For the first time since its early centuries the church found itself in a "pluralistic" environment, and this new situation raised some thorny new questions.

Could Catholicism, seeing itself as the only true church, accept in principle a situation in which all religions were granted equal status? Could—and would—American Catholics whole-heartedly support complete religious toleration even if they were to become a majority?

Simply put, can one be a completely loyal Catholic and a completely loyal American at the same time? From the dawn of American history many non-Catholics were convinced that one could not, and some Catholics themselves seemed uncertain.

In the years following the Civil War, as Catholic intellectual life blossomed, answers to these questions began to emerge. Cardinal James Gibbons, Archbishop John Ireland and Bishop Denis O'Connell, among others, proclaimed that the American tradition of separation of church and state not only was fully compatible with Catholic doctrine but also resulted in less interference with the church's functioning than was the case in Europe.

Some Europeans, both friends and foes of Catholicism, took this to mean that the American constitutional provisions regarding religion should be imitated on the continent.

That line of thought provoked a fateful reaction. In the first papal letter ever written to the American church (*Longinqua Oceani,* 1895), Leo XIII declared it erroneous to teach that American-style separation of church and state is the ideal situation or that it would be good for church and state to be separated everywhere.

He felt compelled to add that the American church would have experienced even greater growth and vitality had it enjoyed not only liberty but governmental recognition and support as well.

Leo followed this with the letter *Testem Benevolentiae* (1899), in which he condemned "Americanism"—in particular, the belief that the church should adapt its teachings to modern conditions and, in order to make Catholicism more appealing to people of other faiths, either de-emphasize those of its doctrines which non-Catholics found particularly objectionable or else reformulate them so as to change the way they had traditionally been understood.

These two letters, plus the condemnation of "Modernism" by Pius X in 1907, sufficed to quash the first real flowering of Catholic intellectual life in America. Analysis of the theological implications of the unique relation between church and state in the United States, an analysis which might have proven extremely useful to the church in its dealings with European governments, was cut short. And American Catholic thinking was plunged into a wilderness of rigidity, sterility, and reaction from which it did not begin to emerge until after the Second World War.

In 1904, roughly halfway between the appearance of *Testem Benevolentiae* and the condemnation of Modernism, John Courtney Murray was born in New York City, the son of an Irish mother and a Scottish father, a lawyer who died when Murray was twelve.

At the age of sixteen Murray entered the Jesuit order; after preliminary studies he taught high school for three years in the Philippines and studied theology at the Jesuit house of studies in Woodstock, Maryland. Upon ordination he attended the Gregorian University in Rome and received a doctorate in theology. In 1937, he returned to Woodstock and taught theology—specializing in grace and the Trinity—until his death thirty years later.

Oh, and there was one thing more. In 1940, the theology faculties of the United States founded a quarterly publication, *Theological Studies,* and the following year Murray became its editor. His enthusiasm for the job, at least in the early years, seems to have been limited—he asked at least twice to be allowed to resign—but eventually Murray turned *Theological Studies* into his forum for commentary on religion and society, and in the process he discovered his life's work.

It was a strange time for America, and a strange time for Catholicism. Old patterns of thinking and living had been broken apart by dislocations of war, with the pieces forming new and unfamiliar shapes. And, as often happens when old structures are disturbed, some ugliness came to light.

The postwar years were the era of McCarthyism and anti-communist hysteria, and the fact that McCarthy happened to be Catholic did nothing to increase non-Catholics' confidence about the church's respect for civil liberties. It was a time when newspapers and magazines across the country debated whether a Catholic could—or should—be elected president, while Catholics argued among themselves about their "ghetto mentality" and wondered why there were no Catholic intellectuals.

This was the background against which John Courtney Murray began to raise his voice.

While others busied themselves with defending the church, Murray counterattacked. To the charge that Catholicism represents a threat to American democracy, he replied, in print and on the lecture platform, that the real danger to American society was not that anyone wanted the United States to become a Catholic country, but that many people wanted it to become a secular country.

What troubled Murray was not the spoken accusation that Catholicism is un-American because it is doctrinally opposed to religious toleration—that, he felt, was easy enough to disprove—but the unstated feeling, all the more pernicious for being unvoiced, that Catholicism is un-American because a democratic state must be a secular state, that religion has no place in public life, that government not only should not favor one religion over another but should take no notice of religious values whatever.

This certainly was not what the founding fathers had in mind—one need only read the Declaration of Independence and the Preamble to the Constitution to realize that—but Murray was convinced that what many advocates of "separation of church and state" really wanted was not freedom *of* religion but freedom *from* religion.

And this secularization of public life Murray considered dangerous because it leads to a monopoly of legitimate authority. Since secularism recognizes no authority higher than human reason, it necessarily holds the civil state to be supreme in the spiritual and moral realms as well as in the political. It must, in principle, deny the legitimacy of any organization which claims authority from a supernatural source.

The state thus becomes the only voice competent to speak out on public issues; the possibility of a moral appeal against unjust laws is eliminated. And in that direction lies the road to tyranny. Recognition of the freedom of religious conscience was, for Murray, not merely a consequence of democracy but a precondition for democracy's continued existence.

In his eyes this made it imperative that Catholics join Jewish and other Christian groups to assert the existence of a moral authority independent of the secular state, and he became a highly visible member of the National Conference of Christians and Jews at a time when such membership was frowned on by many Catholic leaders as implying that all religions are equally valid.

But how can people from different cultural and religious traditions agree on a common ethical and political theory? The only answer, according to Murray, was to use the same method the founding fathers had used—to appeal to natural law, to reason toward conclusions which all can accept because they are based on the Judeo-Christian conception of human nature, a conception radically opposed to that of the secular humanists.

And it was here, he felt, that Catholicism could make a unique contribution to the preservation of a truly pluralistic society. Since natural law is an integral part of the Catholic philosophical tradition, Catholics are particularly well equipped to assist in working out a natural law justification for nonsecular pluralism.

Murray's arguments found a wide audience outside Catholic circles, and he rapidly earned a reputation as one of the country's leading theologians. He received lecture invitations from a number of Ivy League colleges, and in 1954 he became the first Catholic priest to serve as a visiting professor at Yale, lecturing on medieval philosophy and culture.

Upon his return to Woodstock, he began to work out a systematic exposition of his views on the relation between church and state, of which the centerpiece was a series of major articles on Leo XIII. Murray was convinced that it was necessary, both in order to counter the worldwide spread of secular humanism and to assuage the fears of non-Catholics in the United States, for the Catholic Church to formally recognize the American constitutional protection of religious pluralism not merely as something to be tolerated as a practical necessity or a temporary expedient, but as a positive good in itself, a condition at least as beneficial to the welfare of the church as is preferential treatment.

But how could this position be reconciled with Leo's *Longinqua Oceani* and other papal pronouncements which seemed to state quite clearly that legal recognition of Catholicism was always the ideal, the goal to be pursued whenever possible?

For more than a decade Murray used the pages of *Theological Studies* to explore this problem. It was an issue which would ultimately involve the very nature of theological reasoning itself, and it would not be settled until the closing session of the Second Vatican Council. Murray lost every battle except the last one, and for a time it seemed that he might suffer the same fate as Teilhard de Chardin.

In 1955, he was ordered by Jesuit officials in Rome first to submit all of his subsequent writings for approval before publication and then simply not to write any more on the subject of church and state—an ironic restriction for someone who was devoting his life to arguing that the church is not an enemy of freedom.

At times the criticism bordered on the ludicrous. When Murray delivered the annual *Critic* magazine lecture on "Censorship in the Fields of Literature and Arts," several bishops complained that he had undermined the principles upon which the Legion of Decency was founded.

Undaunted, Murray continued his involvement in public affairs. He served as a consultant to the Atomic Energy Commission and was an advisor on constitutional issues to John Kennedy during his presidential campaign. In 1960, he published his first book, *We Hold These Truths,* and was awarded the American journalistic equivalent of canonization, an appearance on the cover of *Time* magazine.

He also paid a price. A crushing workload, compounded by his inability to refuse requests for his assistance and his habit of letting work rob him of needed sleep, kept him often on the edge of exhaustion. For this his superiors were at least partly responsible.

At the end of 1946 Murray, suffering from extreme fatigue and on the verge of a collapse, asked for a third time to be relieved of his *Theological Studies* duties, and again was refused. Less than a year later, illness prevented him from delivering a major address to a meeting of the Catholic Theological Society of America. In 1953, he was hospitalized for fatigue and cardiac problems, and for the rest of his life he suffered from a weak heart.

And as his strength slowly ebbed, demands on his time increased.

One who works in the realm of ideas is not often given a chance to confront his or her principal adversaries directly, to

settle an important issue once and for all, with the whole
world as an audience. That chance was given to Murray;
then, excruciatingly, it was snatched away. And then it was
given back.

When the Second Vatican Council began in 1962, Murray
was teaching at Woodstock, having been, as he put it, "dis-
invited." Although kept informed, by fellow Jesuits and
friends in the American hierarchy, of the behind-the-scenes
maneuvering to secure approval of a Declaration on Religious Freedom, he was forced to watch the fight for which he
had been training all his life begin without him.

As it happened, he did not miss much. The opening rounds
—the first of the Council's four sessions—consisted mostly
of shadow-boxing. A liberal draft was introduced by Cardinal Bea of the Secretariat for Christian Unity, and a conservative draft by the all-powerful Cardinal Alfredo Ottaviani,
head of the Theological Commission. A committee was
formed to reconcile them, and it failed.

When the second session opened in 1963 Murray was there,
at the insistence of New York's Cardinal Spellman. A draft
supporting Murray's general position was approved in comit-
tee at a dramatic face-to-face confrontation with Ottaviani
and other conservative leaders, but it was not submitted to
the whole Council. It had become apparent that there was a
great deal of opposition to its passage.

To the outside world, which saw the issue simply as a yes-
or-no vote on religious freedom, it looked, no doubt, as
though a substantial part of the church was unwilling to
acknowledge a basic human right. In fact what was causing
the delay was not disagreement with the general intent of the
declaration but rather concern about a fundamental theological problem. And the research Murray had done and the concepts he had developed in the preceding two decades were
precisely what were required to solve it.

At issue was a well-entrenched teaching which held that the Catholic Church, as the only religious body founded by God, the only true church, has a right to protection and support by civil government. In practice, this teaching led to different theories about church-state relations in different places.

Where Catholics formed an overwhelming majority—in Italy, for example, or in Spain—the church accepted and sometimes insisted on preferential treatment. At times this led to restrictions on the rights of non-Catholics, particularly on the right to proselytize. Where Catholics were in the minority, however, the church for practical reasons acquiesced in a policy of equal treatment for all religions but still held that legal recognition of the rights it claimed would be the theoretical ideal. The American situation, according to this way of thinking, was neither unjust nor evil, but it was decidedly second-best.

Murray was pressing for rejection of this two-tiered theory in favor of a single statement on religious freedom, based on natural law, which would be applicable everywhere.

The theological problem this caused was that the church, like the American Supreme Court, does not like to contradict itself. The overwhelming majority of the Council had no problem in voting to recognize full religious freedom, but how could this be done without seeming to repudiate earlier papal statements? And why was it necessary to abandon the traditional two-tiered theory, which had been endorsed by several popes?

Murray replied, first, that the proposed declaration was not a contradiction of previous teaching but a development of it—that the tenets of natural law evolve over time because natural law itself is evolving—and, second, that the two-tiered theory was an anachronistic relic of times long past, never truly a part of church doctrine but the result of historical circumstances and a large dose of muddled thinking.

How can natural law evolve? Because it is based on our understanding of human nature, and that understanding grows with time. Slavery, for example, is defended in the bible and in many medieval treatises on natural law but is now condemned by all natural law writers. Human nature did not change over that period, but our awareness of what it means to be human changed.

In a similar fashion, the universal human conscience now recognizes freedom of religion as a right intrinsic to human nature itself, and so this right has become part of the natural law. This is not a new right, merely a newly recognized right —recognized in part because revulsion at the horrors of twentieth-century totalitarianism led to a deeper and more explicit appreciation of the dignity of the human person.

Religious freedom in the modern sense was not a part of traditional church teaching—even though it is perfectly consistent with that teaching—for the excellent reason that it is a relatively new idea.

The two-tiered theory also must be understood historically. The fundamental teaching contained in papal pronouncements must be distinguished from historically conditioned statements which may be valid only for their own time. This is essentially analogous to the distinction which we saw earlier between the form of a theological statement and its content. The content may express an eternal truth, but this truth may be formulated at one moment in history in one way and differently at another.

But this idea was abhorrent to Council conservatives. They saw it as tantamount to reinterpreting church doctrine in order to make it more palatable to non-Catholics, the same "Americanist" error which Leo XIII had condemned in *Testem Benevolentiae*. (It may seem remarkable that theologians who accept the principles of historical exegsis when it comes to scripture would protest applying them to papal declarations, but such was—and sometimes still is—the case.)

Murray countered by arguing, in effect, that his position simply reflected the original teaching of the church—the two cities concept held by Augustine and many others—which had subsequently been lost sight of.

How and why had this way of looking at things been abandoned?

Early Christians viewed church and state just as Augustine had described them, as two separate communities, representing two different orders of reality, with little or nothing in common. Establishment of "Christian" states, however, led to development of a different perspective. The civil and the religious came to be understood not as separate societies but as two functions of a single society, mutually supportive and, therefore, mutually dependent.

Under these circumstances, where there is but one religion and that religion is seen as conferring legitimacy on the civil order, the maintenance of religious unity becomes necessary to the preservation of public order. And preservation of public order is the first responsibility of civil government.

Repression of religious error thus became not merely a means for secular rulers to strengthen their own power, but a positive moral duty, and heresy becomes virtually equivalent to treason.

When it became necessary to find an ethical justification for repression, one was discovered in the concept that "error has no rights." Since, according to this theory, only orthodox Catholicism is the true religion, it alone has a right to exist which is founded in the objective order of things. Heresy, like an outlaw, has no right to exist—it could and should be hunted down and destroyed.

This outlook was not materially changed by the Reformation. Religious liberty was not usually recognized on an individual basis; most principalities established, in one form or another, a state religion. In Protestant England as in Catholic France and Spain, church and state were inseparably intertwined.

But if on the continent an established religion was considered a necessary support for civil government, the precise opposite was true in America. The founding fathers separated the civil and the religious at least in part because that was the best way, perhaps the only way, to establish political unity in the face of religious diversity. In a pluralistic environment, individual conscience had to be respected in order to prevent loyalty to one's conscience from competing with loyalty to the state.

The Vatican had opposed "separation of the church and state" in the eighteenth and nineteenth centuries because, naturally enough, it had understood this concept in the light of the European experience; and such separation in Europe was usually promoted by those hostile to religion. (That this need not be the case was shown by the American experience —but then, as we have seen, theological analysis of the American experience had been stifled almost as soon as it began.) For this reason the church had kept legal support of Catholicism as the theoretical ideal.

But this ideal had nothing to do with church doctrine. It was simply an outdated way of thinking resulting from the circumstances of European history.

In fact, said Murray, the church does not require legal privileges. It merely requires—and this is the basic doctrinal teaching contained in papal pronouncements on church and state—freedom to perform its spiritual mission. The state, in the modern world, has no business trying to promote the spiritual unity of the church; and the church has no business trying to exert influence in the political order except by appealing to the consciences of individual believers.

And, like the boy who cried out what everyone else could

see, that the emperor was wearing no clothes, Murray pointed out what should have been obvious to any thinking person —that the hoary adage "error has no rights" is a palpable sophism, nonsensical on its face. Of course, error has no rights; neither does truth. Only people have rights, and it is with the rights of people that discussion of religious freedom should begin.

One of the main reasons why the church had not found a satisfactory solution to the problem of church and state was that the question had not been properly posed.

These arguments, presented to the Council primarily through speeches by American bishops, prevailed. When the Council's third session began, Murray was appointed to head the committee which wrote the revised draft of the Declaration on Religious Freedom. And during the fourth session— in December, 1965—this Declaration received final approval by a vote of 2,308 to 70.

But Murray was left a broken man. He had suffered a severe heart attack in January of 1964, and another in December. In October, 1965—two weeks after the Council had voted to close debate on the Declaration, thus assuring its passage—he was hospitalized with a collapsed lung.

He devoted his final months to such issues as ecumenism, racial problems, and atheism. He served on a presidential commission studying the Selective Service law, and he and Kingman Brewster, president of Yale, were the only two of its twenty-four members to vote in favor of the right of selective conscientious objection—a positon which followed logically from Murray's belief that natural law theory can distinguish between just and unjust wars.

Murray's life, begun in New York, had a most typically New York ending. He died of a heart attack in a cab while returning to Manhattan from his sister's home in Queens.

His passing in August of 1967 left a void, for the real

significance of his work lies not so much in the conclusions he reached as in the methods he used. Murray's historically based analysis of theological problems, and his application to social and political issues of a natural law rooted not in static, supposedly eternal metaphysical abstractions but in our evolving awareness of what it means to be human, are still sorely needed.

Chapter 19
KARL RAHNER

ABOUT two hundred years ago Immanuel Kant initiated a line of inquiry which has led, in our own time, to the most thorough and far-reaching reformulation of Catholic theology since at least the age of Aquinas.

Starting with the fact that we seem to have knowledge which does not come from experience but with which all experience must agree (mathematics and metaphysics being the most notable examples), Kant determined to discover how such a thing is possible.

To take a trivial example, we know before we ever see an armadillo (or even if we never see one) that three armadillos and two armadillos will equal five armadillos, and we are certain of this even if we do not know what an armadillo is. In a similar fashion we feel confident that the propositions of geometry, although not derived from experience, will never be contradicted by experience.

But how can we be certain of this a priori (prior to experience)? If the knowledge does not come from experience, where does it come from? And how can we be certain ahead of time that it will conform to all possible sense experience if and when we have it?

In a way, this is similar to the question Plato had faced: if we have never experienced a real (that is, a geometric) circle, how can we have knowledge of it—knowledge which is prior to and more certain than the evidence of our senses?

Plato, since he could find no other answer to the question, concluded that we must acquire this knowledge before birth. And, in order to explain how mathematical and metaphysical knowledge is possible, he constructed a theory of forms which had, as we have seen, the most profound impact on the

247

development of Christian thought from Augustine's time to the present. Kant, by turning the problem on its head, as it were, formulated a radically different answer.

It would be possible, he said, for us to have absolutely certain knowledge which does not come from experience, and yet which is true of all possible experience, if that knowledge is founded upon the preconditions of our having experience at all. In other words, our *a priori* knowledge is based, not on the nature of things we know, but on the nature of our way of knowing things.

To take a somewhat analagous case, I can be absolutely certain ahead of time that anything which I see will reflect color. This I know, not by analyzing the objects of my vision, but simply because I am aware that my eyes are constructed in such a way that they cannot perceive anything which does not reflect color.

Just as we can see things only if and to the extent that they are compatible with our specifically human way of seeing, so we can know things only if they are compatible with our specifically human way of knowing. And examination of that way of knowing, and of the preconditions for knowing which careful analysis reveals, can give us *a priori* knowledge to which we can be sure ahead of time that the objects of our experience will conform—for the simple reason that if they do not conform to these preconditions, we will be incapable of experiencing them.

In particular, according to Kant, space and time are not things which exist objectively in the physical world outside ourselves: they are simply subjective preconditions of our human way of knowing things. Our minds are built in such a way that we cannot experience things which are not presented in space and time, any more than we can see things which do not reflect light. Space and time are like mental constructions which we bring to the physical world and which allow us to experience it.

The *a priori* knowledge of mathematics, therefore—and of metaphysics, if there is such a thing as true metaphysical knowledge—must come from an analysis of these mental constructions. Since geometry, for example, does nothing more than express the intrinsic rules of space, and since we cannot experience anything except as given in space, we can be certain ahead of time that anything we will ever experience —or ever could experience—anywhere in the universe will obey the laws of geometry. (The development of non-Euclidian geometries has created certain difficulties for this conception.) This is true, not because of the way things themselves are, but simply because we are incapable of experiencing anything for which it is not true.

(An inescapable implication of this is that we can never know things as they are "in themselves"—that is, without reference to the way in which they must be presented to us in order for us to be able to experience them. But that is a problem for another day.)

Kant went on to say a great many other extremely interesting things, but what is important for us at the moment is his method, not his specific conclusions. The most fundamental thing Kant did—and it was one of the great milestones in the history of philosophy—was to shift the focus of philosophical inquiry from reasoning about experience to reasoning about the subjective preconditions of having experience.

Kant called this methodology "transcendental philosophy," and it was this approach which a Belgian Jesuit named Joseph Marechal tried, in the early decades of this century, to combine with Thomistic epistemology. What was missing in Kant, Marechal felt, was an appreciation of the dynamic nature of intellection (the Thomistic agent intellect) and the fact that the fundamental orientation of the human intellect is not toward the objects of sensible experience but toward absolute being itself—toward God.

But Marechal, who was on the threshold of the synthesis which came to be known as transcendental Thomism, became discouraged by ill health and the lack of an enthusiastic reception for his ideas. To put the matter bluntly, he gave up. He wrote four volumes of historical analysis and one volume of commentary on Kant; his own position, he promised, would appear in a sixth volume.

But Marechal died in 1944 without ever writing that final volume, without ever realizing what momentous results his work would lead to.

A truly outstanding theologian functions, in a sense, like a translator—a translator not from one language to another but from one worldview to another. He or she extracts the meaning of a theological teaching from the particular formulation it was given at one point in history and re-expresses it in terms which are meaningful to the people of his or her own time, all the while remaining scrupulously faithful to the spirit of the original.

That is what Augustine did; that is what Aquinas did. And that is what Karl Rahner was doing until his death in 1984.

Such an undertaking requires a thorough grounding in philosophy, particularly the best philosophical thinking of one's own time, as well as extensive knowledge of church doctrine and the history of its development. For a theologian, being familiar with only one philosophical tradition—and not even a contemporary one at that—is roughly equivalent to knowing only one language, a language not comprehensible to one's contemporaries. With that kind of background it might be possible to become a literary critic, but not a translator.

Yet few people have solid training in both philosophy and theology, perhaps because few people set out to become truly outstanding theologians. In Rahner's case it came about almost by accident.

Karl Rahner seems to have been fated, at least in his early years, to follow in the footsteps of his older brother Hugo. In 1922, when he was eighteen, he entered the Jesuit novitiate in Feldkirch, Austria—like his brother Hugo three years earlier. He showed a special interest in philosophy: during three years of required Thomistic studies he kept private notebooks filled with excerpts from the writings of Kant and Marechal, and he was eventually sent back to his native town of Freiburg-im-Breisgau, in Germany's Black Forest region, to study for a doctorate.

Erasmus had once lived in Freiburg and had been forced to move—he claimed the church bells interrupted his studies. Rahner faced a more formidable obstacle.

Freiburg was the center of some of Europe's most advanced philosophical thinking. No less a personage than Martin Heidegger was teaching there, having taken over the chair previously held by Edmund Husserl, the founder of phenomenology. But although he attended as many of Heidegger's lectures as he possibly could—he later said that while he had studied under many excellent professors, Heidegger was the only one he thought of as his teacher— Rahner was assigned to do research under the direction of a different Martin: Martin Honecker, who might be described as something of a paleoscholastic.

When Rahner presented a doctoral dissertation expounding Thomistic epistemology from a transcendental viewpoint —similar in many respects to the project which Marechal had begun and then abandoned—Honecker flatly refused to accept it. This meant that Rahner could not be awarded a doctorate.

Being stabbed in the back by one's own dissertation director is a trauma which can be appreciated only by those who
have experienced it. But living well, as the saying goes, is the
best revenge. Rahner simply had the rejected manuscript published as a book, *Spirit in the World,* which received instant
and enthusiastic acclaim. One reviewer called it "undoubtedly one of the most important books on scholastic philosophy
to appear in recent times."

Honecker's fate, a punishment worthy of Dante at his most
malicious, was to disappear from human memory, except for
disparaging references in books and articles praising Rahner.

Rahner himself, in the meantime, switched fields and became a theologian—like his brother Hugo. In 1937, he was
assigned to teach at the University of Innsbruck—like his
brother Hugo.

But before long, Europe was convulsed by another war. In
1939, following the Nazi invasion of Austria, the Jesuit house
at Innsbruck was closed and Rahner was ordered to leave the
region. He spent the war years first in Vienna and later in
several small towns near Munich. In 1948, he returned to the
University of Innsbruck and later taught at Munich and
Munster.

At the time, Rahner's misadventure with Honecker must
have seemed a frustrating setback. The end result of his years
at Freiburg, however, was that he began his theological
studies not only with a thorough training in philosophy in
general and contemporary philosophy in particular, but also,
as a result of having written *Spirit in the World,* with a
philosophical position of his own. This enabled him to take
an unusually creative view of the theologian's task.

Theology is usually conceived as understanding and explaining the contents of revelation, not as providing the
answers to philosophical questions about the human condition. Rahner, however, was superbly well equipped to ap-

proach theology in precisely this way. Even more important, he was the first to apply the transcendental method to theological topics.

Rahner's second book, for example, *Hearers of the Word,* explores a standard theological topic—divine revelation. But his method was to ask what are the *a priori* conditions of the possibility of revelation at all. What do the particular human preconditions for knowing tell us about the form which revelation must take in order for God to be able to communicate with us? In *Spirit in the World* he asked what, if anything, our human way of knowing tells us about God and about our relation to God.

This is not simply a new theological outlook; it is a totally new theological science. It is transcendental theology.

The primary objective of this transcendental theology is to provide a Christian interpretation of human experience, not to teach us about things beyond our present knowledge but to point out what is implicit, presupposed, in what we already know. Seen from this viewpoint, the real purpose of the Gospel message is not to bring us news about some exterior reality, but to help us understand more fully who and what we are. And the validation of theology—and of revelation —occurs when one recognizes that this interpretation of his or her inner experience is true.

Rahner's starting point—following Kant, Marechal, and Heidegger (and, for that matter, Descartes)—is an analysis of human spiritual activity. And this analysis, he says, reveals two major and interrelated facts: human transcendence and the existence of God.

To transcend literally means "to climb over," to surpass. It comes from the same Latin root from which "escalator" is derived. And we are transcendent beings because we are able to "climb over" our immediate experience and therefore to surpass ourselves. We can transcend the limitations of our environment; we are, as Marechal pointed out, dynamically oriented toward infinity, toward absolute being.

This is demonstrated most clearly in the phenomenon of human knowledge. We do not blindly accept the objects of sensation as simple facts, to be accepted at face value. We constantly evaluate, compare, question them. We are capable not only of knowing limited objects but also of knowing that limited objects are limited, which presupposes at least an implicit knowledge of the unlimited. The unlimited, the infinite, is a sort of background against which objects must appear in order for us to be able to see them as limited.

And this background of unlimitedness is, like Kant's *a priori* transcendentals, something which we do not find in experience but which we are somehow able to bring to experience.

We can know our knowledge as imperfect only against a background of perfect knowledge; we can recognize ourselves as unfulfilled only against the background of complete fulfillment. In acknowledging ourselves as limited, we see ourselves as particular manifestations of being—which presupposes at least an implicit awareness of absolute being.

Human knowledge, therefore, is a transcendental activity —as are love and every other consciously spiritual act. The key question is, what *a priori* fact about ourselves do these transcendental experiences point to? And Rahner's answer is that we can have such experiences only if there is a transcendental reality in us.

This *a priori* transcendental reality is what we call God. God is the precondition which makes human spiritual experiences possible. God is not identical with me but is intimately present to me, giving me the ability to express—and thus to experience—my spirituality.

Whereas traditional arguments for God proceed as though trying to prove the existence of something of which people have had no previous experience, Rahner insists that all of us have actually experienced God many times—for experience of God is inseparable from our experience of ourselves. When we are most aware of ourselves, we place ourselves most completely in the presence of God.

(It is because he believes that the presence of God is presupposed in our everyday actions, and that it is the duty of the theologian to elucidate this fact, that Rahner has written essays on the theological implications of such commonplace activities as walking, sitting, eating, and going to bed. He has also written on the Beatles—because, as he put it, one cannot understand one's world without listening to its popular music. Parents, please take note.)

The reality of God is not something which we do not already know; it is already implicit, presupposed, in our interior life. It is something in the background of our most profound experiences, something which we usually neglect to focus on. And it is precisely because God is a precondition of our having transcendental experience, not a direct object of experience, that it is possible to deny God's existence.

The beginning of religion, for Rahner, is one's acceptance of himself or herself as a radically open, transcendent being. (From this point of view, contemporary existentialism—which sees human nature as containing, paradoxically, the ability to go beyond one's own nature and which defines the human person as that being which no definition can encompass—is, even in its atheistic forms, a step toward a truly religious attitude.) Acceptance of one's transcendence leads to an awareness of oneself as already fundamentally oriented toward the unlimited, toward absolute being, toward God.

But the fact that we are oriented toward God does not necessarily mean that we have been accepted by God. It is this which makes us "Hearers of the Word," searching history for some sign that God has communicated with us. (Such a sign need not have been given. It is quite possible, after all, for the redemption to have taken place without our having been informed about it—Jesus was in no way obliged to reveal his supernatural identity.)

But the Christian believes that history does in fact provide evidence of such communication, that it furnishes a basis for the knowledge and faith that one has been accepted by God through Jesus Christ.

Yet this faith in God cannot resolve life's problems. It cannot reveal the meaning or purpose of existence, or solve any philosophical puzzles. Indeed, according to Rahner, the Christian is "the most radical of all skeptics," for he or she believes that nothing but God can be the complete answer to anything, and that God himself is the question which has no answer.

As we have seen, most Catholic thinking from the church's early centuries to our own day has taken place within the intellectual framework of Platonism—a way of thinking developed more than two thousand years ago primarily to explain the phenomenon of change in a prescientific age. And Christianity was explained in Platonic terms, by Augustine and by others, not because that was the best possible worldview for the purpose, but because it was the only one available at the time.

The result of this has been a fundamental dualism at the heart of Christianity, a division of reality into two radically opposed principles. This dualism assumed many different forms—material versus spiritual, body versus soul, temporal versus eternal, sensation versus intellection—but in each case one principle was seen as evil, or at least less good, and the human person was seen as torn between the two.

Moral goodness was strongly associated, if not actually equated, with the rejection of the material world, including one's own body. At times the ideal of Christian living resembled the disembodied intelligence of Descartes.

But it was Plato, not Jesus, who taught that.

By basing his work on a contemporary worldview, and espeially on one which has as its starting point a unified phenomenon (the human capacity for spiritual activity) rather than the opposition of contrary principles, Rahner has opened the door to something truly revolutionary: the development of a non-Platonic, non-dualistic Catholic theology. His significance lies principally in the fact that he is, in effect, attacking the basic presuppositions which have guided the mainstream of Catholic theology since the time of Augustine.

Freeing Catholic doctrine from Platonism makes it possible to see even the most familiar teachings in a totally new light. It also makes some of them appear much more reasonable—and probably much closer to what the first followers of Jesus believed.

Concupiscence, for example—the fact that our appetites are not totally under the control of our will—is traditionally explained as a struggle between our sensible appetite and our spiritual appetite, our "higher" and our "lower" selves, a punishment for Adam's sin, something it would be much better not to have.

His transcendental method enabled Rahner to approach the matter quite differently.

Since the human spirit is the act of the total person, body as well as soul, it is the total person, soul and body, who contacts the world. There is no purely spiritual knowledge or desire, and none which is purely sensible—every act of knowing and desiring is a spiritual-sensible activity. It is because all our desires, even the most spiritual, have a sensible content that they are not totally subject to the will. The result is that humans cannot make a total, absolutely unchangeable commitment to anything, as angels (who are pure spirits) can. Thus it sometimes happens that we abandon our best intentions.

But if this is a consequence of Adam's sin, it is also the *a*

258<author>William A. Herr</author>

priori condition of the possibility of our redemption.

Since pure spirits are constructed in such a way that their wills remain totally committed to what they choose, the fallen angels can never repent. But we are built differently, which is what makes it possible for even the worst sinner to accept God's grace. It is our fundamental metaphysical structure, the way we are put together, which makes it possible for us to turn away from sin. This need not have been true. God could just as well have made us, as he made the angels, without the capacity to accept salvation.

And salvation, according to Rahner, is not a kind of posthumous spiritual reward for good behavior, granted to some and withheld from others; it is simply a continuation of what has taken place during one's life, a sharing in God to the extent that each person has developed a capacity for it through the practice of faith, hope and love. Heaven and hell are, in a sense, the same thing—remaining whatever you have made of yourself, forever.

Even in death, we will not be separate from our bodies—we will not spend eternity with a group of other immaterial "souls"—but we will in some way become related to all of material reality.

If the idea that eternity will be a physical as well as a spiritual experience seems strange, recall that Jesus never said that our souls are immortal—that is a Platonic notion. What Jesus said was that our bodies would rise.

However bizarre some of Rahner's ideas may appear at first glance—bizarre because they are based on a different worldview than the one we are used to—he has always managed to stay within the boundaries of orthodoxy. This is because he has not denied any church doctrine. He has simply explained. He has translated. This is the fundamental difference between Rahner and Hans Kung (whose position does not represent nearly as radical a reformulation of dogma as does Rahner's).

One reason for Rahner's enormous influence has been his prodigious output (over 3,500 books and articles); another was his practice of organizing cooperative efforts—dictionaries, encyclopedias, series of monographs—which harness the energies of dozens of talented collaborators to spread his basic ideas.

His great moment of triumph came, as did Murray's, at the Second Vatican Council (like Murray, he ran afoul of Cardinal Ottaviani, who pleaded with the pope—unsuccessfully —to send Rahner back to Austria). But whereas Murray managed to get the Council to pass one declaration, the entire work and spirit of Vatican II was a vindication of Rahner's way of doing theology.

He has often been compared with Thomas Aquinas. But it is notoriously difficult to judge the importance of one's contemporaries. It may be that Rahner's real role is to be the Albert for some Thomas yet to come. Or he may turn out to be another John Scotus Erigena, an astoundingly brilliant ninth-century thinker whose work was never followed up, a road which was never taken.

Or he may in fact be the person who single-handedly set Catholic thinking on a totally new course.

Chapter 20
BERNARD LONERGAN
EDWARD SCHILLEBEECKX
HANS KUNG

BY ITS very nature, epistemology, the philosophical study of human knowledge, tends to be a convoluted discipline. It is basically thinking about thinking—or, if one prefers, it is thought thinking about itself—and it is filled with such conundrums as "Can I be certain that I am certain?" and "How do I know that I know that I know?"

And yet it is as crucial for theologians as for philosophers to understand the process of thinking, for that process is one of the basic tools of their trade. And theology, if it desires to be considered a science in the full sense of the word, must proceed according to a truly scientific method.

In recent years a Canadian Jesuit named Bernard Lonergan has made major contributions to both these objectives by developing a method for conducting theology which is based, he says, on an analysis of the way in which every human mind necessarily operates.

Lonergan, who was born in the province of Quebec in 1904 and received his doctorate from Rome's Gregorian University, is best known for a massive volume called *Insight: A Study of Human Understanding,* published in 1957.

Insight is an exposition of neo-Thomistic epistemology monumental in its scope and mind-numbing in its stylistic opacity. Reading it has been, for many people, an experience opposite to the one Goethe reported having while reading Kant: it has been like having darkness flood into a lighted room.

Yet Lonergan's basic purpose in *Insight* is not difficult to understand. He tries to describe, through introspection and by examining sample cases of problem-solving, the activity of knowing—that is, to determine what, specifically, I am doing when I know something. Then he attempts to explain exactly what that something which I know is.

This investigation was not prompted by idle curiosity. Lonergan states at the beginning of *Insight*—and then again, just for good measure, at the end—that if one thoroughly understands what understanding is, then he or she will have grasped the general outlines of everything which can be understood. Put another way, this means that by an analysis of how one thinks, one can determine the rules according to which the mind necessarily functions, and thereby discover the structure which underlies all true sciences.

This goal is reminiscent in many ways of the dream of Descartes. While they differ in many other respects, Lonergan shares Descartes' belief that the individual sciences are, or at least should be, founded on one common method which is not arbitrary or culturally conditioned but is simply a formal expression of the way the human mind naturally works.

Of the great mass of data and observations contained in *Insight,* what is particularly relevant for our purposes is Longergan's identification of four levels, or stages, in the knowing process.

First is the level of experience, or the gathering of data; then follow understanding and judgment.

Finally comes the level of deliberation (a concept developed more in Lonergan's later work than in *Insight*)—the realm of evaluation and responsibility, the determination of whether or not a particular fact or situation calls for personal involvement and commitment.

As expounded in *Insight,* these concepts have no particular applicability to religious discourse. They are simply presented as the necessary underlying structure of all forms of inquiry.

It was in *Method in Theology* (1970) that, as the book's title suggests, Lonergan specifically considered the implications of his position for theological research.

Method in Theology also shows a much greater concern with subjectivity and the receptivity of the knower than does Lonergan's earlier work. This may be explained in part as a moving away from a strictly neo-Thomistic viewpoint toward a greater appreciation of the existential worldview, as commentators of Lonergan have suggested.

But it is also true that, whether one likes it or not, Christian theology is fundamentally different from other branches of knowledge, not only in its starting point, but also in its objectives.

Other sciences may pursue knowledge strictly for its own sake; theology, properly understood, may not. For theology is involved not only with understanding things—in the manner, let us say, of physics or biology—but also with a message whose accurate and effective transmission it believes to be of the utmost importance. The theologian must be concerned with the subjective conditions of a statement's acceptance as well as the objective conditions of its verification. He or she cannot be indifferent to whether or not people are receptive to the word of God.

(This fact may even have influenced Lonergan's style: *Method* is a much more readable book than is *Insight*.)

Lonergan proposes an eight-step analysis of theological research in *Method in Theology* that is based on the levels of knowing we have just discussed. Four levels are involved in determining what the message of Christianity is, and four are required to apply or transmit that message.

The process begins with an empirical investigation of events and texts, a determination of the facts (the level of experience). Then come the interpretation of what these events and texts mean (understanding) and an appreciation of the historical circumstances in which the texts were written and the events took place (judgment). Finally there is the dialectical process (deliberation) of evaluating different explanations of the facts to determine which explanations can be accepted and harmonized and which must be rejected.

Communicating the Christian message to someone is, in a sense, the opposite of the process of learning it, so here the four steps occur in inverse order.

First there must be a personal conviction on the part of the theologian (deliberation), and then an investigation of the doctrinal implications of this conviction (judgment). This is followed by a search for the proper systematic framework, the appropriate philosophical worldview, to explain his or her conclusions (understanding). The final step is communication, the process of expressing one's conclusions in a reasonable and effective manner, so that the listener sees them as worthy of his or her acceptance. This brings us back to the realm of empirical facts, the level of experience.

This analysis serves several useful functions. It breaks down the somewhat nebulous concept of "doing theology" into a limited number of specific objectives. It indicates what work must be done in order to ensure that a given issue has received thorough and systematic consideration. By specifying how the eight steps in theological research relate to one another, it provides a program for effective collaboration among theologians specializing in different fields.

Finally, since it claims to be based on the steps through which the mind naturally progresses in its search for truth, it is the appropriate method for examining any theological question whatsoever.

What is most significant—and therefore what must be considered most carefully—in Lonergan's work, as in that of Descartes, is not his specific conclusions but his claim to have discovered the proper procedure for conducting investigations. Lonergan has developed a program to guide the direction of all future theological research. And he claims, at least implicitly, not merely that his program will produce better results than some other way of doing theology, but that it is, objectively considered, the only proper way to go about things because it is the only way which is completely compatible with the structure of the human mind.

That is a very strong claim indeed.

And while Lonergan has attracted a large and extremely enthusiastic following, some serious questions do suggest themselves. How can anyone be certain that there is one way of thinking or of solving problems which is "natural" for the human mind, across all times and all cultures, even into the future? And if there is no way to be certain that there is, does not a program such as Lonergan's, if strictly adhered to, run the risk of seriously restricting and distorting future theological investigation?

Ultimately Lonergan's dream, like that of Descartes, must be—and will be—judged by the results to which it leads. The dreams of two other contemporary theologians, however, have already been judged.

When the Second Vatican Council opened in 1962 in an atmosphere of hope and humility—a willingness to acknowledge past mistakes and a joyful exploration of the possibilities opened up by new ways of thinking—among those in attendance were Edward Schillebeeckx (pronounced ShhhKILL-a-bakes), then 48, and Hans Kung, 34.

Schillebeeckx, a shy, scholarly Dominican from Antwerp, Belgium, was destined to become the chief theological advisor to the Dutch Bishops' Conference and the principal consultant on doctrine for the near-revolutionary *New Dutch Catechism*. He was already credited with having promoted a revival of sacramental theology through his presentation of the sacraments as personal encounters with Jesus, a concept which was incorporated into Vatican II's official decrees.

Kung, an articulate, somewhat flamboyant Swiss diocesan priest who had studied in London, Amsterdam, Berlin and Madrid, who held two degrees from the Gregorian University and a doctorate from the Institut Catholique in Paris, had created a sensation by writing a book entitled *The Council, Reform, and Reunion,* in which he argued that if Catholicism and Protestantism would each reform itself in the spirit of the Gospels, then the dream of Christian unity would become a practical reality.

Such was the excitement raised by Kung's proposals in those ecumenically-minded days that Episcopal Bishop James Pike of San Francisco ordered a copy of the book for every priest in his diocese.

When Vatican II began, Schillebeeckx and Kung were considered two of the most creative and promising theologians in the church. Today, twenty years later, each is known primarily for having written one book. And for having been called back to Rome, not this time to offer theological advice, but to defend himself for having written it.

What Schillebeeckx was trying to do can be understood only against the background of the "historical Jesus" controversy, the contention by a number of influential scholars that the existence of the Jesus Christ of traditional Christian belief cannot be substantiated by solid historical evidence.

In his book *Jesus: An Experiment in Christology,* Schillebeeckx claimed that modern biblical scholarship has made it possible to do precisely that, to identify the historically verifiable words and actions which led the followers of Jesus to proclaim him to be the Son of God, and to determine what they meant when they did so.

This is a much more complex matter than it might seem. For one thing, it means temporarily putting aside, so to speak, the classical Christological definitions of church councils—without denying them—in order to recapture, as far as possible, the apostles' own experience of meeting and following the human person called Jesus of Nazareth. One need not deny that Jesus was "consubstantial with the Father," for example, in order to assert that his disciples did not think of him in those terms. It is a safe bet that Peter, Andrew, or Thomas would have been hard-pressed even to spell "consubstantial," let alone to define it.

Another problem is that the New Testament itself was not composed until long after the death of Jesus. What Schillebeeckx was trying to reach was the beliefs of the Palestinian church before the Gospels in their present form were written.

What makes this possible, at least in theory, is the fact that textual research has shown that the Gospels are not unified, continuous narratives but stratified collections of material from different sources. The layers can be peeled away, as at an archeological site, to reveal the oldest, the most original Christological statements still extant. The oldest parts of the Gospels, in other words, contain the oldest statements of Christian belief.

And the oldest part of the Gospels, or so the biblical experts say, is the recounting of Jesus' passion and death. This was followed by the resurrection and post-resurrection narratives, and then by stories of Jesus' ministry—his miracles and teachings. The last parts of the Gospels to be written, and therefore the parts which the earliest Christians presumably considered least important, are the nativity stories.

Indeed, the emphasis of the gospels, or at least of the synoptics—Matthew, Mark and Luke, the three oldest Gospels—is almost the exact opposite of the emphasis of the dogmatic Christological definitions.

The councils of Chalcedon and Nicaea, because of their desire to clarify orthodox beliefs in the face of heretical teachings, were primarily concerned with who Jesus was. They produced philosophical—neoplatonic, to be specific —definitions of his nature and his relation with the first person of the Trinity. Their declarations, and the traditional creeds, almost completely ignore Jesus' ministry.

The Gospels, on the other hand, which are not theological propositions but the story of salvational encounters between humanity and divinity, are much more interested in what Jesus came for, in what differences his life and work made in the world.

This difference in emphasis parallels the distinction Schillebeeckx makes between dogmatic "Christology from above," which tries to explain what is meant by saying that God became a human person, and the earlier, more biblical "Christology from below," which tries to express and rejoice in the wondrous fact that a human person was exhalted to the status of the Son of God.

But what did the apostles mean by calling Jesus "the Son of God?" Indeed, what did Jesus himself mean?

Schillebeeckx finds the key to answering this question in the absolutely unprecedented fact that Jesus used the term "Abba" to refer to God—a word which is usually translated as "Father," but which literally means something much closer to "Daddy."

In a culture in which it was strictly forbidden even to speak the name of God, Jesus' unique "Abba experience," as Schillebeeckx calls it, reflected his feeling of total intimacy with the divinity. Jesus, in other words, in his humanity, was so closely and completely united with God that by virtue of that union he may properly be called the Son of God.

What, then, of the resurrection, of the event which for St. Paul, and for many others both before and after him, was the cornerstone and guarantee of the Christian faith? Did Jesus or did he not really rise from the dead?

In this area as in others, Schillebeeckx proceeds by trying to identify the original experience which led the disciples of Jesus to proclaim that he had risen. And that experience, he says, had nothing to do with an empty tomb, or with conversations with Jesus after his death. These pious stories came later.

The original and fundamental Easter-event was a conversion experience on the part of the apostles, a spiritual transformation which absolutely convinced them that Jesus, despite having been crucified, was now truly alive with God. That conviction, that experience of the living presence and power of Jesus, became the foundation of their faith in Jesus Christ as Lord. That faith did not depend in any way on whether or not Jesus' physical body was still in his tomb.

By skillfully weaving together the results of an enormous amount of scriptural research, Schillebeeckx was able to draw a picture of Jesus as he was experienced by his contemporaries. And many of his readers found that this Jesus— Jesus as he was known and loved by those who first believed in him—was a much more appropriate object of faith than the metaphysical entity described by the definitions of Chalcedon and Nicaea.

But it was primarily because his book omitted mention of the definitions of Chalcedon and Nicaea—an omission which was required by his objective and his method—that Schillebeeckx was summoned back to Rome.

What Hans Kung was trying to do is more difficult to determine.

At least as eary as 1960, in *The Council, Reform,* and *Reunion,* Kung had called for re-examination of a number of issues separating Catholics from other Christian groups, particularly Anglicans and Lutherans. One of these problem areas was the concept of papal infallibility.

In later works he attempted to lessen the divisive impact of infallibility by refuting misconceptions about what the doctrine really means. Thus in his 1964 book *Structures of the Church* he denied that the pope can define a dogma against the consensus of the church, and in *The Church* (1967) he pointed out that even according to the wording of the decree of infallibility itself, the power of the pope is not absolute, arbitrary, or unlimited.

Then, in *Infallible? An Inquiry* (1971), he proceeded to assert precisely what he had previously denied. And he proposed that the notion of papal infallibility be replaced by the concept of the "indefectability" of the church as a whole—a concept he had earlier described, correctly, as a Protestant idea. What made him change his position so drastically?

The issuing of the notorious birth control encyclical, *Humanae Vitae,* by Pope Paul VI, against the recommendations of his own study commission and to the consternation of many bishops and theologians and the utter dismay of a large percentage of the faithful, apparently, was the most important factor.

Humanae Vitae may well have contradicted the consensus of the church, and it might reasonably be construed as an arbitrary act. Considering, however, that no responsible person ever claimed that it met the conditions of an infallible pronouncement, *Humanae Vitae* was a poor springboard from which to jump into the murky waters of the infallibility issue.

But jump Kung did.

Infallibility? begins with a long list of doctrinal issues on which, Kung claims, the church has changed its official position at one time or another. These include recognition of the right of religious liberty and of the legitimacy of applying techniques of textual criticism to the scriptures, and acknowledgment that Christian baptism creates a common ecumenical bond and that baptized non-Catholics are part of the Mystical Body. But it is *Humanae Vitae* more than anything else, according to Kung, which shows that the church is capable of making enormous errors on matters of faith and morals.

How can this demonstrated ability to err be reconciled with belief that the holy Spirit will maintain the church in truth?

Kung's answer is based on an analogy with the interpretation of scripture. One may believe that the church as a whole unfailingly communicates truth despite its mistakes in the same way that he or she may believe that the whole bible is the inspired word of God and that every part of it teaches truth, even though the text itself contains many factual errors.

That is to say, through the church as through the bible, God communicates his truth despite the fact that the humans through whom he speaks sometimes make colossal blunders. Put another way, the truth of the church's teaching does not depend on the truth of each and every one of its individual statements.

This being the case, Kung concludes, it is time to repudiate the traditional doctrine of papal infallibility.

There is an old saying that bad cases make bad law; it is probably equally true that bad issues make bad theology. By presenting his discussion of infallibility as a response to supposed errors the church has made and by adopting an aggressively belligerent tone, Kung—who in some ways resembles a modern-day Abelard—actually made a poor case for his own position.

Even his supporters conceded that *Infallible?* fell far short of Kung's previous books in the quality of its research and the clarity and depth of its thought. At the same time, his detractors—most of them, at least—were forced to admit that he had opened up a long-overdue discussion of an issue which badly needed discussing.

For the fact is that infallibility is not exclusively a Roman Catholic issue. Every Christian church maintains, in some form, that it cannot err in the fundamental sense of leading its members away from the true teachings of Jesus Christ. And it is also a fact that the concept of infallibility is very poorly understood even within the church. That much became clear after *Humanae Vitae,* when many Catholics were astounded (as well as relieved) to hear their own theologians telling them that not every papal declaration on faith and morals is an infallible statement.

One reason infallibility is poorly understood is that it is not at all clear what infallibility means. We have seen, for example, that a given religious truth can be expressed in different ways and given different interpretations. Does the doctrine of infallibility necessarily say anything more than that no solemnly defined dogma, including that of infallibility itself, is incapable of being given at least one "true" interpretation—meaning, presumably, at least one interpretation consistent with scripture? And if this is all infallibility means, would anyone really have a problem in accepting it?

There is even a serious question about whether the notion of infallibility has any meaning at all in a religious context.

Kung argues, convincingly, that when the First Vatican Council defined papal infallibility, it presupposed a rationalistic conception of truth—that is, it assumed that all truth can be expressed in propositions whose contradictions are false. But the fact is that religious language is not propositional; it is analogical. The great religious teachers have always spoken in symbols, allegories, parables; and the true / false dichotomy does not apply to this kind of communication as it does to ordinary language.

Even Aquinas would admit—would insist—that it would be as true to say that God is not good as it would be to say that God is good. "Goodness" can properly be applied to God only analogously. The story of the Good Samaritan, to use an example of Gregory Baum, teaches a profound

religious truth, and one which is central to the meaning of
Christianity; but is there a single sentence of that story which
anyone would wish to claim is infallibly true?

But to say all this is not the same as to say that the doctrine
of papal infallibility is false, that the church must repudiate
the declarations of Vatican I.

Things are considerably more nuanced than that, as
Abelard, were he still alive, would quickly point out. One
need not assert that the church has ever adopted a false
dogma in order to suggest that it may have proposed some inappropriate or meaningless ones—or some which, over the
course of time, might come to be recognized as inappropriate
or meaningless.

In other words, infallibility as it has been traditionally
understood may come to be seen by Catholics and non-Catholics alike as neither a true concept nor a false concept, but
simply as a concept which a more sophisticated understanding of the nature of language has shown cannot validly be
applied to religious discourse.

In that case, a thoughtful, well-reasoned re-examination of
what it means for religious statements to be true may well
contribute to Kung's original goal of hastening Christian reunion. And Kung's sensational polemics, and the difficulties
which they caused for him and for others in the church, may
turn out to have been unnecessary.

In the latter part of 1979, Schillebeeckx was asked by the
Vatican to take part in a "conversation" in Rome about his
theological work with representatives of the Congregation for
the Doctrine of the Faith, the successor to the Holy Office as
guardian of the purity of Catholic doctrine. The unstated
purpose of the meeting was to help in determining whether or
not his ideas were heretical. Schillebeeckx went.

For three days he answered questions. More than a year
later, he was asked by the Vatican to make several clarifica-

tions in his future writings—clarifications which Schillebeeckx had already said he had intended to make all along.
The case, apparently, was closed.

If one accepts that the church has a responsiblity to ensure
that what is taught by Catholic theologians is in fact compatible with Catholic doctrine, then the inquisitorial procedure,
for all its much-publicized shortcomings, seems in this instance to have performed its principal function reasonably
well.

Hans Kung had been asked to participate in a similar "conversation" eleven years before Schillebeeckx. He had refused
to do so except under his own conditions, which were not
accepted. A similar request was refused by Kung in 1971, the
same year he began an "exchange of views" with the German
Bishops' Conference which dragged on and on without
result.

In 1973 and again in 1975 the CDF declared that some of
Kung's teachings, particularly on infallibility, contradicted
church doctrine. More meetings were proposed and rejected.
Finally on December 15, 1979, the same day Schillebeeckx
ended his three-day interrogation—and in the same building
—Cardinal Franjo Seper, Prefect of CDF, signed a statement
previously approved by Pope John Paul II which declared
that Kung was no longer recognized by the church as a Catholic theologian. The German Bishops' Conference issued a
similar statement the same day.

Kung's response was that he was ashamed of the church,
that not since the time of Luther had the Vatican fought so
bitterly against one person, that he would fight on until the
injustice done to him had been rectified, that the younger
clergy and many students were behind him.

It was the kind of reply Abelard might have given.

It was not an encouraging sign.

CONCLUSION

LOOKING back at almost two thousand years of Christian thinking—the many worldviews we have discussed, and the many others we have passed over—is a bit like standing on the edge of the Grand Canyon.

Over the course of centuries the Colorado River has carved a massive complex of channels through solid rock simply by flowing along the path of least resistance. Sometimes that meant following one channel, sometimes another. What made the Grand Canyon was the fact that no single channel was sufficient to contain the river's fullness.

In a somewhat similar fashion, no single intellectual structure has ever been sufficient to contain the fullness of the Christian message, and none ever will be.

Every worldview focuses on a different aspect of reality, and no one viewpoint can adequately encompass the totality of things. Just as one cannot fully appreciate a work of architecture by looking at it from only one position, so it is only when one looks at the world from a succession of different viewpoints, and concentrates on a number of different aspects, that its richness and fullness begin to emerge.

The problem comes when one mistakes the view from a particular vantage point for the entire edifice.

Just as it must always be possible in principle to reconcile religion and science, so the Christian message must also be compatible in principle with the worldview—or views—of every age and every culture.

If we grant that the Christian message is not tied to a particular time—that it is not necessary, in order to understand Christianity, for one to think like a thirteenth-century schoolman, let alone like a fourth-century B.C. Athenian—is it not also true that this message is not tied to any particular culture? If it was possible for Europeans to become Chris-

276 William A. Herr

tians without learning to think like Israelites, is it not possible for Asians or Africans to become Christians without learning to think like Europeans?

And must all Europeans—or Americans—necessarily think alike?

In short, is it not possible for many theologies, expressions of Christianity based on many different worldviews, to coexist on terms of equality within the church?

Karl Rahner went so far as to call the decrees of Vatican II on the use of modern languages in the liturgy a welcome step away from a culturally monolithic church and toward the development of many smaller churches, all professing the same doctrine but each expressing that belief in a different cultural form.

Whether or not this prediction is fulfilled, it is well to remember that the definitive formulation of Catholic doctrine has not yet been written, and that it will not be written before the Judgment Day.

And then—when we are all able to see, as St. Paul put it, face to face—it will not be necessary.

Index

Abelard, Peter, 57-62, 128; and Hans Kung, 270, 272, 273; influence of, 61; use of Aristotle's logical works, 84

Adeodatus (Augustine's son), 30, 31, 32

Adrian VI, Pope, 154

Aeterni Patris (Pope Leo XIII), 197, 204

Agent intellect, 79-80, 85, 95, 133, 249

Albert the Great, St., 87-89, 91, 97

Alcuin, 52

Alexander II, Pope, 52

Alexander IV, Pope, 66, 68

Alexander of Hales, 97

Ambrose, St., 31, 32, 143

Americanism, 234, 242

Analogy, 155-56, 271

Angels, nature of, 107

Anselm, St., 52-57; and the ontological argument, 55-57, 119, 188; life of, 52-54; on the redemption, 54-55; writings of, 54-55

Aquinas, Thomas. *See* Thomas Aquinas

Aristotelianism: Church's attitude toward, 93-94; in the West, 82-86; opposition to, 85-86, 93-96

Aristotle, 75-86; and unchanging species, 220; influence of, 206; life of, 75; relation of to Plato, 76

Augustine, St., 28-48, 143; and concept of sin, 38-40, 42-45; and love, 41-42, 45, 192; and monasticism, 32; and origin of civil government, 158, 159-60; and Protestant theology, 33; and sacramental theology, 33,

and sexual morality, 38-39, 47; and "Two Cities" theory, 160, 243; conversion of, 31-32; influence of, 45-48; life of, 29-35; on relation of faith and reason, 200; refutation of skepticism, 186; writings of, 31, 32-33, 34-35

Averroes, 85, 86, 95

Averroists, Latin, 96, 99

Bacon, Roger, 97

Banez, Domingo, 163, 170-71

Barth, Karl, 57

Baum, Gregory, 271

Bea, Cardinal, 240

Beatific vision, 110, 128, 178

Bede, St., 52

Being, hierarchy of, 37-38

Bellarmine, Robert, St., 163

Benedict XII, Pope, 129

Benedict XV, Pope, 197

Bergson, Henri, 201, 221-22; and Teilhard de Chardin, 230

Bernard of Clairvaux, St., 60; and doctrine of the Immaculate Conception, 123

Birth control: and Aquinas, 106; and Augustine, 47

Boethius, 52, 83, 84

Bologna, University of, 154

Bonaventure, St., 66-74, 91; and creation dispute, 94; and ontological argument, 56; attitude of toward Aristotelianism, 93; death of, 89; influence of, 74; life of, 66-69; on the nature of angels, 107; teachings of, 69-74

Book of Foundations (Teresa of Avila), 177

Buber, Martin, 217

Cajetan, 153-56; and study of
analogy, 155-56
Calvin, John, 33
Cambridge, University of, 143
Carmelites, 167; Discalced, 171
Chalcedon, Ecumenical Council
of, 266
Change, philosophical analysis
of, 24-25, 37-38, 76-77, 120
Chicago, University of, 201
Christian philosophy, concept of,
199-201
Christianity, legalism in, 15
Christina, Queen of Sweden, 185
Christology, 15, 265-68
Church and State, relation be-
tween, 23, 34, 160; and John
Courtney Murray, 236-37, 238,
241-45; in the United States,
234, 235
City of God, The (Augustine),
34, 38, 41, 46
Clement IV, Pope, 68
Clement VI, Pope, 129
Clement VII, Pope, 150
Clement VIII, Pope, 164-66
Clement of Alexandria, 17-18, 22
College de France, 198, 201, 222,
226
Columbia University, 201
Confessions (St. Augustine), 29,
31, 33, 38, 42
Congregation for the Doctrine of
the Faith, 272-73
*Council, Reform, and Reunion,
The* (Kung), 265, 268
Creation from all eternity, 94-95
Cur Deus Homo (Anselm), 54

Dark Night of the Soul, The
(John of the Cross), 176
Darwin, Charles, 221
De auxiliis controversy, 161-66
Defense of the Seven Sacraments
(Henry VIII), 149-50

Democracy, Catholic theory of,
159
Descartes, Rene, 182-89, 195,
208, 211, 223; and anthropo-
centrism, 218-19; and Gilson,
198; and Lonergan, 261, 263,
264; and ontological argument,
56, 188; and Pascal, 190, 192;
and Suarez, 157; starting point
of, 185-86, 253; works of, 184
Discourse on Method
(Descartes), 184
Divine Milieu, The (Teilhard
de Chardin), 226
Docetism, 15
Dominicans, 66, 137, 153, 161-66
Donatism, 33
Duns Scotus, John, 113-125; and
doctrine of the Immaculate
Conception, 123; and formal
distinctions, 119-20; and
proofs for God's existence,
118-19; life of, 113-114;
significance of, 123-25

Erasmus, Desiderius, 140-45,
251; and Luther, 143, 144; and
Thomas More, 151; works of,
142-44
Ethical theory: of Augustine, 37-
40; of Duns Scotus, 115-18; of
William of Ockham, 135
Evolution, biological, 206, 220-
21, 225; and original sin, 205
Existentialism, 218, 255

Faith and reason, relation between, 22-23, 194, 196; in
Clement of Alexandria, 17-18;
in Gilson, 199-200; in Origen,
19-20; in Pascal, 192; in Tertullian, 14, 16
Feudalism, 51-52
Fisher, John, St., 141, 143,
151-52

Franciscans, 66, 67-68, 127
Free will, 20-21, 33, 44-45, 162-66, 191
Freedom in the Modern World (Maritain), 203

Gibbons, James, Cardinal, 234
Gilson, Etienne, 195, 198-202; works of, 199
God, experience of, 69-70, 168-69. *See also* Mysticism
God, nature of: in Aquinas, 104-05; in Duns Scotus, 115
God, our knowledge of: in Bonaventure, 69-73
God, proofs for the existence of: in Anselm, 55-57, 119, 188; in Aquinas, 101-04; in Descartes, 187-88, 189; in Duns Scotus, 118-19; in Maritain, 203; in Ockham, 131; in Pascal, 192; in Rahner, 254-55; in Suarez, 157-58. *See also* Ontological argument
Grace, 162-66; in Augustine, 44
Greek philosophy: effects of on Christianity, 23, 45-47, 256-7; relation of to Christianity, 10, 13-23
Gregorian University, 235, 260, 265
Gregory X, Pope, 66, 69
Grotius, Hugo, 160

Haecceitas, 120-21, 133
Handbook of a Christian Knight (Erasmus), 142
Hearers of the Word (Rahner), 253
Hegel, G. W. F., 195
Heidegger, Martin, 251, 253
Heidelberg, University of, 201
Heloise, 59, 60, 62-63
Henry VIII, King of England, 144, 146, 149, 150

Holy Office, 272
Homo Viator (Marcel), 209
Honecker, Martin, 251-52
Human nature: evolving awareness of, 246; in Aquinas, 105-07, 186-87; in Aristotle, 78, 186-87; in Descartes, 186; in Ockham, 131; in Plato, 26-27, 40, 186
Humanae Vitae (Paul VI), 269, 271
Hume, David, 188, 195
Husserl, Edmund, 251

Immaculate Conception, doctrine of the, 123, 137
Infallibility, papal, 268-72
Infallible? An Inquiry (Kung), 269-70
Innocent IV, Pope, 91
Insight (Lonergan), 260-61, 262
Institut Catholique, 201, 265
Interior Castle, The (Teresa of Avila), 177
Intersubjectivity, 216-17
Ireland, John, Cardinal, 234

Jansen, Cornelius, Bishop, 191
Jansenism, 33, 191
Jerome, St., 33, 143; biblical translation of, 142, 154-55
Jesuits, 153, 161-66, 197; and Jansenism, 191; and Pascal, 192
Jesus: An Experiment in Christology (Schillebeeckx), 265
John Paul II, Pope, 154, 73
John Scotus Erigena, 52, 259
John XXI, Pope, 97
John XXII, Pope, 127-28
John di Fidanza (St. Bonaventure), 66
John of the Cross, St., 172-76, 180

Kant, Immanuel, 188, 195, 219, 247-49, 253; and Karl Rahner, 251
Kirkegaard, Soren, 217
Kung, Hans, 258, 264-65, 268-73; and ontological argument, 57

Lamark, Jean Baptiste, 220, 221
Lanfranc, 52, 53
Leibnitz, Gottfried, 157; and ontological argument, 56
Leo XI, Pope, 166
Leo XIII, Pope, 197, 234, 232; and revival of Thomism, 197, 204-05
Levy-Bruhl, Lucien, 198
Living Flame of Love, The (John of the Cross), 176
Locke, John, 195
Lonergan, Bernard, 260-64
Longinqua Oceani (Leo XIII), 234, 238
Louvain, University of, 143-44
Love: in Aquinas, 109; in Augustine, 41-42, 45, 192; in Bonaventure, 73; in Duns Scotus, 115; in Teilhard de Chardin, 229
Luther, Martin, 33, 140, 153; and Cajetan, 154; and Erasmus, 143, 144; and William of Ockham, 136
Lyons II, Ecumenical Council of, 89

Man and the State (Maritain), 203
Manicheanism, 30, 31, 33, 37, 46-47
Marcel, Gabriel, 195, 208-19
Marechal, Joseph, 249-50, 251, 253, 254
Maritain, Jacques, 195, 201-06; political theory of, 201-03

Marriage, purpose of, 47
Marx, Karl, 195
Meditations on First Philosophy (Descartes), 184
Metaphysical Journal (Marcel), 211
Method in Theology (Lonergan), 262
Michael of Cesena, 127, 129
Mind's Journey to God, The (Bonaventure), 73
Modernism, 235
Molina, Luis de, 163-66
Monica, St., 29, 31
Montmayor, Prudentio de, 162-63
More, Thomas, 141, 145-52, 168; and Erasmus, 141, 148, 151, 152
Murray, John Courtney, 235-46, 259
Mysticism, 73; and Pascal, 191; stages of, 177-79. *See also* God, experience of

Naples, University of, 90, 154
Natural law, 161, 237-38, 241-42
Natural rights, 159
Neoplatonism, 19, 37; Christian, 71
New Dutch Catechism, 264
Nicaea, Ecumenical Council of, 266
Notre Dame University, 201

O'Connell, Denis, Bishop, 234
O'Connell, William, Cardinal, 226
Ockham's Razor, 132-33
Ontological argument, 55-57, 119, 188
Origen, 18-21, 22, 143; and doctrine of the Immaculate Conception, 123

Original sin, 42-44, 193; and evolution, 205
Ottaviani, Alfredo, Cardinal, 240, 259
Oxford, University of, 113, 126, 145

Paris, University of, 65-66, 87, 91, 93, 113, 141, 191. *See also* Sorbonne
Pascal, Blaise, 189-94, 223
Pascal's Wager, 193-94
Passions of the Soul, The (Descartes), 184
Paul V, Pope, 166
Paul VI, Pope, 269
Pelagianism, 33
Pensees (Pascal), 192
Peter of Alcantara, 169, 171
Phenomenon of Man, The (Teilhard de Chardin), 226
Philosophy, political. *See* Political philosophy
Philosophy and theology, relation between, 200-01. *See also* Faith and reason, relation between
Philosophy of Existentialism, The (Marcel), 218
Pike, James, Bishop, 265
Pius IV, Pope, 169
Pius X, Pope, 197, 235
Plato, 24-28; and *a priori* knowledge, 247-48; and involuntary nature of evil, 42-43; influence of, 45; on relation of goodness and being, 56; relation of to Aristotle, 76
Platonism: Augustine's use of, 71; Bonaventure's use of, 69, 71; effect of on Christianity, 45-46
Plotinus, 19, 31
Political philosophy, 159-60, 201-03

Pontifical Institute of Medieval Studies, 198, 201
Potentiality, concept of, 76-77, 101
Praise of Folly, The (Erasmus), 143, 152
Predestination, 191
Prime mover: in Aristotle, 81; in Aquinas, 101-03, 157-58; in Suarez, 157-58
Princeton University, 201
Principles of Philosophy (Descartes), 184
Proslogion (Anselm), 55
Provincial Letters (Pascal), 191

Questiones Disputatae (Aquinas), 99

Rahner, Karl, 250-59, 276; influence of, 257-59
Reason, value of: in Aquinas, 111. *See also* Faith and reason, relation between
Retractions (Augustine), 34-35

Salamanca, University of, 172
Schillebeeckx, Edward, 264-68, 272-73
Scholastic metaphysics, 157-58
Scholasticism: decline of, 123-24; revival of, 157. *See also* Thomism
Schopenhauer, Arthur, 157
Sentences of Peter Lombard, 91, 113, 127, 154, 155
Seper, Franjo, Cardinal, 273
Sexual morality: in Augustine, 38-39, 47
Sic et Non (Abelard), 59-60
Sin, concept of: in Augustine, 38-40, 42-45
Sin, original. *See* Original sin
Society of Jesus. *See* Jesuits
Socrates, 73, 89

Sorbonne, 59, 73, 198, 209, 225
Soul, human: in Aquinas, 106
Spellman, Francis, Cardinal, 240
Spinoza, Benedict, 56
Spirit in the World (Rahner),
  252, 253
*Spirit of Medieval Philosophy,
  The* (Gilson), 199
Spiritual Canticle (John of the
  Cross), 176
Story of My Misfortunes, The
  (Abelard), 58
Suarez, Francisco, 157-61, 163,
  197; and international law,
  160-61; political philosophy of,
  158-60
Summa Contra Gentiles
  (Aquinas), 93, 98, 227
Summa Theologiae (Aquinas),
  93, 97-98, 100-01, 197;
  Cajetan's commentary on,
  154, 155; literary form of, 92,
  97-98

Teilhard de Chardin, Pierre, 195
  223-32; life of, 223-27; relation
  of to Thomas Aquinas, 227;
  significance of, 230-32
Tempier, Etienne, Bishop, 69, 97
Tertullian, 14-16, 22
Testem Benevolentiae (Leo XIII),
  234, 242
Theological Studies, 235, 238,
  239
Theology, Christian, origin of,
  12, 13, 22
Theology and philosophy, relation between, 200-01
Teresa of Avila, St., 168-80;
  mystical experiences of,
  168-69; significance of, 179
Thomas Aquinas, 66, 89-112;
  and analogy, 271; and concept
  of grace, 162; and creation
  dispute, 94-95; and doctrine of

the Immaculate Conception,
  123; and Maritain, 201; and
  proofs for God's existence,
  101-04; and translation of
  Aristotle's *Metaphysics,* 86;
  condemnation of teachings of,
  97; life of, 89-93, 96-97; on
  the nature of angels, 107; relation of to Teilhard de Chardin, 227; significance of, 100,
  111-12; works of, 97-99
Thomas a Becket, St., 54
Thomism: influence of on Pope
  Leo XIII, 204; revival of,
  195-206; stagnation of, 196;
  transcendental, 250; value of,
  111-12. *See also* Scholasticism
Tillich, Paul, 57
Transcendental method, 249-53
Trent, Ecumenical Council of,
  107, 145, 161, 162, 169, 171,
  195
"Two Cities" of Augustine, 41
  160

*Unity of Philosophical Experi-
  ence, The* (Gilson), 199
Universals, problem of, 119-20,
  122, 131-32
Universities, medieval, 63-65,
  92-93
Utopia (Thomas More), 147-48

Vatican I, Ecumenical Council
  of, 271
Vatican II, Ecumenical Council
  of, 238, 240-45, 259, 276
Vestigia Dei, 70
Vio, Giacomo de. *See* Cajetan
Voltaire, Francois Marie Arouet
  de, 140, 223

Way of Perfection, The
  (Teresa of Avila), 176

We Hold These Truths (John Courtney Murray), 239

Will, freedom of the. *See* Free will

William of Champeaux, 58

William of Ockham, 126-37; and divine omnipotence, 130-31, 135; and rise of empirical science, 134; influence of on Luther, 136; life of, 126-29; significance of, 136-37

Wolsey, Thomas, Cardinal, 150

Women, Christian attitude toward, 15

Suggested Readings

All of the following books are available in paperback editions unless otherwise noted, and all paperbacks listed here are in print as of this writing.

General Sources: Frederick Copleston's *A History of Philosophy*, a multi-volume work published by Doubleday (Image Books), and *A History of Christian Philosophy in the Middle Ages* by Etienne Gilson (New York: Random House, 1955, hardcover) provide good introductions to most of the philosophers and theologians mentioned in *Catholic Thinkers*. *The Catholic Encyclopedia* has information on almost all of the people and events discussed in this book, and *The Encyclopedia Britannica* contains in-depth essays on many of them.

Chapter 1: Information on Tertullian, Clement of Alexandria, and Origen can be found in *The Catholic Encyclopedia* and Gilson's *A History of Christian Philosophy in the Middle Ages.*

Chapter 2: *The Republic,* one of the most influential (and readable) masterpieces of Western literature, is available in innumerable editions, often bound together with one or more of Plato's other works. All of the Platonic dialogs are rewarding reading for those who enjoy intellectual give-and-take. The best life of St. Augustine is the one which he himself wrote, *The Confessions,* which is available as a Doubleday Image Book and in many other editions.

Chapter 3: Augustine's *City of God* can be found in both Penguin and Doubleday (Image Book) editions. *Augustine of Hippo: Selected Writings* (published by the Paulist Press) provides a good introduction to some of his other works.

Chapter 4: Anselm is best known for the *Proslogion,* which contains his arugment for the existence of God. It, plus *Cur Deus Homo* and several other works, is contained in *Saint Anselm: Basic Writings,* published by Open Court. *Abelard and Heloise* by D.W. Robertson, Jr., is a readable and very informative account of Abelard's life, work,

284

and relationship with Heloise (New York: The Dial Press, 1972, hardcover).

Chapter 5: The most accessible of St. Bonaventure's works is the short treatise called *The Mind's Journey to God,* published as a booklet by Bobbs-Merrill. Its contention that the divine reality may be experienced through the senses by means of "God's footprints" in the physical world, rather than by arguments and proofs, gives an indication of how Bonaventure's general orientation differed from that of Aquinas.

Chapter 6: Mortimer J. Adler's book *Aristotle for Everybody* (published by Macmillan) is a general introduction to the man who has been called the most influential teacher in history. *The Philosophy of Aristotle,* edited by Renford Bambrough, a Mentor paperback, contains selections from seven of Aristotle's works. Probably the single most interesting work of Aristotle for the average reader is the *Nichomachean Ethics,* available from Penguin and many other publishers.

Chapter 7: Gilson's *A History of Christian Philosophy in the Middle Ages* contains a substantial amount of information on Albert the Great. There are many lives of Thomas Aquinas on library shelves, but *The Life and Spirit of Thomas Aquinas* by L.H. Petitor, O.P. (Chicago: The Priory Press, 1966, hardcover) is something slightly different: an intellectual and spiritual biography.

Chapter 8: F.C. Copleston's *Aquinas,* a Pelican paperback, is a good one-volume overview of Thomas's thought. *Introduction to St. Thomas Aquinas,* part of Random House's Modern Library series (hardcover), is a selection of passages from the *Summa Theologica* and the *Summa contra Gentiles* edited by Anton C. Pegis. The entire *Summa contra Gentiles* has been published in four paperback volumes by Notre Dame Press. *A Tour of the Summa* by Paul J. Glenn (St. Louis: B. Herder Book Co., 1960, hardcover), which contains paraphrases of the "reply" sections of the *Summa Theologica,* question by question and article by article, presents the basic content of the entire work in a volume of manageable size.

Chapter 9: An extended discussion of Duns Scotus (seventy-five pages worth) may be found in Copleston's *A History of Philosophy*.

Chapter 10: Two chapters in F.C. Copleston's *Medieval Philosophy*, one dealing with William of Ockham himself and the other dealing with his followers, summarize Ockham's teachings and explain their significance. Published as a Harper Torchbook.

Chapter 11: *The Praise of Folly* by Erasmus and Thomas More's *Utopia* both are available from Penguin and several other publishers. Both may be disappointing to modern readers unless they are considered not only as literary works but also as historically important documents. Jasper Ridley's *Statesman and Saint* (New York: The Viking Press, 1982, hardcover) is a controversial but enlightening re-evaluation of More's career.

Chapter 12: *The Cahtolic Encyclopedia* provides good introductions to both Cajetan and Suarez. In addition, its entry "Congregatio de Auxiliis" gives an extended account of the long and disedifying dispute between Dominicans and Jesuits on the subject of grace.

Chapter 13: Teresa of Avila's *The Interior Castle* and *The Way of Perfection*, as well as St. John of the Cross's *The Dark Night of the Soul*, have been published by Doubleday (Image Books). *St. Teresa of Avila* by Stephen Clissold (London: Sheldon Press, 1979, hardcover) is a readable biography of Teresa which also contains a good deal of information about St. John of the Cross.

Chapter 14: The *Discourse on Method* and *Meditations on First Philosophy* of Rene Descartes are available in many editions. *A History of Modern Philosophy* by James Collins (Milwaukee: Bruce Publishing Company, 1954, hardcover) contains a long and informative discussion of Descartes. Pascal's *Pensees* and *Provincial Letters* both have been published as Penguin paperbacks.

Chapter 15: Etienne Gilson's *The Unity of Philosophical Experience* has been published by Christian Classics and *God and Philosophy* by Yale University Press. Jacques Maritain's *Man and the State* is available from The University of Chicago Press, his *The Person and the Common Good* from The University of Notre Dame Press.

Chapter 16: Two of Gabriel Marcel's works, *Man Against Mass Society* and *The Mystery of Being* (the latter in two volumes) are available from University Presses of America.

Chapter 17: *The Divine Milieu* and *The Phenomenon of Man* by Pierre Teilhard de Chardin both have been published as Harper Torchbooks. Two hardcover biographies provide readable accounts of Teilhard's life: *The Life of Teilhard de Chardin* by Robert Speaight (New York: Harper and Row, 1967) and *Teilhard: The Man, the Priest, The Scientist* by Mary Lukas and Ellen Lukas (Garden City, NY: Doubleday and Company, 1977).

Chapter 18: *We Hold these Truths* by John Courtney Murray is available in a Sheed and Ward edition.

Chapter 19: Karl Rahner's *Spirit in the Church, The Practice of Faith, The Love of Jesus and the Love of Self,* and *A Dictionary of Theology* are all available from Crossroads. *I Remember: An Autobiographical Interview with Meinold Krauss* (New York: Crossroad, 1985, hardcover) is a good source of information on Rahner's life.

Chapter 20: Bernard Lonergan's *Insight* is published by Harper and Row. *Jesus: An Experiment in Christology, Christ: The Experience of Jesus as Lord,* and *The Schillebeeckx Reader* all are available from Crossroad. Hans Kung's *On Being a Christian, The Chruch,* and *Infallible: An Inquiry* all are published by Doubleday, the last only in a hardcover edition.